普通高等学校规划教材

《灰色童话书》"译"问
How to Translate *The Grey Fairy Book*

曹顺发　主　编
陈福宇　谭雯文　副主编

人民交通出版社股份有限公司
China Communications Press Co., Ltd.

内 容 提 要

本书包括17个英语童话及参考译文，内容很是生动，语言十分地道。每则故事有编者用下划线和斜体字标明的"重点提示"，指出应注意或需要思考的英语用法或汉译技巧。

本书可供普通大专院校英语专业的学生阅读使用，而且对英语爱好者和翻译工作者也不失为上佳的学习参考材料。

图书在版编目(CIP)数据

《灰色童话书》"译"问：中文、英文/曹顺发主编．—北京：人民交通出版社股份有限公司，2014.8
ISBN 978-7-114-11554-7

Ⅰ．①灰… Ⅱ．①曹… Ⅲ．①英语—口语 Ⅳ．①H319.9

中国版本图书馆CIP数据核字(2014)第160815号

书　　　名：	《灰色童话书》"译"问
著　作　者：	曹顺发　陈福宇　谭雯文
责任编辑：	刘永芬
出版发行：	人民交通出版社股份有限公司
地　　　址：	(100011)北京市朝阳区安定门外外馆斜街3号
网　　　址：	http://www.ccpress.com.cn
销售电话：	(010)59757969，59757973
总 经 销：	人民交通出版社股份有限公司发行部
经　　　销：	各地新华书店
印　　　刷：	北京市密东印刷有限公司
开　　　本：	787×1092　1/16
印　　　张：	10.75
字　　　数：	275千
版　　　次：	2014年8月　第1版
印　　　次：	2014年8月　第1次印刷
书　　　号：	ISBN 978-7-114-11554-7
定　　　价：	26.00元

(有印刷、装订质量问题的图书由本公司负责调换)

前　言

本书原文精选自1900年出版的The Grey Fairy Book(汉译名:灰色童话故事书),作者Andrew Lang(1844—1912)(汉译名:安德鲁·兰);全书分别由长度不等的17个故事组成,靠前的相对简短易懂,靠后的则相对偏长费神一些,最后两则实属"故事中的故事"。

鉴于全书均为"很久很久以前"的童话,在读者中自然会出现"有人喜欢有人忧"的现象,但故事中语言十分地道,有时甚至精妙到无以言表的地步,这对语言学习者(尤其是翻译专业学生或爱好者)不失为上佳的练习材料。需说明的是,国内的翻译从业者(包括爱好者),对英译汉的喜好远胜过汉译英。但不能忽略的是,缺乏充足的英语材料作支撑,其汉译英的作品,多半也只能使其读者"看一遍就无心看二遍"。

为方便读者,编者以为重要或值得注意的词汇或句式下用"下划线"或/和"斜体"标出,且用汉语明确提示,以免读者不慎而误译。

每则故事后列有一"思考题",参考译文集中附后。

总之,该书有教材的效果,有读物的趣味,也有练习的功能,若阅读、翻译每则故事并稍事总结,读者定能受益匪浅,即便是教师使用,或许也要认真思考,且借助语法书籍、词典等方可消化原文中的难点。因此,该书有助于各层次、各专业的翻译从业者或爱好者边阅读边翻译,以巩固甚至提高自己的语法知识。

书中瑕疵或错误难免,我们欢迎任何形式的批评和建议!

编　者

2014年6月于山城家中

Table of Contents

1. The Goblin Pony 1
2. The Partnership of the Thief and the Liar 3
3. The Goat-faced Girl 8
4. The Story of Bensurdatu 13
5. The Story of the Queen of the Flowery Isles 19
6. The White Wolf 24
7. The Simpleton 29
8. The Street Musicians 34
9. The Twin Brothers 37
10. Cannetella 43
11. The Daughter of Buk Ettemsuch 48
12. Laughing Eye and Weeping Eye, or the Limping Fox 55
13. Donkey Skin 59
14. A Fairy's Blunder 67
15. What Came of Picking Flowers 76
16. The Story of the Three Sons of Hali 80
17. The Story of the Fair Circassians 97

Chinese Translation for Reference 107

References 165

1. The Goblin Pony

'Don't <u>stir from</u> the fireplace tonight,'①said <u>old</u> Peggy, 'for the wind is blowing so violently that the house shakes; besides, this is Hallow-e'en, when the witches are abroad, and the goblins, who are their servants, are wandering about <u>in all sorts of disguises</u>, doing harm to the children of men.'

重点提示：各下划线应如何译成汉语？其中 Peggy 的口气需留意！

'Why should I stay here?' said <u>the eldest of the young people</u>. 'No, I must go and see what the daughter of *old* Jacob, the rope-maker, is doing. She wouldn't close her blue eyes all night if I didn't visit her father <u>before the moon had gone down</u>.'

重点提示：第一处下划线译为"年龄最大的那个孩子"可取吗？若不恰当，怎样处理更妥？斜体字一定得处理成"老"吗？第二处下划线直译好吗？

'I must go and catch lobsters and crabs,' said <u>the second</u>, 'and <u>not all</u> the witches and goblins in the world shall hinder me.'

重点提示：这两处下划线又如何处理？

So they all determined to <u>go on their business or pleasure</u>, and scorned the wise advice of old Peggy. Only <u>the youngest child</u> hesitated a minute, when she said to him, 'You stay here, my <u>little Richard</u>, and I will <u>tell you beautiful stories</u>.'

重点提示：查看第一处下划线的词义，二、三、四处怎么译更妥？

But he wanted to pick a bunch of wild thyme and some blackberries by moonlight, and ran out after the others. When they got outside the house they <u>said</u>: '<u>The old woman</u> talks of wind and storm, but never was the weather finer or the sky more clear; see how majestically the moon <u>stalks</u> through the transparent clouds!'

重点提示：第一处下划线译成"说"好吗？二、三处怎么译更有味呢？

Then all of a sudden they noticed <u>a little black pony</u> close beside them.

重点提示：下划线怎么译更妙？

'Oh, ho!' they said, 'that is <u>old</u> Valentine's pony; it must have escaped from its stable, and is going down to drink at the horse-pond.'

重点提示：此处的下划线又该怎么处理呢？

'My <u>pretty</u> little pony,' said the eldest, patting the creature with his hand, 'You mustn't run too far; I'll take you to the pond myself.' With these words he jumped on the pony's back and was quickly followed by his second brother, then by the third, and so on, till at last they were all astride the little beast, down to the *small* Richard, who didn't like to be left behind.

重点提示：如何翻译下划线？替换斜体字。

---

①常见的直接引语一般用双引号，此处的单引号在旧时英国英语中十分流行，因此，为维持作品原貌，故保留此类单引号。（后同）——编者注。

On the way to the pond they met several of their companions, and they invited them all to mount the pony, which they did, and the little creature did not seem to mind the extra weight, but trotted merrily along.

The quicker it trotted the more the young people enjoyed the fun; they <u>dug their heels into the pony's sides</u> and called out, 'Gallop, little horse, you have never had such brave riders on your <u>back before</u>!'

重点提示：如何译出两处下划线的真实意思？

In the meantime the wind had risen again, and the waves began to howl; but the pony did not seem to mind the noise, and instead of going to the pond, <u>cantered gaily</u> towards the seashore.

重点提示：从前面内容中找出下划线的同义部分！

Richard began to <u>regret</u> his thyme and blackberries, and the eldest brother seized the pony by the mane and tried to make it turn round, for he remembered the blue eyes of Jacob the rope-maker's daughter. But he <u>tugged and pulled</u> in vain, for the pony galloped straight on into the sea, till the waves met its forefeet. As soon as it felt the water it <u>neighed lustily</u> and capered about with glee, advancing quickly into the foaming billows. When the waves had covered the children's legs they repented their careless behaviour, and cried out: 'The cursed little black pony is bewitched. If we had only listened to old Peggy's advice we shouldn't have been lost.'

重点提示：尽量使下划线处译得生动些！

The further the pony advanced, the higher rose <u>the sea</u>; at last the waves covered the children's heads and they were all drowned.

重点提示：下划线的真实意思是什么？

Towards morning old Peggy went out, for she was <u>anxious about the fate of her grandchildren</u>. She sought them <u>high and low</u>, but could not find them anywhere. She asked all the neighbours if they had seen the children, but no one knew anything about them, except that the eldest had not been with the blue-eyed daughter of Jacob the rope-maker.

重点提示：查阅第一处下划线之意；留心 old Peggy 与故事中几个男孩的关系，并翻译第二处；用类似表达法替换第三处！

As she was going home, <u>bowed with grief</u>, she saw a little black pony coming towards her, springing and curveting in every direction. When it got quite near her it neighed loudly, and galloped past her so quickly that in a moment it was out of her sight.

重点提示：下划线在句中是什么成分？如何翻译？

思考题：

三处人名前的 old 如何处理更恰当一些？

2. The Partnership of the Thief and the Liar

There was once upon a time a thief, who, being out of a job, was wandering by himself up and down the seashore. As he walked he passed a man who was standing still, looking at the waves.

重点提示：琢磨第一处下划线（失业的小偷？）；如何理解第二处呢？

'I wonder,' said the thief, addressing the stranger, 'if you have ever seen a stone swimming?'

'Most certainly I have,' replied the other man, 'and, what is more, I saw the same stone jump out of the water and fly through the air.'

'This is capital,' replied the thief. 'You and I must go into partnership. We shall certainly make our fortunes. Let us start together for the palace of the king of the neighbouring country. When we get there, I will go into his presence alone, and will tell him the most startling thing I can invent. Then you must follow and back up my lie.'

重点提示：各下划线中，第二处可用四个字概括，第四、五处措辞应考究！

Having agreed to do this, they set out on their travels. After several days' journeying, they reached the town where the king's palace was, and here they parted for a few hours, while the thief sought an interview with the king, and begged his majesty to give him a glass of beer.

重点提示：第一处下划线怎么译才言简意赅？琢磨第二处的措辞！

'That is impossible,' said the king, 'as this year there has been a failure of all the crops, and of the hops and the vines; so we have neither wine nor beer in the whole kingdom.'

重点提示：用两个字处理下划线！

'How extraordinary!' answered the thief. 'I have just come from a country where the crops were so fine that I saw twelve barrels of beer made out of one branch of hops.'

'I bet you three hundred florins that is not true,' answered the king.

'And I bet you three hundred florins it is true,' replied the thief.

Then each staked his three hundred florins, and the king said he would decide the question by sending a servant into that country to see if it was true.

So the servant set out on horseback, and on the way he met a man, and he asked him whence he came. And the man told him that he came from the self-same country *to* which the servant was at that moment *bound*.

重点提示：替换两处下划线；同时用斜体部分造句！

'If that is the case,' said the servant, 'you can tell me how high the hops grow in your country, and how many barrels of beer can be brewed from one branch?'

'I can't tell you that,' answered the man, 'but I happened to be present when the hops were being gathered in, and I saw that it took three men with axes three days to cut down one branch.'

重点提示：替换下划线！

Then the servant thought that he might save himself a long journey; so he gave the man ten florins, and told him he must repeat to the king what he had just told him. And when they got back to the palace, they came together into the king's presence.

重点提示：下划线在句中是什么成分？

And the king asked him: 'Well, is it true about the hops?'

'Yes, sire, it is,' answered the servant; 'and here is a man I have brought with me from the country to confirm the tale.'

重点提示：如何翻译下划线更妥帖？

So the king paid the thief the three hundred florins; and the partners once more set out together in search of adventures. As they journeyed, the thief said to his *comrade*: 'I will now go to another king, and will tell him something still more startling; and you must follow and back up my lie, and we shall get some money out of him; just see if we don't.'

重点提示：下划线的真实意思需细细琢磨！替换斜体字。

When they reached the next kingdom, the thief presented himself to the king, and requested him to give him a cauliflower. And the king answered: 'Owing to a blight among the vegetables we have no cauliflower.'

重点提示：如何处理两处下划线更恰当？

'That is strange,' answered the thief. 'I have just come from a country where it grows so well that one head of cauliflower filled twelve water-tubs.'

重点提示：留意下划线的表达法，删除哪两个单词仍能留住原义？

'I don't believe it,' answered the king.

'I bet you six hundred florins it is true,' replied the thief.

'And I bet you six hundred florins it is not true,' answered the king. And he sent for a servant, and ordered him to start at once for the country whence the thief had come, to find out if his story of the cauliflower was true. On his journey the servant met with a man. Stopping his horse he asked him where he came from, and the man replied that he came from the country to which the other was travelling.

'If that is the case,' said the servant, 'you can tell me to what size cauliflower grows in your country? Is it so large that one head fills twelve water-tubs?'

'I have not seen that,' answered the man. 'But I saw twelve waggons, drawn by twelve horses, carrying one head of cauliflower to the market.'

And the servant answered: 'Here are ten florins for you, my man, for you have saved me a long journey. Come with me now, and tell the king what you have just told me.'

重点提示：怎么译下划线才更合原意？

'All right,' said the man, and they went together to the palace; and when the king asked the servant if he had found out the truth about the cauliflower, the servant replied: 'Sire, all that you heard was perfectly true; here is a man from the country who will tell you so.'

So the king had to pay the thief the six hundred florins. And the two partners set out once more on their travels, with their nine hundred florins.

When they reached the country of the neighbouring king, the thief entered the royal presence, and began conversation by asking if his majesty knew that in an adjacent kingdom there was a town with a church steeple on which a bird had alighted, and that the steeple was so high, and the bird's beak so long, that it had pecked the stars till some of them fell out of the sky.

重点提示：从本文中找出下划线的类似表达法。

'I don't believe it,' said the king.

'Nevertheless I am prepared to bet *twelve hundred* florins that it is true,' answered the thief.

重点提示：用当今的英语表达法替换斜体字。

'And I bet twelve hundred florins that it is a lie,' replied the king. And he <u>straightway</u> sent a servant into the neighbouring country to find out the truth.

重点提示：替换下划线！

As he rode, the servant met a man <u>coming in the opposite direction</u>. So he hailed him and asked him where he came from. And the man replied that he came out of the very town to which the man was bound. Then the servant asked him if the story they had heard about <u>the bird with the long beak</u> was true.

重点提示：如何才能将两处下划线处理得更简洁？

'I don't know about that,' answered the man, 'as I have never seen the bird; but I once saw twelve men shoving <u>all their might and main</u> with brooms to push <u>a monster egg</u> into a cellar.'

重点提示：查实两处下划线，并给出适当的译文！

'That is capital,' answered the servant, <u>presenting</u> the man <u>with</u> ten florins. 'Come and tell your tale to the king, and you will save me a long journey.'

重点提示：用一个单词替代两处下划线！

So, when the story was repeated to the king, there was nothing for him to do but to pay the thief the twelve hundred florins.

Then the two partners set out again with their <u>ill-gotten gains</u>, which they proceeded to divide into two equal shares; but the thief kept back three of the florins that belonged to the liar's half of the booty. Shortly afterwards they each married, and settled down in homes of their own with their wives. One day the liar discovered that he had been <u>done out of</u> three florins by his partner, so he went to his house and <u>demanded them from him</u>.

重点提示：查词典，恰当翻译三处下划线内容！

'Come next Saturday, and I will give them to you,' answered the thief. But as he had no intention of giving the liar the money, when Saturday morning came he <u>stretched himself out stiff and stark</u> upon the bed, and told his wife she was to say he was dead. So the wife rubbed her eyes with an onion, and when the liar appeared at the door, <u>she met him in tears</u>, and told him that as her husband was dead he could not be paid the three florins.

重点提示：细心琢磨并翻译两处下划线（特别留意 stiff and stark）！

But the liar, who knew his partner's tricks, instantly suspected the truth, and said: 'As he has not paid me, I will pay him out with <u>three good lashes</u> of my riding whip.'

重点提示：下划线中的 good 为何意？用 bad 一词替换行吗？

At these words the thief <u>sprang to his feet</u>, and, appearing at the door, promised his partner that if he would return the following Saturday he would pay him. So the liar went away <u>satisfied</u> with this promise.

重点提示：替换第一处下划线；请问第二处在句中作什么成分？

But when Saturday morning came the thief got up early and hid himself under a truss of hay in the hay-loft.

When the liar appeared to demand his three florins, the wife met him *with tears in her eyes*, and told him that her husband was dead.

重点提示：用两个（甚至一个）单词替掉斜体字。

'Where have you buried him?' asked the liar.

'In the hay-loft,' answered the wife.

'Then I will go there, and take away some hay in payment of his debt,' said the liar. And proceeding to the hay-loft, he began to toss about the hay with a pitchfork, prodding it into the trusses of hay, till, in terror of his life, the thief crept out and promised his partner to pay him the three florins on the following Saturday.

重点提示：思考并翻译两处下划线！

When the day came he got up at sunrise, and going down into the crypt of a neighbouring chapel, stretched himself out quite still and stiff in an old stone coffin.

重点提示：查阅第一处下划线，给出恰当译文；细品第二处的精妙地方（即 still and stiff），并试着译成汉语。

But the liar, who was quite as clever as his partner, very soon bethought him of the crypt, and set out for the chapel, confident that he would shortly discover the hiding-place of his friend. He had just entered the crypt, and his eyes were not yet accustomed to the darkness, when he heard the sound of whispering at the grated windows. Listening intently, he overheard the plotting of a band of robbers, who had brought their treasure to the crypt, meaning to hide it there, while they set out on fresh adventures.

重点提示：请仔细琢磨下划线处，再给出译文！

All the time they were speaking they were removing the bars from the window, and in another minute they would all have entered the crypt, and discovered the liar. Quick as thought he wound his mantle round him and placed himself, standing stiff and erect, in a niche in the wall, so that in the dim light he looked just like an old stone statue. As soon as the robbers entered the crypt, they set about the work of dividing their treasure.

重点提示：请思考第一处下划线，再看怎么译第二处更简便？

Now, there were twelve robbers, but by mistake the chief of the band divided the gold into thirteen heaps. When he saw his mistake he said they had not time to count it all over again, but that the thirteenth heap should belong to whoever among them could strike off the head of the old stone statue in the niche with one stroke. With these words he took up an axe, and approached the niche where the liar was standing. But, just as he had waved the axe over his head ready to strike, a voice was heard from the stone coffin saying, in sepulchral tones: '*Clear out of this*, or the dead will arise from their coffins, and the statues will descend from the walls, and you will be driven out *more dead than alive*.'

重点提示：查阅两处斜体部分的真实意思，并译成汉语。

And with a bound the thief jumped out of his coffin and the liar from his niche, and the robbers

6

were so terrified that they ran helter-skelter out of the crypt, leaving all their gold behind them, and vowing that they would never put foot inside *the haunted place* again. So the partners divided the gold between them, and carried it to their homes; and history tells us no more about them.

重点提示： 细品下划线中的两个谐音词,能用同样的方法处理吗？斜体部分是什么意思？

思考题：
本文哪几个词或词组最吸引你？能否借助例证造句？

3. The Goat-faced Girl

There was once upon a time a peasant called Masaniello who had twelve daughters. They were exactly like the steps of a staircase, for there was just a year between each sister. It was all the poor man could do to bring up such a large family, and in order to provide food for them he used to dig in the fields all day long. In spite of his hard work he only just succeeded in keeping the wolf from the door, and the poor little girls often went *hungry* to bed.

重点提示：第一处下划线需认真措辞，第二处有汉语现成说法（怎么说简洁、妥当？），第三处可查词典获得其意！斜体字在句中作什么成分？

One day, when Masaniello was working at the foot of a high mountain, he came upon the mouth of a cave which was so dark and gloomy that even the sun seemed afraid to enter it. Suddenly a huge green lizard appeared from the inside and stood before Masaniello, who nearly went out of his mind *with* terror, for the beast was as big as a crocodile and quite as fierce looking.

重点提示：替换第一处并翻译第二、三处下划线，且举例说明斜体字（with）的含义。

But the lizard sat down beside him in the most friendly manner, and said: 'Don't be afraid, my good man, I am not going to hurt you; on the contrary, I am most anxious to help you.'

重点提示：下划线怎么译更妥？

When the peasant heard these words he knelt before the lizard and said: 'Dear lady, for I know not what to call you, I am in your power; but I beg of you to be merciful, for I have twelve wretched little daughters at home who are dependent on me.'

'That's the very reason why I have come to you,' replied the lizard. 'Bring me your youngest daughter tomorrow morning. I promise to bring her up as if she were my own child, and to look upon her as the apple of my eye.'

重点提示：恰当处理下划线！

When Masaniello heard her words he was very unhappy, because he felt sure, from the lizard's wanting one of his daughters, the youngest and tenderest too, that the poor little girl would only serve as dessert for the terrible creature's supper. At the same time he *said to himself*, 'If I refuse her request, she will certainly eat me up on the spot. If I give her what she asks she does indeed take part of myself, but if I refuse she will take the whole of me. What am I to do, and how in the world am I to get out of the difficulty?'

重点提示：替换第一处下划线；翻译第二处；如何巧断第三处的真实意思？斜体部分能直译吗？

As he kept muttering to himself the lizard said, 'Make up your mind to do as I tell you at once. I desire to have your youngest daughter, and if you won't comply with my wish, I can only say it will be the worse for you.'

重点提示：揣摩并翻译两处下划线！

Seeing that there was nothing else to be done, Masaniello set off for his home, and arrived there looking so white and wretched that his wife asked him at once: 'What has happened to you, my dear husband? Have you quarrelled with anyone, or has the poor donkey fallen down?'

'*Neither the one nor the other*,' answered her husband, 'but something far worse than either. A terrible lizard has nearly <u>frightened me out of my senses</u>, for she threatened that if I did not give her our youngest daughter, she would make me repent it. My head is <u>going round like a millwheel</u>, and I don't know what to do. I am indeed <u>between the Devil and the Deep Sea</u>. You know how dearly I love Renzolla, and yet, if I fail to bring her to the lizard tomorrow morning, I must <u>say farewell to life</u>. Do advise me what to do.'

重点提示：细心琢磨各下划线（尤其最后一处）方可动手翻译！如何翻译斜体部分最简洁？

When his wife had heard all he had to say, she said to him: 'How do you know, my dear husband, that the lizard is really our enemy? May she not be <u>a friend in disguise</u>? And your meeting with her may be the beginning of better things and the end of all our misery. Therefore go and take the child to her, for <u>my heart</u> tells me that you will never repent doing so.'

重点提示：巧译第一处下划线！第二处好译吗？

Masaniello was much comforted by her words, and next morning as soon as it was light he took his little daughter by the hand and led her to the cave.

The lizard, who was <u>awaiting</u> the peasant's arrival, came forward to meet him, and taking the girl by the hand, she gave the father a sack full of gold, and said: 'Go and <u>marry</u> your other daughters, and give them dowries with this gold, and <u>be of good cheer</u>, for Renzolla will <u>have both father and mother in me</u>; it is a great piece of luck for her that she has fallen into my hands.'

重点提示：替换第一处（见本文）下划线；留意第二处（国人常出错）；琢磨第三处的含义；第四处怎么译更像汉语？

Masaniello, quite overcome with gratitude, thanked the lizard, and returned home to his wife.

As soon as it was known how rich the peasant had become, <u>suitors for the hands of his daughters</u> were *not wanting*, and very soon he <u>married them all off</u>; and even then there was enough gold left to <u>keep</u> himself and his wife <u>in comfort and plenty</u> all their days.

重点提示：品味各下划线内容（考虑第二处中 off 可删除否）；琢磨并替换斜体部分！

As soon as the lizard was left alone with Renzolla, she changed the cave into a beautiful palace, and led the girl inside. Here she brought her up like a little princess, and the child <u>wanted for nothing</u>. She gave her sumptuous food to eat, beautiful clothes to wear, and a thousand servants to wait on her.

重点提示：下划线是什么意思？如何翻译更佳？

Now, it happened, one day, that the king of the country was hunting in a wood close to the palace, and was <u>overtaken by the dark</u>. Seeing a light shining in the palace he sent one of his servants to ask if he could get a night's lodging there.

重点提示：斜体字在句中起什么作用？能翻译出来吗？如何处理下划线？

When the *page* knocked at the door the lizard changed herself into a beautiful woman, and opened it herself. When she heard the king's request she sent him a message to say that she would be delighted to see him, and give him all he wanted.

重点提示：查阅斜体字的意思并替换。

The king, on hearing this kind invitation, instantly *betook himself* to the palace, where he was received *in the most hospitable manner*. A hundred pages with torches came to meet him, a hundred more waited on him at table, and another hundred waved big fans in the air to keep the flies from him. Renzolla herself poured out the wine for him, and, so gracefully did she do it, that his Majesty could not take his eyes off her.

重点提示：各用一个单词替换两处斜体字；能用肯定及否定方式分别处理该下划线吗？

When the meal was finished and the table cleared, the king retired to sleep, and Renzolla drew the shoes from his feet, at the same time drawing his heart from his breast. So desperately had he fallen in love with her, that he called the fairy to him, and asked her for Renzolla's hand in marriage. As the kind fairy *had* only the girl's welfare *at heart*, she willingly gave her consent, and not her consent only, but a wedding portion of seven thousand golden guineas.

重点提示：品味第一处下划线的修辞；翻译第二处；对斜体部分造句。

The king, full of delight *over* his good fortune, prepared to take his departure, accompanied by Renzolla, who *never so much as* thanked the fairy for all she had done for her.

重点提示：两处斜体字为何意？请举例说明！

When the fairy saw such a base want of gratitude she determined to punish the girl, and, cursing her, she turned her face into a goat's head.

重点提示：如何再现下划线之意？

In a moment Renzolla's pretty mouth stretched out into a snout, with a beard a yard long at the end of it, her cheeks sank in, and her shining plaits of hair changed into two sharp horns.

重点提示：下划线未必好处理，请留意！

When the king turned round and saw her he thought he must have taken leave of his senses. He burst into tears, and cried out: 'Where is the hair that bound me so tightly, where are the eyes that pierced through my heart, and where are the lips I kissed? Am I to be tied to a goat all my life? No, no! Nothing will induce me to become the laughing-stock of my subjects for the sake of a goat-faced girl!'

重点提示：如何理解下划线部分？

When they reached his own country he shut Renzolla up in a little turret chamber of his palace, with a waiting-maid, and gave each of them ten bundles of flax to spin, telling them that their task must be finished by the end of the week.

The maid, obedient to the king's commands, set at once to work and combed out the flax, wound it round the spindle, and sat spinning at her wheel so diligently that her work was quite done by Saturday evening.

But Renzolla, who had been spoilt and petted in the fairy's house, and was quite unaware of the change that had taken place in her appearance, threw the flax out of the window and said: 'What is the king thinking of that he should give me this work to do? If he wants shirts he can buy them. It isn't even *as if he had picked me out of the gutter*, for he ought to remember that I brought him seven thousand golden guineas as my wedding portion, and that I am his wife and not his slave. He must be mad to treat me like this.'

重点提示:怎么理解下划线？能给出斜体字的"等值"汉语吗？

All the same, when Saturday evening came, and she saw that the waiting-maid had finished her task, she took fright lest she should be punished for her idleness. So she hurried off to the palace of the fairy, and confided all her woes to her. The fairy embraced her tenderly, and gave her a sack full of spun flax, in order that she might show it to the king, and let him see what a good worker she was. Renzolla took the sack without one word of thanks, and returned to the palace, leaving the kind fairy very indignant over her want of gratitude.

重点提示:仔细琢磨下划线(尤其是后两者)的含义,尽力给出恰当的译文!

When the king saw the flax all spun, he gave Renzolla and the waiting-maid each a little dog, and told them to look after the animals and train them carefully. The waiting-maid brought hers up with the greatest possible care, and treated it almost as if it were her son. But Renzolla said：'I don't know what to think. Have I come among a lot of lunatics? Does the king imagine that I am going to comb and feed a dog with my own hands?' With these words she opened the window and threw the poor little beast out, and he fell on the ground as dead as a stone.

重点提示:下划线怎么译更生动？

When a few months had passed the king sent a message to say he would like to see how the dogs were getting on. Renzolla, who felt very uncomfortable in her mind at this request, hurried off once more to the fairy.

This time she found an old man at the door of the fairy's palace, who said to her：'Who are you, and what do you want?'

重点提示:下划线翻译起来如此"简单",是吗？试试看！

When Renzolla heard his question she answered angrily：'Don't you know me, old Goat-beard? And how dare you address me in such a way?'

重点提示:下划线怎么处理更恰当？

'The pot can't call the kettle black,' answered the old man, 'for it is not I, but you who have a goat's head. Just wait a moment, you ungrateful wretch, and I will show you to what a *pass* your want of gratitude has brought you.'

重点提示:查阅第一处下划线的出处,并作恰当处理;用一个单词替代第二处;举例说明斜体字的意思。

With these words he hurried away, and returned with a mirror, which he held up before Renzolla. At the sight of her ugly, hairy face, the girl nearly fainted with horror, and she broke into loud sobs at seeing her countenance so changed.

Then the old man said：'You must remember, Renzolla, that you are a peasant's daughter, and that the fairy turned you into a queen; but you were ungrateful, and never as much as thanked her for all she had done for you. Therefore she has determined to punish you. But if you wish to lose your long white beard, throw yourself at the fairy's feet and implore her to forgive you. She has a tender heart, and will, perhaps, take pity on you.'

Renzolla, who was really sorry for her conduct, took the old man's advice, and the fairy not only gave her back her former face, but she dressed her in a gold embroidered dress, presented her with a beautiful carriage, and brought her back, accompanied by a host of servants, to her husband.

When the king saw her looking as beautiful as ever, he fell in love with her once more, and bitterly repented having caused her so much suffering. So Renzolla lived happily ever afterwards, for she loved her husband, honoured the fairy, and was grateful to the old man for having told her the truth.

思考题：
请列举文中的精彩词句，同时模仿举出两个自己满意的例证。

4. The Story of Bensurdatu

There was once <u>a king and a queen</u> who had three *wonderfully beautiful daughters*, and their one thought, from morning till night, was how they could make the girls happy.

重点提示：划掉第一处下划线的某个单词可保证原文大意不变,请指出;思考"下划线+斜体字"部分,比较一下"全译"和"半译"效果!

One day the princesses said to the king, '*Dear father*, we want so much to <u>have a picnic, and eat our dinner in the country.</u>'

重点提示：如何处理斜体字才像常见汉语?怎么翻译下划线更简便且不失其大意?

'Very well, dear children, let us have a picnic by all means,' answered he, and gave orders that everything should be got ready.

When luncheon was prepared it was put into a cart, and the royal family stepped into a carriage and drove right away into the country. After a few miles they reached *a house and garden belonging to the king*, and close by was their favourite place for lunch. The drive had made them very hungry, and they ate <u>with a hearty appetite</u>, till almost all the food had disappeared.

重点提示：斜体字是何意?怎么处理更简便?用一个副词替换下划线!

When they had quite done, they said to their parents: 'Now we should like to wander about the garden a little, but when you want to *go home*, just call to us.' <u>And they ran off, laughing, down a green glade</u>, which led to the garden.

重点提示：如何翻译斜体字才能反映出原意?认真处理下划线!

But no sooner had they stepped across the fence, than a dark cloud came down and covered them, and <u>prevented them seeing</u> whither they were going. Meanwhile <u>the king and queen</u> sat lazily among the heather, and an hour or two <u>slipped away</u>. The sun was <u>dropping towards the horizon</u>, and they began to think it was time to go home. So they called to their daughters and called again, but no one answered them.

重点提示：第一处下划线可添加哪个单词?第二处如何翻译更简便?用两个汉语成语处理最后两处!

Frightened at the silence, they searched every corner of the garden, the house, and the neighbouring wood, but no trace of the girls was to be found anywhere. The earth seemed to have swallowed them up. The poor parents were in despair. The queen wept all the way home, and for many days after, and the king <u>issued</u> a proclamation that whoever should bring back his lost daughters should *have* one of them *to wife*, and should, after his death, reign in his stead.

重点提示：恰当翻译下划线;用一个单词替换斜体字部分!

Now two young generals were at that time living at the court, and when they heard the king's declaration, they said one to the other: 'Let us go in search of them; perhaps we shall be the lucky persons.' And they set out, <u>each mounted on a strong horse</u>, taking with them a change of *raiment* and some money.

重点提示:判断下划线的句子成分！猜猜斜体字并替换！

But though they inquired at every village they rode through, they could hear nothing of the princesses, and by-and-by their money was all spent, and they were forced to sell their horses, or give up the search. Even this money only lasted a little while longer, and *nothing but their clothes lay between them and starvation*. They sold the spare garments that were bound on their saddles, and went in the coats they stood up in to the inn, to beg for some food, as they were really starving. When, however, they had to pay for what they had eaten and drank, they said to the host: 'We have no money, and <u>naught</u> but the clothes <u>we stand up in</u>. Take these, and give us instead some old rags, and let us stay here and serve you.' And the innkeeper was content with the bargain, and the generals remained, and were his servants.

重点提示:替换第一处下划线;查词典弄清第二处的意思！请仔细思考斜体字的含义,然后翻译。

All this time the king and queen remained in their palace <u>hungering for</u> their children, but not a word was heard of either of them or of the generals who had gone to seek for them.

重点提示:用一个单词替换下划线！

Now there was living in the palace a faithful servant of the king's called Bensurdatu, who had served him for many years, and when Bensurdatu saw how grieved the king was, he lifted up his voice and said to him: 'Your majesty, let me go and seek your daughters.'

'No, no, Bensurdatu,' replied the king. 'Three daughters have I lost, and two generals, and shall I lose you also?'

But Bensurdatu said again: 'Let me now go, your majesty; trust me, and I will bring you back your daughters.'

Then the king *gave way*, and Bensurdatu set forth, and rode on till he came to the inn, where he dismounted and asked for food. It was <u>brought</u> by the two generals, whom he knew at once <u>in spite of</u> their miserable clothes, and, much astonished, asked them how <u>in the world</u> they came there.

重点提示:替换斜体字;第一、二处下划线是什么意思？第三处起何作用？能省略吗？

They told him all their adventures, and he <u>sent for the innkeeper</u>, and said to him: 'Give them back their garments, and I will pay everything that they owe you.'

重点提示:下划线怎么处理更妥帖？

And the innkeeper did as he was *bid*, and when the two generals were <u>dressed in their proper clothes</u>, they declared they would join Bensurdatu, and with him seek for the king's daughters.

重点提示:替换斜体字;下划线的真实意思是什么？细思后才可恰当处理！

The three companions rode on for many miles, and at length they came to a wild place, without sign of a human being. It was getting dark, and fearing to be lost on this desolate spot they pushed on their horses, and at last saw a light in the window of a tiny hut.

'<u>Who comes there</u>?' asked a voice, as they knocked at the door.

重点提示:思考下划线如何处理为好。

'Oh! Have pity on us, and give us a night's shelter,' replied Bensurdatu; 'we are three tired travellers who have lost our way.'

Then the door was opened by a very old woman who stood back, and beckoned them to enter. 'Whence do you come, and whither do you go?' said she.

重点提示:几处下划线该怎么处理才像样呢?(老妇人是普通人吗?猜猜!)

'Ah, *good woman*, we have a heavy task before us,' answered Bensurdatu, 'we are bound to carry the king's daughters back to the palace!'

重点提示:斜体字不可直译,那该如何处理为好?

'Oh, unhappy creatures,' cried she, 'you know not what you are doing! The king's daughters were covered by a thick cloud, and no one knows where they may now be.'

'Oh, tell us, if you know, my good woman,' entreated Bensurdatu, 'for with them lies all our happiness.'

'Even if I were to tell you,' answered she, 'you could not rescue them. To do that you would have to go to the very bottom of a deep river, and though certainly you would find the king's daughters there, yet the two eldest are guarded by two giants, and the youngest is watched by a serpent with seven heads.'

The two generals, who stood by listening, were filled with terror at her words, and wished to return immediately; but Bensurdatu stood firm, and said: 'Now we have got so far we must carry the thing through. Tell us where the river is, so that we may get there as soon as possible.' And the old woman told them, and gave them some cheese, wine, and bread, so that they should not *set forth starving*; and when they had eaten and drunk they laid themselves down to sleep.

重点提示:替换斜体字部分。

The sun had only just risen above the hills next morning before they all woke, and, taking leave of the wise woman who had helped them, they rode on till they came to the river.

'I am the eldest,' said one of the generals, 'and it is my right to go down first.'

So the others fastened a cord round him, and gave him a little bell, and *let him down* into the water. But scarcely had the river closed above his head when such dreadful rushing sounds and peals of thunder came crashing round about him that he lost all his courage, and rang his bell, if perchance it might be heard amidst all this clamour. Great was his relief when the rope began slowly to pull him upwards.

重点提示:用一个单词替换斜体部分。

Then the other general plunged in; but he fared no better than the first, and was soon on dry ground again.

'*Well, you are a brave pair*!' said Bensurdatu, as he tied the rope round his own waist; 'let us see what will happen to me.' And when he heard the thunder and clamour round about him he thought to himself, 'oh, make as much noise as you like, it won't hurt me!' When his feet touched the bottom he found himself in a large, brilliantly lighted hall, and in the middle sat the eldest princess, and in front of her lay a huge giant, fast asleep. Directly she saw Bensurdatu she nodded to him, and *asked with her eyes* how he had come there.

重点提示:揣摩并译出两处斜体字的口吻。

For answer he drew his sword, and was about to cut off the giant's head, when she stopped him quickly, and made signs to hide himself, as the giant was just beginning to wake. 'I smell the flesh of a man!' murmured he, stretching his great arms.

'Why, how in the world could any man get down here?' replied she, 'you had better go to sleep again.'

So he turned over and went to sleep. Then the princess signed to Bensurdatu, who drew his sword and cut off the giant's head with such a blow that it flew into the corner. And the heart of the princess leapt within her, and she placed a golden crown on the head of Bensurdatu, and called him her deliverer. 'Now show me where your sisters are,' he said, 'that I may free them also.'

重点提示:猜猜下划线的意思:能再添一个单词而不改其意吗?

So the princess opened a door, and led him into another hall, wherein sat her next sister, guarded by a giant who was fast asleep. When the second princess saw them, she made a sign to them to hide themselves, for the giant was showing symptoms of waking.

重点提示:请琢磨并翻译两处下划线!

'I smell man's flesh!' murmured he, sleepily.

'Now, how could any man get down here?' asked she, 'go to sleep again.'

And as soon as he closed his eyes, Bensurdatu stole out from his corner, and struck such a blow at his head that it flew far, far away. The princess could not find words to thank Bensurdatu for what he had done, and she too placed in his hand a golden crown.

重点提示:下划线是"偷"的意思吗?

'Now show me where your youngest sister is,' said he, 'that I may free her also.'

'Ah! That I fear you will never be able to do,' sighed they, 'for she is in the power of a serpent with seven heads.'

'Take me to him,' replied Bensurdatu. 'It will be a splendid fight.'

Then the princess opened a door, and Bensurdatu passed through, and found himself in a hall that was even larger than the other two. And there stood the youngest sister, chained *fast* to the wall, and before her was stretched a serpent with seven heads, horrible to see. As Bensurdatu came forward it twisted all its seven heads in his direction, and then made a quick dart to snatch him within its grasp. But Bensurdatu drew his sword and *laid about him*, till the seven heads were rolling on the floor. Flinging down his sword he rushed to the princess and broke her chains, and she wept for joy, and embraced him, and took the golden crown *from off* her head, and placed it in his hand.

重点提示:第一处斜体字跟速度有关吗? 第二处斜体字的两个单词可交换位置吗? 如何简洁再现下划线?

'Now we must go back to the upper world,' said Bensurdatu, and led her to the bottom of the river. The other princesses were waiting there, and he tied the rope round the eldest, and rung his bell. And the generals above heard, and drew her gently up. They then unfastened the cord and threw it back into the river, and in a few moments the second princess stood beside her sister.

重点提示:有更可接受的单词(以时下英语的用法为例)替换下划线吗?

So now there were left only Bensurdatu and the youngest princess. 'Dear Bensurdatu,' said she, 'do me a kindness, and let them draw you up before me. I dread the treachery of the generals.'

重点提示:第一处下划线怎么译更恰当? 第二处好译吗?

'No, no,' replied Bensurdatu, 'I certainly will not leave you down here. There is nothing to fear from my comrades. '

重点提示:下划线怎么处置更可信?

'If it is your wish I will go up then; but first I swear that if you do not follow to marry me, I shall stay single for the rest of my life. ' Then he bound the rope round her, and the generals drew her up.

重点提示:细心揣摩并翻译下划线!

But instead of lowering the rope again into the river, envy at the courage and success of Bensurdatu so filled the hearts of the two generals, that they turned away and left him to perish. And, more than that, they threatened the princesses, and forced them to promise to tell their parents that it was the two generals who had set them free. 'And if they should ask you about Bensurdatu, you must say you have never seen him,' they added; and the princesses, fearing for their lives, promised everything, and they rode back to court together.

重点提示:两处下划线怎样措辞更合适?

The king and queen *were beside themselves with joy* when they saw their dear children once more. But when the generals had told their story, and the dangers they had run, the king declared that they had gained their reward, and that the two eldest princesses should become their wives.

重点提示:替换下划线!

And now we must see what poor Bensurdatu was doing.

重点提示:查阅斜体字部分,再举例强化该用法;下划线为何意?怎样翻译好一点呢?

He waited patiently a long, long time, but when the rope never came back he knew he had been right, and that his comrades had betrayed him. 'Ah, now I shall never reach the world again,' murmured he; but being a brave man, and knowing that moaning his fate would profit him nothing, he rose and began to search through the three halls, where, perhaps, he might find something to help him. In the last one stood a dish, covered with food, which reminded him that he was hungry, and he sat down and ate and drank.

重点提示:请用(两个)成语翻译下划线!

Months passed away, when, one morning, as he was walking through the halls, he noticed a purse hanging on the wall, which had never been there before. He took it down to examine it, and nearly let it fall with surprise when a voice came from the purse saying: 'What commands have you?'

重点提示:下划线可以删除吗?

'Oh, take me out of this horrible place, and up into the world again;' and in a moment he was standing by the river bank, with the purse tightly grasped in his hand.

'Now let me have the most beautiful ship that ever was built, all manned and ready for sea. ' And there was the ship, with a flag floating from its mast on which were the words, 'King with the three crowns. '

重点提示:下划线如何处置更像样?

Then Bensurdatu climbed on board, and sailed away to the city where the three princesses dwelt; and when he reached the harbour he blew trumpets and beat drums, so that every one ran to the doors and windows.

重点提示：如何准确再现下划线？

And the king heard too, and saw the beautiful vessel, and said to himself: 'That must indeed be a mighty monarch, for he has three crowns while I have only one.' So he hastened to greet the stranger, and invited him to his castle, for, thought he, 'this will be a fine husband for my youngest daughter.' Now, the youngest princess had never married, and had turned a deaf ear to all her wooers.

Such a long time had passed since Bensurdatu had left the palace, that the king never guessed for a moment that the splendidly *clad* stranger before him was the man whom he had so deeply mourned as dead. 'Noble lord,' said he, 'let us feast and make merry together, and then, if it seems good to you, do me the honour to take my youngest daughter to wife.'

重点提示：斜体字的原形是什么？可用什么单词替换？

And Bensurdatu was glad, and they all sat down to a great feast, and there were great rejoicings. But only the youngest daughter was sad, for her thoughts were with Bensurdatu. After they arose from the table the king said to her, 'Dear child, this mighty lord does you the honour to ask your hand in marriage.'

重点提示：下划线如何直译？

'Oh, father,' answered she, 'spare me, I pray you, for I desire to remain single.'

Then Bensurdatu turned to her, and said: 'And if I were Bensurdatu, would you give the same answer to me?'

And as she stood silently gazing at him, he added: 'Yes, I am Bensurdatu; and this is my story.'

The king and queen had their hearts stirred within them at the tale of his adventures, and when he had ended the king stretched out his hand, and said: 'Dear Bensurdatu, my youngest daughter shall indeed be your wife; and when I die my crown shall be yours. As for the men who have betrayed you, they shall leave the country and you shall see them no more.' And the wedding feast was ordered, and rejoicings were held for three days over the marriage of Bensurdatu and the youngest princess.

重点提示：如何理解两处下划线？

思考题：
如何再现本文中不同人物的口吻？举例说明。

5. The Story of the Queen of the Flowery Isles

There once lived a queen who ruled over the Flowery Isles, whose husband, <u>to her extreme grief</u>, died a few years after their marriage. On being left a widow she devoted herself almost entirely to the education of the two charming princesses, her only children. The elder of them was so lovely that as she grew up her mother greatly feared she would excite the jealousy of the Queen of all the Isles, who <u>prided herself on</u> being the most beautiful woman in the world, and insisted on all rivals bowing before her charms.

重点提示：第一处下划线在句中作什么成分？如何再现第二处？

In order the better to *gratify* her vanity she had urged the king, her husband, to make war on all the surrounding islands, and as his greatest wish was to please her, the only condition he imposed on any newly-conquered country was that each princess of every royal house should attend his court as soon as she was fifteen years old, and do homage to the <u>transcendent beauty</u> of his queen.

重点提示：替换斜体字！如何翻译下划线的意思？

The queen of the Flowery Isles, well aware of this law, was fully determined to present her daughter to the proud queen as soon as her fifteenth birthday was past.

The queen herself had heard a rumour of the young princess's great beauty, and awaited her visit with some anxiety, which soon developed into jealousy, for when the interview took place it was impossible not to be dazzled by such radiant charms, and she was obliged to admit that she had never beheld anyone so exquisitely lovely.

Of course she thought in her own mind 'excepting myself!' for nothing could have made her believe it possible that anyone could <u>eclipse</u> her.

重点提示：替换下划线！

But the outspoken admiration of the entire court soon <u>undeceived</u> her, and made her so angry that she pretended illness and retired to her own rooms, so as to avoid witnessing the princess's triumph. She also sent word to the Queen of the Flowery Isles that she was sorry not to be well enough to see her again, and advised her to return to her own *states* with the princess, <u>her daughter</u>.

重点提示：第一处下划线需细思量：可直译吗？猜猜斜体字是怎么回事儿？第二处下划线需要翻译吗？

This message was entrusted to <u>one of the great ladies of the court</u>, who was an old friend of the Queen of the Flowery Isles, and who advised her not to wait to take a formal leave but to go home as fast as she could.

重点提示：下划线怎样处理成汉语更妥帖？

The queen was <u>not slow to take the hint</u>, and lost no time in obeying it. Being <u>well</u> aware of the magic powers of the incensed queen, she warned her daughter that she was threatened by some great danger if she left the palace for any reason whatever during the next six months.

重点提示："正译"下划线！

19

The princess promised obedience, and *no pains* were *spared* to make the time pass pleasantly for her.

重点提示：将斜体部分还原成词组，并造句！

The six months were nearly at an end, and on the very last day a splendid fête was to take place in a lovely meadow quite near the palace. The princess, who had been able to watch all the preparations from her window, implored her mother to let her go as far as the meadow; and the queen, thinking all risk must be over, consented, and promised to take her there herself.

The whole court was delighted to see their much-loved princess at *liberty*, and everyone set off in high glee to join in the fête.

The princess, overjoyed at being once more in the open air, was walking a little in advance of her party when suddenly the earth opened under her feet and closed again after swallowing her up!

The queen fainted away with terror, and the younger princess burst into floods of tears and could hardly be dragged away from the fatal spot, *whilst* the court was overwhelmed with horror at so great a calamity.

重点提示：如何再现下划线中的内容？请替换斜体字部分。

Orders were given to *bore the earth to a great depth*, but *in vain*; not a trace of the vanished princess was to be found.

重点提示：替换两处斜体字部分；请为下划线找个恰当的汉语说法！

She sank right through the earth and found herself in a desert place with nothing but rocks and trees and no sign of any human being. The only living creature she saw was a very pretty little dog, who ran up to her and at once began to caress her. She took him in her arms, and after playing with him for a little put him down again, when he started off in front of her, looking round from time to time as though begging her to follow.

She let him lead her on, and *presently* reached a little hill, from which she saw a valley full of lovely fruit trees, bearing flowers and fruit together. The ground was also covered with fruit and flowers, and in the middle of the valley rose a fountain surrounded by a velvety lawn.

重点提示：替换斜体字；品味下划线并恰当重现。

The princess hastened to this charming spot, and sitting down on the grass began to think over the misfortune which had befallen her, and burst into tears as she reflected on her sad condition.

The fruit and clear fresh water would, she knew, prevent her from dying of hunger or thirst, but how could she escape if any wild beast appeared and tried to devour her?

重点提示：两处替换下划线！

At length, having thought over every possible evil which could happen, the princess tried to distract her mind by playing with the little dog. She spent the whole day near the fountain, but as night drew on she wondered what she should do, *when* she noticed that the little dog was pulling at her dress.

She paid no heed to him at first, but as he continued to pull her dress and then run a few steps in one particular direction, she at last decided to follow him; he stopped before a rock with a large opening in the centre, which he evidently wished her to enter.

The princess did so and discovered a large and beautiful cave lit up by the brilliancy of the stones with which it was lined, with a little couch covered with soft moss in one corner. She lay down on it and the dog at once nestled at her feet. Tired out with all she had gone through she soon fell asleep.

Next morning she was awakened very early by the songs of many birds. The little dog woke up too, and sprang round her in his most caressing manner. She got up and went outside, the dog as before running on in front and turning back constantly to take her dress and draw her on.

She let him have his way and he soon led her back to the beautiful garden where she had spent part of the day before. Here she ate some fruit, drank some water of the fountain, and felt as if she had made an excellent meal. She walked about amongst the flowers, played with her little dog, and at night returned to sleep in the cave.

In this way the princess passed several months, and as her first terrors died away she gradually became more resigned to her fate. The little dog, too, was a great comfort, and her constant companion.

重点提示:将下划线译成汉语成语！斜体字表达出什么语义？请举例说明。

One day she noticed that he seemed very sad and did not even caress her as usual. Fearing he might be ill she carried him to a spot where she had seen him eat some particular herbs, hoping they might do him good, but he would not touch them. He spent all the night, too, sighing and groaning as if in great pain.

At last the princess fell asleep, and when she awoke her first thought was for her little pet, but not finding him at her feet as usual, she ran out of the cave to look for him. As she stepped out of the cave she caught sight of an old man, who hurried away so fast that she had barely time to see him before he disappeared.

重点提示:(从前面故事中)找词替换下划线！

This was a fresh surprise and almost as great a shock as the loss of her little dog, who had been so faithful to her ever since the first day she had seen him. She wondered if he had strayed away or if the old man had stolen him.

Tormented by all kinds of thoughts and fears she wandered on, when suddenly she felt herself wrapped in a thick cloud and carried through the air. She made no resistance and before very long found herself, to her great surprise, in an avenue leading to the palace in which she had been born. No sign of the cloud anywhere.

重点提示:下划线可删除且不改变原义,说明理由！

As the princess approached the palace she perceived that everyone was dressed in black, and she was filled with fear as to the cause of this mourning. She hastened on and was soon recognised and welcomed with shouts of joy. Her sister hearing the cheers ran out and embraced the wanderer, with tears of happiness, telling her that the shock of her disappearance had been so terrible that their mother had only survived it a few days. Since then the younger princess had worn the crown, which she now resigned to her sister to whom it by *right* belonged.

But the elder wished to refuse it, and would only accept the crown on condition that her sister should share in all the power.

The first acts of the new queen were to do honour to the memory of her dear mother and to shower every mark of generous affection on her sister. Then, being still very grieved at the loss of her little dog, she had a careful search made for him in every country, and when nothing could be heard of him she was so grieved that she offered half her kingdom to whoever should restore him to her.

重点提示:用凝练措辞处理下划线！猜猜斜体字部分的意思。

Many gentlemen of the court, tempted by the thought of such a reward, set off in all directions in search of the dog; but all returned empty-handed to the queen, who, in despair announced that since life was unbearable without her little dog, she would give her hand in marriage to the man who brought him back.

The prospect of such a prize quickly turned the court into a desert, nearly every courtier starting on the quest. Whilst they were away the queen was informed one day that a very ill-looking man wished to speak with her. She desired him to be shown into a room where she was sitting with her sister.

重点提示:第一处下划线是直译好还是意译好？第二处是"生病之人"吗？说说理由！替换第三处。

On entering her presence he said that he was prepared to give the queen her little dog if she on her side was ready to keep her word.

重点提示:下划线为何不用 meeting her 替代呢？

The princess was the first to speak. She said that the queen had no right to marry without the consent of the nation, and that on so important an occasion the general council must be summoned. The queen could not say anything against this statement; but she ordered an apartment in the palace to be given to the man, and desired the council to meet on the following day.

Next day, accordingly, the council assembled in great state, and by the princess's advice it was decided to offer the man a large sum of money for the dog, and *should he refuse it*, to banish him from the kingdom without seeing the queen again. The man refused the price offered and left the hall.

The princess informed the queen of what had passed, and the queen approved of all, but added that as she was her own mistress she had made up her mind to abdicate her throne, and to wander through the world till she had found her little dog. The princess was much alarmed by such a resolution, and implored the queen to change her mind.

重点提示:如何翻译下划线更妥？

Whilst they were discussing the subject, one of the chamberlains appeared to inform the queen that the bay was covered with ships. The two sisters ran to the balcony, and saw a large fleet in full sail for the port. In a little time they came to the conclusion that the ships must come from a friendly nation, as every vessel was decked with gay flags, streamers, and pennons, and the way was led by a small ship flying a great white flag of peace.

重点提示:能用两个汉字表达、翻译下划线吗？

The queen sent a special messenger to the harbour, and was soon informed that the fleet belonged to the Prince of the Emerald Isles, who *begged leave* to land in her kingdom, and to present his humble respects to her. The queen at once sent some of the court dignitaries to receive the prince and bid him welcome. She awaited him seated on her throne, but rose on his appearance, and went a few steps to meet him; then begged him to be seated, and for about an hour kept him in close conversation.

重点提示：查阅斜体字部分的用法；认真思考三处下划线之意，以免译文不伦不类！

The prince was then conducted to a splendid suite of apartments, and the next day he asked for a private audience. He was admitted to the queen's own sitting-room, where she was sitting alone with her sister.

重点提示：细品下划线！

After the first greetings the prince informed the queen that he had some very strange things to tell her, which she only would know to be true.

'Madam,' said he, 'I am a neighbour of the Queen of all the Isles; and a small isthmus connects part of my states with hers. One day, when hunting a stag, I had the misfortune to meet her, and not recognising her, I did not stop to salute her with all proper ceremony. You, Madam, know better than anyone how revengeful she is, and that she is also a mistress of magic. I learnt both facts to my cost. The ground opened under my feet, and I soon found myself in a far distant region transformed into a little dog, under which shape I had the honour to meet your Majesty. After six months, the queen's vengeance not being yet satisfied, she further changed me into a hideous old man, and in this form I was so afraid of being unpleasant in your eyes, Madam, that I hid myself in the depths of the woods, where I spent three months more. At the end of that time I was so fortunate as to meet a benevolent fairy who delivered me from the proud queen's power, and told me all your adventures and where to find you. I now come to offer you a heart which has been entirely yours, Madam, since first we met in the desert.'

重点提示：按常规方式翻译第一处下划线显然不当，怎么处理更妥？替换第二处！第三处也不易处理，务必小心以待！

A few days later a herald was sent through the kingdom to proclaim the joyful news of the marriage of the Queen of the Flowery Isles with the young prince. They lived happily for many years, and ruled their people well. As for the bad queen, whose vanity and jealousy had caused so much mischief, the Fairies took all her power away *for* a punishment.

重点提示：替换斜体字！

思考题：
本故事中哪几个词或词组与"国王、王后、王宫"等相关？明白这一点与翻译有多大的关联度？

6. The White Wolf

Once upon a time there was a king who had three daughters; they were all beautiful, but the youngest was *the fairest of the three*.

重点提示: 如何理解斜体字?

Now it happened that one day their father had to set out for a tour in a distant part of his kingdom. Before he left, his youngest daughter made him promise to bring her back *a wreath of wild flowers*. When the king was ready to return to his palace, he <u>bethought himself</u> that he would like to take home presents to each of his three daughters; so he went into a 's shop and bought a beautiful necklace for the eldest princess; then he went to a rich merchant jeweler's and bought a dress embroidered in gold and silver thread for the second princess, but in none of the flower shops nor in the market could he find the wreath of wild flowers that his youngest daughter had <u>set her heart on</u>. So he had to set out on his homeward way without it. Now his journey led him through a thick forest. While he was still about four miles distant from his palace, he noticed a white wolf squatting on the roadside, and, behold! On the head of the wolf, there was a wreath of wild flowers.

重点提示: 斜体部分一定得译成"野花做成的花环"吗? 请用当今的英语(单词)替换第一处下划线;请举例说明第二处的含义!

Then the king called to the coachman, and ordered him to get down from his seat and fetch him the wreath from the wolf's head. But the wolf heard the order and said: 'My lord and king, I will let you have the wreath, but I must have something in return.'

'What do you want?' <u>answered</u> the king. 'I will gladly give you rich treasure in exchange for it.'

重点提示: 下划线能译成"回答"吗?

'I do not want rich treasure,' replied the wolf. 'Only promise to give me the first thing that meets you on your way to your castle. In three days I shall come and fetch it.'

And the king thought to himself: 'I am still a *good* long way from home, I am sure to meet a wild animal or a bird on the road, it will be quite safe to promise.' So he consented, and carried the wreath away with him. But all along the road he met no living creature till he turned into the palace gates, where his youngest daughter was waiting to welcome him home.

重点提示: 下划线怎么译? 其中的斜体字起什么作用?

That evening the king was very sad, remembering his promise; and when he told the queen what had happened, she too shed bitter tears. And the youngest princess asked them why they both looked so sad, and why they wept. Then her father told her what a price he would have to pay for the wreath of wild flowers he had brought home to her, for in three days a white wolf would come and claim her and carry her away, and they would never see her again. But the queen thought and thought, and at last she <u>hit upon a plan</u>.

重点提示: 下划线是什么意思?

There was in the palace a servant maid *the same age* and the same height as the princess, and the queen dressed her up in a beautiful dress belonging to her daughter, and determined to give her to the white wolf, who would never know the difference.

On the third day the wolf *strode into the palace* yard and up the great stairs, to the room where the king and queen were seated.

重点提示:请思考下划线及斜体字的要义,并翻译!

'I have come to claim your promise,' he said. 'Give me your youngest daughter.'

重点提示:汉译下划线!

Then they led the servant maid up to him, and he said to her: 'You must mount on my back, and I will take you to my castle.' And with these words he swung her on to his back and left the palace.

When they reached the place where he had met the king and given him the wreath of wild flowers, he stopped, and told her to dismount that they might rest a little. So they sat down by the roadside.

'I wonder,' said the wolf, 'what your father would do if this forest belonged to him?'

And the girl answered: 'My father is a poor man, so he would cut down the trees, and saw them into planks, and he would sell the planks, and we should never be poor again; but would always have enough to eat.'

Then the wolf knew that he had not got the real princess, and he swung the servant-maid on to his back and carried her to the castle. And he strode angrily into the king's chamber, and spoke, 'Give me the real princess at once. If you deceive me again I will cause such a storm to burst over your palace that the walls will fall in, and you will all be buried in the ruins.'

重点提示:酌情处置下划线!

Then the king and the queen wept, but they saw there was no escape. So they sent for their youngest daughter, and the king said to her: 'Dearest child, you must go with the white wolf, for I promised you to him, and I must keep my word.'

So the princess got ready to leave her home; but first she went to her room to fetch her wreath of wild flowers, which she took with her. Then the white wolf swung her on his back and bore her away. But when they came to the place where he had rested with the servant-maid, he told her to dismount that they might rest for a little at the roadside. Then he turned to her and said: 'I wonder what your father would do if this forest belonged to him?'

重点提示:给出下划线的原级,并替换之!

And the princess answered: 'My father would cut down the trees and turn it into a beautiful park and gardens, and he and his courtiers would come and wander among the glades in the summer time.'

'This is the real princess,' said the wolf to himself. But aloud he said: 'Mount once more on my back, and I will bear you to my castle.' And when she was seated on his back he set out through the woods, and he ran, and ran, and ran, till at last he stopped in front of a stately courtyard, with massive gates.

'This is a beautiful castle,' said the princess, as the gates swung back and she stepped inside. 'If only I were not so far away from my father and my mother!'

But the wolf answered: 'At the end of a year we will pay a visit to your father and mother.' And at these words the white <u>furry skin</u> slipped from his back, and the princess saw that he was not a wolf at all, but a beautiful youth, tall and stately; and he gave her his hand, and led her up the castle stairs.

重点提示:查阅下划线的意思!

One day, at the end of half a year, he came into her room and said: 'My dear one, you must get ready for a wedding. Your eldest sister is going to be married, and I will take you to your father's palace. When the wedding is over, I shall come and fetch you home. I will whistle outside the gate, and when you hear me, pay no heed to what your father or mother say, leave your dancing and feasting, and come to me at once; for if I have to leave without you, you will never find your way back alone through the forests.'

When the princess was ready to start, she found that he had put on his white fur skin, and was changed back into the wolf; and he swung her on to his back, and set out with her to her father's palace, where he left her, while he himself returned home alone. But, in the evening, he went back to fetch her, and, standing outside the palace gate, he gave a long, loud whistle. In the midst of her dancing the princess heard the sound, and at once she went to him, and he swung her on his back and bore her away to his castle.

Again, at the end of half a year, the prince came into her room, *as the white wolf*, and said: 'Dear <u>heart</u>, you must prepare for the wedding of your second sister. I will take you to your father's palace today, and we will remain there together till tomorrow morning.'

重点提示:如何理解斜体字部分?替换并再现下划线的大意!

So they went together to the wedding. In the evening, when the two were alone together, he dropped his fur skin, and, ceasing to be a wolf, became a prince again. Now they did not know that the princess's mother was hidden in the room. When she saw the white skin lying on the floor, she crept out of the room, and sent a servant to fetch the skin and to burn it in the kitchen fire. The moment the flames touched the skin there was a fearful clap of thunder heard, and the prince disappeared out of the palace gate *in a whirlwind*, and returned to his palace alone.

But the princess was heart-broken, and spent the night weeping bitterly. Next morning she set out to find her way back to the castle, but she wandered through the woods and forests, and she could find no path or track to guide her. For fourteen days she roamed in the forest, sleeping under the trees, and living upon wild berries and roots, and at last she reached a little house. She opened the door and went in, and found the wind seated in the room all by himself, and she spoke to the wind and said: 'Wind, have you seen the white wolf?'

And the wind answered: 'All day and all night I have been blowing round the world, and I have only just come home; but I have not seen him.' But he gave her a pair of shoes, in which, he told her, she would be able to walk a hundred miles with every step.

Then she walked through the air till she reached a star, and she said: 'Tell me, star, have you seen the white wolf?'

And the star answered: 'I have been shining all night, and I have not seen him.' But the star gave her a pair of shoes, and told her that if she put them on she would be able to walk two hundred miles at a stride.

So she drew them on, and she walked to the moon, and she said: 'Dear moon, have you not seen the white wolf?'

重点提示:替换下划线！斜体字中的同义词使用有何目的？

But the moon answered, 'All night long I have been sailing through the heavens, and I have only just come home; but I did not see him.' But he gave her a pair of shoes, in which she would be able to cover four hundred miles with every stride.

So she went to the sun, and said: 'Dear sun, have you seen the white wolf?'

And the sun answered, 'Yes, I have seen him, and he has chosen another bride, for he thought you had left him, and would never return, and he is preparing for the wedding. But I will help you. Here are a pair of shoes. If you put these on you will be able to walk on glass or ice, and to climb the steepest places. And here is a spinning-wheel, with which you will be able to spin moss into silk. When you leave me you will reach a glass mountain. Put on the shoes that I have given you and with them you will be able to climb it quite easily. At the summit you will find the palace of the white wolf.'

重点提示:说说两处下划线的联系:若换掉其中一处,另一处会怎样呢？

Then the princess set out, and *before long* she reached the glass mountain, and at the summit she found the white wolf's palace, as the sun had said.

重点提示:斜体字是什么意思？交换位置会怎样？

But no one recognized her, as she had disguised herself as an old woman, and had *wound* a shawl round her head. Great preparations were going on in the palace for the wedding, which was to take place next day. Then the princess, still disguised as an old woman, took out her spinning-wheel, and began to spin moss into silk. And as she spun the new bride passed by, and seeing the moss turn into silk, she said to the old woman: 'Little mother, I wish you would give me that spinning-wheel.'

重点提示:斜体字的原级是什么？下划线怎么译更妥？

And the princess answered, 'I will give it to you if you will allow me to sleep tonight on the mat outside the prince's door.'

And the bride replied, 'Yes, you may sleep on the mat outside the door.'

So the princess gave her the spinning-wheel. And that night, winding the shawl all round her, so that no one could recognize her, she lay down on the mat outside the white wolf's door. And when everyone in the palace was asleep she began to tell the whole of her story. She told how she had been one of three sisters, and that she had been the youngest and the fairest of the three, and that her father had betrothed her to a white wolf. And she told how she had gone first to the wedding of one sister, and then with her husband to the wedding of the other sister, and how her mother had ordered the servant to throw the white fur skin into the kitchen fire. And then she told of her wanderings through the forest; and of how she had sought the white wolf weeping; and how the wind and star and moon and sun had befriended her, and had helped her to reach his palace.

And when the white wolf heard all the story, he knew that it was his first wife, who had sought him, and had found him, after such great dangers and difficulties. But he said nothing, for he waited till the next day, when many guests—kings and princes from <u>far countries</u> —were coming to his wedding. Then, when all the guests were assembled in the banqueting hall, he spoke to them and said: '<u>Hearken to me</u>, ye kings and princes, for I have something to tell you. I had lost the key of my treasure casket, so I ordered a new one to be made; but I have since found the old one. Now, which of *these* keys is the better?'

重点提示：三处下划线的用词均需思考！斜体字是否一定得译出来？

Then <u>all the kings and royal guests</u> answered: 'Certainly the old key is better than the new one.'

重点提示：如何处理下划线更好？

'Then,' said the wolf, 'if that is so, my former bride is better than my new one.'

And he sent for the new bride, and he <u>gave her in marriage to one of the princes who was present</u>, and then he turned to his guests, and said: 'And here is my former bride' — and the beautiful princess was led into the room and seated beside him on his throne. 'I thought she had forgotten me, and that she would never return. But she has sought me everywhere, and now we are together once more we shall never part again.'

重点提示：下划线如何措辞更恰当？

思考题：

综合前面故事的内容,列举几个与"结婚"相关的词汇(词或词组)。

7. The Simpleton

There lived, once upon a time, <u>a man who was as rich as he could be</u>; but as no happiness in this world is ever quite complete, he had an only son who was such a simpleton that he could barely *add two and two together*. At last his father determined to <u>put up with</u> his stupidity no longer, and giving him a purse full of gold, he sent him off to seek his fortune in foreign lands, mindful of the adage:

How much a fool that's sent to <u>roam</u>.
Excels a fool that stays at <u>home</u>.

重点提示：下划线中的第一处应注意译文的措辞；替换第二处；翻译第三、四处时，roam 和 home 的韵脚需努力再现；斜体字可直译否？

Moscione, for this was the youth's name, mounted a horse, and set out for Venice, hoping to find a ship there that would take him to Cairo. After he had ridden for some time he saw a man standing *at the foot of a poplar tree*, and said to him: 'What's your name, my friend; where do you come from, and what can you do?'

重点提示：用一个单词替换斜体字部分！

The man replied, 'My name is *Quick-as-Thought*, I come from *Fleet-town*, and <u>I can run like lightning</u>.'

重点提示：两处斜体字大有专有名词之意，需认真措辞；请翻译下划线！

'I should like to see you,' returned Moscione.

'Just wait a minute, then,' said Quick-as-Thought, 'and I will soon show you that I am speaking the truth.'

The words were *hardly* out of his mouth *when* a young doe ran right across the field they were standing in.

重点提示：留意斜体字部分的搭配（思考类似搭配）！

Quick-as-Thought let her run on a short distance, in order to give her a start, and then pursued her so quickly and so lightly that *you* could not have tracked his footsteps if the field had been strewn with flour. In a very few <u>springs</u> he had overtaken the doe, and had so impressed Moscione with his fleetness of foot that he begged Quick-as-Thought to go with him, promising at the same time to <u>reward him handsomely</u>.

重点提示：替换斜体字部分！恰当处理两处下划线！

Quick-as-Thought agreed to his proposal, and they continued on their journey together. They had hardly gone a mile when they met a young man, and Moscione stopped and asked him: 'what's your name, my friend; where do you come from, and what can you do?'

The man *thus addressed* answered promptly, 'I am called <u>Hare's-ear</u>, I come from <u>Curiosity Valley</u>, and if I lay my ear on the ground, <u>without moving from the spot</u>, I can hear everything that goes on in the world, the plots and intrigues of court and cottage, and all the plans of mice and men.'

重点提示：解释斜体字的成分及大意；琢磨三处下划线，并译成汉语！

'If that's the case,' replied Moscione, 'just tell me what's going on in my own home at present.'

The youth laid his ear to the ground and at once reported: 'An old man is saying to his wife, "Heaven be praised that we have got rid of Moscione, for perhaps, when he has been out in the world a little, he may gain some common sense, and return home less of a fool than when he set out."'

'*Enough, enough,*' cried Moscione. 'You speak the truth, and I believe you. Come with us, and *your fortune's made.*'

The young man consented; and after they had gone about ten miles, they met a third man, to whom Moscione said: 'what's your name, my brave fellow; where were you born, and what can you do?'

重点提示：如何恰当处置两处斜体字的口吻？

The man replied, 'I am called *Hit-the-Point*, I come from the city of *Perfect-aim*, and I draw my bow so exactly that I can shoot a pea off a stone.'

重点提示：两处斜体字部分应小心以对！

'I should like to see you do it, if you've no objection,' said Moscione.

The man at once placed a pea on a stone, and, drawing his bow, he shot it in the middle *with the greatest possible ease.*

重点提示：揣摩斜体字的表达法！

When Moscione saw that he had spoken the truth, he immediately asked Hit-the-Point to *join his party*. After they had all travelled together for some days, they *came upon* a number of people who were digging a trench in the blazing sun.

重点提示：恰当处理两处斜体字！

Moscione felt so sorry for them, that he said: 'My dear friends, how can you endure working so hard <u>in heat</u> that would cook an egg in a minute?'

重点提示：如何处理下划线？

But one of the workmen answered: 'We are <u>as fresh as daisies</u>, for we have a young man among us who *blows* on our backs *like the west wind.*'

重点提示：查阅词典关于下划线的比喻；请用一个动词替换斜体字部分！

'Let me see him,' said Moscione.

The youth was *called*, and Moscione asked him: 'what's your name; where do you come from, and what can you do?'

重点提示：替换斜体字！

He answered: 'I am called *Blow-Blast*, I come from *Wind-town*, and with my mouth I can make any winds you please. If you wish a west wind I can raise it for you in a second, but if you prefer a north wind I can blow these houses down *before your eyes.*'

重点提示：如何处置前两处斜体字中的专有名词？怎样理解第三处斜体字部分？

'Seeing is believing,' returned the cautious Moscione.

Blow-Blast at once began to convince him of the truth of his assertion. First he blew so softly that it seemed like the gentle breeze <u>at evening</u>, and then he turned round and raised such a mighty storm, that he blew down a whole row of oak trees.

重点提示：注意下划线的用法！

When Moscione saw this he was delighted, and begged Blow-Blast to join his *company*. And as they went on their way they met another man, whom Moscione addressed as usual：'what's your name：where do you come from, and what can you do？'

重点提示：替换斜体字（见前）！

'I am called *Strong-Back*；I come from *Power-borough*, and I possess such strength that I can take a mountain on my back, and it seems a feather to me.'

重点提示：品味并恰当再现两处斜体字中的专有名词！

'If that's the case,' said Moscione, 'you are a clever fellow；but I should <u>like</u> some proof of your strength.'

重点提示：如何处理下划线（能直译吗）？

Then Strong-Back loaded himself with great boulders of rock and trunks of trees, so that a hundred waggons could not have taken away all that he carried on his back.

When Moscione saw this he <u>prevailed on</u> Strong-Back to join his *troop*, and they all continued their journey till they came to a country called *Flower Vale*.

重点提示：恰当处理下划线；替换斜体字部分！第三处斜体字的汉译需把握分寸！

Here there reigned a king whose only daughter ran as quickly as the wind, and so lightly that she could *run over a field of young oats without bending a single blade*. The king had <u>given out a proclamation</u> that anyone who could <u>beat</u> the princess <u>in a race</u> should <u>have her for a wife</u>, but that <u>all who failed in the competition should lose their head</u>.

重点提示：本段惜墨如金，下划线和斜体字即为其精华部分，欲再现需仔细琢磨！

As soon as Moscione heard of the <u>Royal Proclamation</u>, he hastened to the king and <u>challenged the princess to race with him</u>. But on the morning appointed for the trial he <u>sent word to</u> the king that he was not feeling well, and that as he could not run himself he would <u>supply someone to take his place</u>.

重点提示：认真琢磨下划线的内容，再谨慎从译！

'It's just the same to me,' said Canetella, the princess,'let anyone come forward <u>that likes</u>, I am quite prepared to meet him.'

重点提示：请解释下划线部分的成分，同时在翻译兼顾公主的口气！

At the time appointed for the race the whole place was crowded with people *anxious to see the contest*, and, *punctual to the moment*, Quick-as-Thought, and Canetella dressed in a short skirt and *very lightly shod*, appeared at the starting-point.

重点提示：说说前两处斜体字的句子成分！后一处是什么意思？

Then a silver trumpet sounded, and the two rivals started on their race, looking <u>for all the world</u> like a greyhound chasing a hare. But Quick-as-Thought, true to his name, <u>outran</u> the princess, and when the *goal* was reached the people all clapped their hands and shouted, '*Long live* the stranger！'

重点提示:第一处下划线起什么作用？替换第二处；如何处理两处斜体字？

Canetella was much depressed by her defeat; but, as the race had to be run a second time, she determined she would not be beaten again. Accordingly she went home and sent Quick-as-Thought a magic ring, which prevented the person who wore it, not only from running, but even from walking, and begged that he would wear it *for her sake*.

重点提示:在不改变原意的基础上删除斜体字中的一个单词！

Early next morning the crowd assembled on the race-course, and Canetella and Quick-as-Thought began their trial afresh. The princess ran as quickly as ever, but poor Quick-as-Thought was like an overloaded donkey, and could not go a step.

Then Hit-the-Point, who had heard all about the princess's deception from Hare's-ear, when he saw the danger his friend was in, seized his bow and arrow and shot the stone out of the ring Quick-as-Thought was wearing. In a moment the youth's legs became free again, and in five *bounds* he had *overtaken* Canetella and won the race.

重点提示:替换两处斜体字！

The king was much disgusted when he saw that he must acknowledge Moscione as his future son-in-law, and summoned <u>the wise men of his court</u> to ask if there was no way out of the difficulty. <u>The council</u> at once decided that Canetella was far too dainty a morsel for the mouth of such a travelling tinker, and advised the king to offer Moscione a present of gold, which no doubt a beggar like him would *prefer to* all the wives in the world.

重点提示:如何处理第一处下划线？第二处指谁？如何恰当表达第三处？替换斜体字！

The king was delighted at this suggestion, and calling Moscione before him, he asked him *what sum of money* he would take instead of his promised bride.

重点提示:替换斜体字！

Moscione first <u>consulted *with*</u> his friends, and then answered: 'I demand as much gold and *precious stones* as my followers can carry away.'

重点提示:查看第一处下划线中斜体字的用法！翻译第二处斜体字！

The king thought he was <u>being let off very easily</u>, and produced coffers of gold, sacks of silver, and chests of precious stones; but the more Strong-Back was loaded with the treasure the straighter he stood.

重点提示:恰当处置下划线！

At last the treasury was quite exhausted, and the king had to send his courtiers to his subjects to collect all the gold and silver they possessed. But nothing was of any *avail*, and Strong-Back only asked for more.

重点提示:替换斜体字！

When the king's counsellors saw <u>the unexpected result of their advice</u>, they said it would be *more than* foolish to let some strolling thieves take so much treasure out of the country, and urged the king to send a troop of soldiers after them, to recover the gold and precious stones.

重点提示:如何处理下划线？替换斜体字！

So the king sent a <u>body</u> of armed men <u>on foot and horse</u>, to take back the treasure Strong-Back was carrying away with him.

重点提示:综合考虑两部分下划线内容,以确保译文更准确、简洁!

But Hare's-ear, who had heard what the counsellors had advised the king, told his companions just as the dust of their pursuers was visible on the horizon.

No sooner had Blow-Blast <u>taken in</u> their danger than he raised such a mighty wind that all the king's army was blown down like so many nine-pins, and as they were quite unable to get up again, Moscione and his companions proceeded on their way without further let or hindrance.

重点提示:细品并查阅词典,力保下划线的大意不变!

As soon as they reached his home, Moscione divided his spoil with his companions, at which they were much delighted. He, himself, stayed with his father, who was obliged at last to acknowledge that his son was not quite such a fool as he looked.

思考题:
说说故事中专有人名的翻译!

8. The Street Musicians

A man once possessed a donkey which had served him faithfully for many years, but at last the poor beast grew old and feeble, and every day his work became more of a burden. As he was no longer of any use, his master made up his mind to shoot him; but when the donkey learnt the fate that was in store for him, he determined not to die, but to run away to the nearest town and there to become a street musician.

重点提示:举例说明下划线的含义!

When he had trotted along for some distance he came upon a greyhound lying on the road, and panting for *dear* life. 'Well, brother,' said the donkey, 'what's the matter with you? You look rather tired.'

'So I am,' replied the dog, 'but because I am getting old and am growing weaker every day, and cannot go out hunting any longer, my master wanted to poison me; and, as life is still sweet, I have taken leave of him. But how I am to earn my own livelihood I haven't a notion.'

重点提示:替换下划线! 斜体线部分起什么作用? 可以删除吗?

'Well,' said the donkey, 'I am on my way to the nearest big town, where I mean to become a street musician. Why don't you take up music as a profession and come along with me? I'll play the flute and you can play the kettle-drum.'

The greyhound was quite pleased at the idea, and the two set off together. When they had gone a short distance they met a cat with a face as long as three rainy days. 'Now, what has happened to upset your happiness, friend puss?' inquired the donkey.

重点提示:试一试直译两处下划线!

'It's impossible to look cheerful when one feels depressed,' answered the cat. 'I am well up in years now, and have lost most of my teeth; *consequently* I prefer sitting in front of the fire to catching mice, and so my old mistress wanted to drown me. I have no wish to die yet, so I ran away from her; *but good advice is expensive*, and I don't know where I am to go to, or what I am to do.'

重点提示:恰当处理下划线;替换第一处斜体字! 说说第二处的真实含义。

'Come to the nearest big town with us,' said the donkey, 'and try your fortune as a street musician. I know what sweet music you make at night, so you are sure to be a success.'

重点提示:试着处理下划线!

The cat was delighted with the donkey's proposal, and they all continued their journey together. In a short time they came to the courtyard of an inn, where they found a cock crowing *lustily*. 'What in the world is *the matter* with you?' asked the donkey. 'The noise you are making is enough to break the drums of our ears.'

重点提示:替换两处斜体字;揣摩并恰当翻译下划线的含义!

'I am only prophesying good weather,' said the cock; 'for tomorrow is a feast day, and just because it is a holiday and a number of people are expected at the inn, the landlady has *given orders for my neck to be wrung* tonight, so that I may be made into soup for tomorrow's dinner.'

重点提示:斜体字怎样处理更简洁明了?

'I'll tell you what, redcap,' said the donkey,'you had much better come with us to the nearest town. You have got a good voice, and could join a street band we are getting up.' The cock was much pleased with the idea, and the party proceeded on their way.

重点提示:适当处理第一处下划线;替换第二处!

But the nearest big town was a long way off, and it took them more than a day to reach it. In the evening they came to a wood, and they made up their minds to go no further, but to spend the night there. The donkey and the greyhound lay down under a big tree, and the cat and the cock got up into the branches, the cock flying right up to the topmost twig, where he thought he would be safe from all danger. Before he went to sleep he looked round the four points of the compass, and saw a little spark burning in the distance. He called out to his companions that he was sure there must be a house not far off, for he could see a light shining.

重点提示:替换第一处下划线;如何处置第二处?

When he heard this, the donkey said at once:'Then we must get up, and go and look for the house, for this is very poor shelter.' And the greyhound added:'Yes? I feel I'd be all the better for a few bones and a scrap or two of meat.'

重点提示:恰当处置下划线!

So they set out for the spot where the light was to be seen *shining faintly in the distance*, but the nearer they approached it the brighter it grew, till at last they came to a brilliantly lighted house. The donkey being the biggest of *the party*, went to the window and looked in.

重点提示:如何再现两处斜体字的大意?

'Well, *greyhead*, what do you see?' asked the cock.

重点提示:斜体字的"洋味"当保留吗?

'I see a *well-covered* table,' replied the donkey, 'with excellent food and drink, and several robbers are sitting round it, enjoying themselves highly.'

重点提示:如何处置斜体字和下划线?

'I wish we were doing the same,' said the cock.

'So do I,' answered the donkey. 'Can't we think of *some* plan for *turning out* the robbers, and taking possession of the house ourselves?'

重点提示:替换两处斜体字!

So they consulted together what they were to do, and at last they arranged that the donkey should stand at the window with his fore-feet on the sill, that the greyhound should get on his back, the cat on the dog's shoulder, and the cock on the cat's head. When they had grouped themselves in this way, at a given signal, they all began their different forms of music. The donkey brayed, the greyhound barked, the cat miawed, and the cock crew. Then they all scrambled through the window into the room, breaking the glass into a thousand pieces as they did so.

重点提示:给出下划线中的象声词之音!

The robbers were all startled by the dreadful noise, and thinking that some evil spirits at the least were entering the house, they rushed out into the wood, their hair standing on end with terror.

The four companions, delighted with the success of their trick, sat down at the table, and ate and drank all the food and wine that the robbers had left behind them.

重点提示:如何处置两处下划线内容?

When they had finished their meal they put out the lights, and each animal chose a suitable sleeping-place. The donkey lay down in the courtyard outside the house, the dog behind the door, the cat in front of the fire, and the cock flew up on to a high shelf, and, as they were all tired after their long day, they soon went to sleep.

Shortly after midnight, when the robbers saw that no light was burning in the house and that all seemed quiet, the *captain of the band* said: 'We were fools to let ourselves be so easily frightened away,' and, turning to one of his men, he ordered him to go and see if all was safe.

重点提示:替换斜体字!

The man found everything in silence and darkness, and going into the kitchen he thought he had better strike a light. He took a match, and mistaking the fiery eyes of the cat for two glowing coals, he tried to light his match with them. But the cat didn't see the joke, and sprang at his face, spitting and scratching him in the most vigorous manner. The man was terrified out of his life, and tried to run out by the back door; but he stumbled over the greyhound, which bit him in the leg. Yelling with pain he ran across the courtyard only to receive a kick from the donkey's hind leg as he passed him. In the meantime the cock had been roused from his slumbers, and feeling very cheerful he called out, from the shelf where he was perched, 'Kikeriki!'

重点提示:细品并适当处理两处下划线。

Then the robber hastened back to his captain and said: 'Sir, there is a dreadful witch in the house, who spat at me and scratched my face with her long fingers; and before the door there stands a man with a long knife, who cut my leg severely. In the courtyard outside lies a black monster, who fell upon me with a huge wooden club; and that is not all, for, sitting on the roof, is a judge, who called out: "Bring the rascal to me." So I fled for dear life.'

重点提示:如何处置三处下划线为宜?

After this the robbers dared not venture into the house again, and they abandoned it for ever. But the four street musicians were so delighted with their lodgings that they determined to take up their abode in the robbers' house, and, *for all I know to the contrary*, they may be living there to this day.

重点提示:翻译下划线;思考斜体字的大意!

思考题:

本故事中有一个象声词,即"kikeriki",译者若遇上不见于词典的这类词该怎么办?

9. The Twin Brothers

Once there was a fisherman who had plenty of money but no children. One day an old woman came to his wife and said: 'What use is all your *prosperity* to you when you have no children?'

'*It is God's will*,' answered the fisherman's wife.

重点提示:两处斜体字部分怎么译好呢?

'*Nay*, my child, it is not God's will, but the fault of your husband; for if he would <u>but</u> catch the little gold-fish you would surely have children. Tonight, when he comes home, tell him he must go back and catch the little fish. He must then cut it in six pieces—one of these you must eat, and your husband the second, and soon after you will have two children. The third piece you must give to the dog, and she will have two puppies. The fourth piece give to the mare, and she will have two foals. The fifth piece bury on the right of the house door, and the sixth on the left, and two cypress trees will spring up there.'

重点提示:替换斜体字和下划线!

When the fisherman came home at evening his wife told him all that the old woman had advised, and he promised to bring home the little gold-fish. Next morning, therefore, he went very early to the water, and caught the little fish. Then they did as the old woman had ordered, and <u>in due time</u> the fisherman's wife had two sons, <u>so like each other that no one could tell the difference</u>. The dog had two puppies exactly <u>alike</u>, the mare had two foals, and on each side of the front door there sprang up two cypress trees precisely similar.

重点提示:请仔细琢磨几处下划线的措辞,且思考如何汉译更简洁到位!

When the two boys were grown up, they were not content to remain at home, though they had wealth in plenty; but they wished to go out into the world, and <u>make a name for themselves</u>. Their father would not allow them both to go at once, as they were the only children he had. He said: 'First one shall travel, and when he <u>is come back</u> then the other may go.'

重点提示:琢磨第一处下划线的含义;替换第二处!

So the one took his horse and his dog, and went, saying to his brother: 'So long as the cypress trees are green, that is a sign that I am <u>alive and well</u>; but if one begins to wither, then make haste and come to me.' So he <u>went forth into the world</u>.

重点提示:如何恰当处理并再现两处下划线的内容?

One day he <u>stopped at</u> the house of an old woman, and as at evening he sat before the door, he perceived in front of him a castle standing on a hill. He asked the old woman to whom it belonged, and her answer was: '<u>My son</u>, it is the castle of <u>the Fairest in the Land</u>!'

重点提示:仔细琢磨第一处下划线的含义;如何处理第二处?第三处的汉译兴许更费心思!

'And I <u>am come</u> here to <u>woo</u> her!'

重点提示:替换两处下划线(其中后者可在下文中找到)!

'*That*, my son, many have <u>sought</u> to do, and have lost their lives in the attempt; for she has cut off their heads and stuck them on the post you see standing there.'

重点提示:斜体字作什么成分用?替换下划线。

'And the same will she do to me, or else I shall be <u>victor</u>, for tomorrow I go there to court her.'

重点提示:下划线是什么成分?

Then he took his zither and <u>played upon it</u> so beautifully that no one in all that land had ever heard <u>the like</u>, and the princess herself came to the window to listen.

重点提示:注意第一处用法;替换第二处!

The next morning the Fairest in the Land sent for the old woman and asked her, 'Who is it that lives with you, and plays the zither so well?'

'It is a stranger, princess, who arrived yesterday evening,' answered the old woman.

And the princess then commanded that the stranger should be brought to her.

When he appeared before the princess she questioned him about his home and his family, <u>and about this and that</u>; and confessed at length that his zither-playing gave her great pleasure, and that she would take him for her husband. The stranger replied that it was with that intent he had come.

重点提示:如何恰当处置下划线?

The princess then said: 'You must now go to my father, and tell him you desire to have me to wife, and when he has put the three problems before you, then come back and tell me.' The stranger then went straight to the king, and told him that he wished to *wed* his daughter.

重点提示:替换斜体字!

And the king answered: 'I shall be well pleased, provided you can do what I impose upon you; if not you will lose your head. Now, listen; out there on the ground, there lies a <u>thick</u> log, which measures more than two fathoms; if you can <u>cleave</u> it in two with one stroke of your sword, I will give you my daughter to wife. If you fail, then it will cost you your head.'

重点提示:如何理解第一处下划线?举例说明;替换第二处。

Then the stranger <u>withdrew</u>, and returned to the house of the old woman *sore distressed*, for he could believe nothing but that next day he must atone to the king with his <u>head</u>. And so full was he of the idea of how to set about cleaving the log that he forgot even his zither.

重点提示:替换两处下划线。说说斜体字在句中作什么成分?

In the evening came the princess to the window to listen to his playing, and *behold* all was still. Then she called to him: 'Why are you so *cast down* this evening, that you do not play on your zither?' And he told her his trouble.

重点提示:替换两处斜体字(前者有误吗?后者可在前面找到)!

But she *laughed at* it, and called to him: 'And you grieve over that? Bring quickly your zither, and <u>play something for my amusement</u>, and early tomorrow come to me.'

重点提示:斜体字是"嘲笑"吗?下划线怎么处理才恰当呢?

Then the stranger took his zither and played the whole evening for <u>the amusement of</u> the princess.

重点提示:下划线有必要译出来吗?

Next morning she took a hair from her <u>locks</u> and gave it to him, saying: 'Take this hair, and wind it round your sword, then you will be able to cleave the log in two.'

重点提示：下划线是什么意思？

Then the stranger went forth, and <u>with one blow</u> cleft the log in two.

重点提示：如何处置下划线？

But the king said: 'I will impose another task upon you, before you can wed my daughter.'

'Speak on,' said the stranger.

'Listen, then,' answered the king, 'you must mount a horse and ride three miles at full gallop, holding in each hand a goblet full of water. If you spill no drop then I shall give <u>you my daughter</u> to wife, but *should you not succeed then I will take your life*.'

重点提示：下划线中的哪一部分是直接宾语？举例说明！说说斜体字部分的结构，并举例。

Then the stranger returned to the house of the old woman, and again he was so troubled as to forget his zither.

In the evening the princess came to the window as before to listen to the music, but again all was still; and she called to him: 'What is the matter *that you do not play on your zither*?'

重点提示：斜体字作什么成分用？

Then he related all that the king had ordered him to do, and the princess answered: '*Do not let yourself be disturbed*, only play now, and come to me tomorrow morning.'

重点提示：替换斜体字！

Then next morning he went to her, and she gave him her ring, saying: 'Throw this ring into the water and it will immediately freeze, so that you will not spill any.' The stranger did as the princess bade him, and carried the water all the way.

Then the king said: 'Now I will give you a third task, and this shall be the last. I have a negro who will fight with you tomorrow, and if you are the *conqueror* you shall wed my daughter.'

重点提示：替换斜体字！

The stranger returned, full of joy, to the house of the old woman, and that evening was so merry that the princess called to him: 'You seem very cheerful this evening; what has my father told you that makes you so glad?'

He answered: 'Your father has told me that tomorrow I must fight with his negro. He is only another man like myself, and I hope to *subdue* him, and to *gain the contest*.'

重点提示：替换两处斜体字！

But the princess answered: 'This is the hardest of all. I myself am the black man, for I swallow a drink that changes me into a negro <u>of unconquerable strength</u>. Go tomorrow morning to the market, buy twelve buffalo hides and wrap them round your horse; fasten this cloth round you, and when I am let loose upon you tomorrow show it to me, that I may hold myself back and may not kill you. Then when you fight me you must try to hit my horse between the eyes, for when you have killed it you have conquered me.'

重点提示：用汉语成语对译下划线！

Next morning, therefore, he went to the market and bought the twelve buffalo hides which he wrapped round his horse. Then he began to fight with the black man, and when the combat had already lasted a long time, and eleven hides were torn, then the stranger hit the negro's horse between the eyes, so that it fell dead, and the black man was defeated.

Then said the king: 'Because you have solved the three problems I take you for my son-in-law.'

But the stranger answered: 'I have some business to *conclude* first; in fourteen days I will return and bring the bride home.'

重点提示：替换斜体字!

So he arose and went into another country, where he came to a great town, and <u>alighted at</u> the house of an old woman. When he had had supper he begged of her some water to drink, but she answered: 'My son, I have no water; a giant has taken possession of the spring, and only lets us draw from it once a year, when we bring him a maiden. He eats her up, and then he lets us draw water; just now it is the lot of <u>the king's daughter</u>, and tomorrow she will be led forth.'

重点提示：替换两处下划线。

The next day accordingly the princess was led forth to the spring, and bound there with a golden chain. After that all the people went away <u>and she was left alone</u>.

重点提示：下划线一定得译出来吗？

When they had gone the stranger went to the maiden and asked her what *ailed* her <u>that</u> she lamented so much, and she answered that the reason was because the giant would come and eat her up. And the stranger promised that he would set her free if she would take him for her husband, and the princess joyfully consented.

重点提示：替换斜体字，且说说下划线的用法。

When the giant appeared the stranger <u>set his dog at him</u>, and <u>it took him by the throat and throttled him till he died</u>; so the princess was set free.

重点提示：如何处理两处下划线？

Now when the king heard of it he gladly consented to the marriage, and the wedding took place with great rejoicings. The young bridegroom abode in the palace *one hundred and one weeks*. Then he began to find it too dull, and he desired to go out hunting. The king would <u>fain</u> have prevented it, but in this he could not succeed. Then he begged his son-in-law at least to take sufficient <u>escort</u> with him, but this, too, the young man evaded, and took only his horse and his dog.

重点提示：斜体字当如何处置更妥？第一处下划线当如何翻译？请查实其意，并举例说明；替换第二处下划线。

He had ridden already a long way, when he saw in the distance a hut, and rode straight towards it in order to get some water to drink. There he found an old woman from whom he begged the water. She answered that first he should allow her to beat his dog with her little wand, that it might not bite her while she fetched the water. The hunter consented; and as soon as she had touched the dog with her wand it immediately turned to stone. Thereupon she touched the hunter and also his horse, and both turned to stone. As soon as that had happened, the cypress trees in front of <u>his father's house</u> began to wither. And when the other brother saw this, he immediately set out in search of his twin.

He came first to the town where his brother had slain the giant, and there fate led him to the same old woman where his brother had lodged. When she saw him she took him for his twin brother, and said to him: <u>'Do not take it amiss of me, my son, that I did not come to wish you joy on your marriage with the king's daughter.'</u>

重点提示：如何处理两处下划线？

The stranger perceived what mistake she had made, but only said: 'That does not matter, <u>old woman</u>,' and rode on, *without further speech*, to the king's palace, where the king and the princess both took him for his twin brother, and called out: '<u>Why have you tarried so long away?</u> We thought something evil had *befallen* you.'

重点提示：第一处下划线怎样译为宜？翻译第二处的用法！替换斜体字。

When night came and he slept with the princess, who still believed him to be her husband, he laid his sword between them, and when morning came he rose early and went out to hunt. Fate led him by the same way which his brother had taken, and from a distance he saw him and knew that he was turned to stone. Then he entered the hut and ordered the old woman to *disenchant* his brother. But she answered: 'Let me first touch your dog with my wand, and then I will free your brother.'

重点提示：替换斜体字！

He ordered the dog, however, to take hold of her, and bite her up to the knee, till she cried out: '<u>Tell your dog to let me go</u> and I will set your brother free!'

重点提示：替换下划线。

But he only answered: 'Tell me the magic words that I may disenchant him myself;' and as she would not he ordered his dog to bite her up to the hip.

Then the old woman cried out: 'I have two wands, with the green one I turn to stone, and with the red one I bring to life again.'

So the hunter took the red wand and disenchanted his brother, also his brother's horse, and his dog, and ordered his own dog to eat the old woman up altogether.

While the brothers went on their way back to the castle of the king, the one brother *related to* the other how the cypress tree had all at once dried up and withered, how he had immediately set out in search of his twin, and how he had come to the castle of his father-in-law, and had claimed the princess as his wife. But the other brother became furious on hearing this, and *smote* him over the forehead till he died, and returned alone to <u>the house of his father-in-law</u>.

重点提示：替换两处斜体字并指出前者的宾语；恰当翻译下划线！

When night came and he was in bed the princess asked him: 'What was the matter with you last night, that you never spoke a word to me?'

Then he cried out: 'That was not me, but my brother, and I have slain him, because he told me *by the way* that he had *claimed you for his wife*!'

重点提示：替换两处斜体字。

'Do you know the place where you slew him?' asked the princess, 'and can you find the body?'

'I know the place exactly.'

'Then tomorrow we shall ride thither,' said the princess. Next morning accordingly they set out together, and when they had come to the place, the princess drew forth a small bottle that she had brought with her, and sprinkled the body with some drops of the water so that immediately he became alive again.

When he stood up, his brother said to him: 'Forgive me, dear brother, that I slew you in my anger.' Then they embraced and went together to <u>the Fairest in the Land</u>, whom the unmarried brother took to wife.

重点提示：恰当处理下划线的内涵！

Then the brothers brought their parents to live with them, and all dwelt together in joy and happiness.

思考题：
兄弟姐妹之间怎么处为好？

10. Cannetella

There was once upon a time a king who <u>reigned over</u> a country called 'Bello Puojo'. He was very rich and powerful, and had everything in the world he could desire except a child. But at last, after he had been married for many years, and was quite an old man, his wife Renzolla <u>presented him with</u> a fine daughter, whom they called Cannetella.

重点提示：替换两处下划线！

She grew up into a beautiful girl, and was as <u>tall and straight</u> as a young fir-tree. When she was eighteen years old her father called her to him and said: 'You are of an age now, my daughter, to marry and settle down; but as I love you more than anything else in the world, and desire nothing but your happiness, I am determined to leave the choice of a husband to yourself. Choose a man *after your own heart*, and you are sure to satisfy me.' Cannetella thanked her father very much for his kindness and consideration, but told him that she had not the slightest wish to marry, and was quite determined to remain single.

重点提示：如何处理下划线的措辞？斜体字在句中起什么作用？

The king, who felt himself growing old and feeble, and longed to see <u>an heir to the throne</u> *before he died*, was very unhappy at her words, and begged her earnestly not to disappoint him.

重点提示：如何翻译下划线？斜体字如何措辞更精准？

When Cannetella saw that the king had <u>set his heart on her marriage</u>, she said: 'Very well, dear father, I will marry to please you, for I do not wish to appear ungrateful for all your love and kindness; but you must find me *a husband handsomer, cleverer, and more charming than anyone else in the world.*'

重点提示：推敲下划线的意思，并恰当行文！斜体字部分如何理解更简洁明了？

The king was overjoyed by her words, and from early in the morning till late at night he sat at the window and looked carefully at all the passers-by, *in the hopes of* finding a son-in-law among them.

One day, seeing a very good-looking man crossing the street, the king called his daughter and said: 'Come quickly, dear Cannetella, and look at this man, for I think he might suit you as a husband.'

They called the young man into the palace, and <u>set a sumptuous feast before him, with every sort of delicacy you can imagine</u>. In the middle of the meal the youth let an almond fall out of his mouth, which, however, he picked up again very quickly and hid under the table-cloth.

重点提示：删除斜体字部分的一个单词而不改其意。注意下划线的措辞，并考虑如何翻译为宜。

When the feast was over the stranger went away, and the king asked Cannetella: 'Well, what did you think of the youth?'

'I think he was a clumsy wretch,' replied Cannetella. 'Fancy a man of his age letting an almond fall out of his mouth!'

When the king heard her answer he returned to his watch at the window, and shortly afterwards a very handsome young man passed by. The king instantly called his daughter to come and see what she thought of the new comer.

'Call him in,' said Cannetella, 'that we may see him close.'

Another splendid feast was prepared, and when the stranger had eaten and drunk as much as he was able, and had taken his departure, the king asked Cannetella how she liked him.

'Not at all,' replied his daughter, 'what could you do with a man who requires at least two servants to help him on with his cloak, because he is too awkward to put it on properly himself?'

重点提示:恰当处置两处下划线内容!

'If that's all you have *against* him,' said the king, 'I see how the land lies. You are determined not to have a husband at all; but marry someone you shall, for I do not mean my name and house to die out.'

重点提示:查阅有关斜体字的意思!揣测下划线的含义!此外,努力再现国王的口吻!

'Well, then, my dear parent,' said Cannetella, 'I must tell you at once that you had better not count upon me, for I never mean to marry unless I can find a man with a gold head and gold teeth.'

重点提示:各下划线似乎表明了公主的脾气,如何传达这一口气?

The king was very angry at finding his daughter so obstinate; but as he always gave the girl her own way in everything, he issued a proclamation to the effect that any man with a gold head and gold teeth might come forward and claim the princess as his bride, and the kingdom of Bello Puojo as a wedding gift.

重点提示:仔细品味并翻译两处下划线!

Now the king had a deadly enemy called Scioravante, who was a very powerful magician. No sooner had this man heard of the proclamation than he summoned his attendant spirits and commanded them to gild his head and teeth. The spirits said, at first, that the task was beyond their powers, and suggested that a pair of golden horns attached to his forehead would both be easier to make and more comfortable to wear; but Scioravante would allow no compromise, and insisted on having a head and teeth made of the finest gold. When it was fixed on his shoulders he went for a stroll in front of the palace. And the king, seeing the very man he was in search of, called his daughter, and said: 'Just look out of the window, and you will find exactly what you want.'

重点提示:恰当处置三处下划线。

Then, as Scioravante was hurrying past, the king shouted out to him: 'Just stop a minute, brother, and don't be in such desperate haste. If you will step in here you shall have my daughter for a wife, and I will send attendants with her, and as many horses and servants as you wish.'

重点提示:如何翻译下划线更可取?

'A thousand thanks,' returned Scioravante; 'I shall be delighted to marry your daughter, but it is quite unnecessary to send anyone to accompany her. Give me a horse and I will carry off the princess in front of my saddle, and will bring her to my own kingdom, where there is no lack of courtiers or servants, or, indeed, of anything your daughter can desire.'

At first the king was very much against Cannetella's departing <u>in this fashion</u>; but finally Scioravante <u>got his way</u>, and placing the princess before him on his horse, he set out for his own country.

重点提示：替换两处下划线！

Towards evening he dismounted, and entering a stable he placed Cannetella in the same stall as his horse, and said to her: 'Now listen to what I have to say. I am going to my home now, and that is a seven years' journey from here; you must wait for me in this stable, and never move from the spot, or let yourself be seen by a living soul. If you disobey my commands, <u>it will be the worse for you</u>.'

重点提示：如何处理下划线更适合说话人的口吻？

The princess answered meekly: '<u>Sir, I am your servant</u>, and will do exactly as you bid me; but I should like to know what I am to live on till you come back?'

重点提示：如何再现下划线？

'You can take what the horses leave,' was Scioravante's reply.

When the magician had left her Cannetella felt very miserable, and <u>bitterly cursed the day she was born</u>. She spent all her time weeping and bemoaning the cruel fate that had driven her from a palace into a stable, <u>from soft down cushions to a bed of straw, and from the dainties of her father's table to the food that the horses left</u>.

重点提示：思考、琢磨下划线内容，以免行文累赘不堪！

She led this wretched life for a few months, and during that time she never saw who fed and watered the horses, for it was all done by invisible hands.

One day, when she was more than usually unhappy, she perceived a little crack in the wall, through which she could see a beautiful garden, with <u>all manner of</u> delicious fruits and flowers growing in it. *The sight and smell of such delicacies were too much for poor Cannetella*, and she said to herself, 'I will slip quietly out, and pick a few oranges and grapes, and I don't care what happens. Who is there to tell my husband what I do? And even if he should hear of my disobedience, *he cannot make my life more miserable than it is already*.'

重点提示：注意下划线的用法并替换；细心观察并翻译两处斜体字的内容！

So she slipped out and <u>refreshed her poor, starved body</u> with the fruit she plucked in the garden.

重点提示：恰当处理下划线！

But a short time afterwards her husband returned unexpectedly, and one of the horses instantly told him that Cannetella had gone into the garden, in his absence, and had stolen some oranges and grapes.

Scioravante was furious when he heard this, and seizing a huge knife from his pocket he threatened to kill his wife for her disobedience. But Cannetella threw herself at his feet and implored him to spare her life, saying that <u>hunger drove even the wolf from the wood</u>. At last she succeeded in so far softening her husband's heart that he said, 'I will forgive you this time, and spare your life; but if you disobey me again, and I hear, on my return, that you have as much as moved out of the stall, I will certainly kill you. So, beware, for I am going away once more, and shall be absent for seven years.'

重点提示:思考下划线来源(参考 keep the wolf from the door)。

With these words he took his departure, and Cannetella <u>burst into a flood of tears</u>, and, <u>wringing her hands</u>, she moaned: 'Why was I ever born to such a hard fate? Oh! Father, how miserable you have made your poor daughter! But, why should I blame my father? *For I have only myself to thank for all my sufferings*. I got the cursed head of gold, and it has brought all this misery on me. I am indeed punished for not doing as my father wished!'

重点提示:第一处下划线容易猜到,那第二处呢? 查阅词典,看 thank 一词的意思有什么"奥秘"?

When a year had gone by, it *chanced*, one day, that the king's cooper passed the stables where Cannetella was kept prisoner. She recognized the man, and called him to come in. At first he did not know the poor princess, and could not make out who it was *that called him by name*. But when he heard Cannetella's <u>tale of woe</u>, he hid her in a big empty barrel he had with him, partly because he was sorry for the poor girl, and, even more, because he wished to gain the king's favour. Then he slung the barrel on a mule's back, and in this way the princess was carried to her own home. They arrived at the palace about four o'clock in the morning, and the cooper knocked loudly at the door. When the servants came in haste and saw only the cooper standing at the gate, they were very indignant, and scolded him <u>soundly</u> for coming at such an hour and waking them all out of their sleep.

重点提示:替换第一处斜体字;说出第二处斜体字的成分;翻译两处下划线!

The king hearing the noise and the cause of it, sent for the cooper, for he felt certain the man must have some important business, to have come and disturbed the whole palace at such an early hour.

The cooper asked permission to unload his mule, and Cannetella crept out of the barrel. At first the king refused to believe that it was really his daughter, for she had changed so terribly in a few years, and had grown so thin and pale, that it was pitiful to see her. At last the princess showed her father a <u>mole</u> she had on her right arm, and then he saw that the poor girl was indeed his long-lost Cannetella. He kissed her <u>a thousand times</u>, and instantly had the choicest food and drink set before her.

重点提示:猜猜第一处下划线的大意;如何处置第二处更妥当、更可信?

After she had *satisfied her hunger*, the king said to her: 'Who would have thought, my dear daughter, to have found you in such a state? What, may I ask, has <u>brought you to this pass</u>?'

重点提示:替换斜体字;琢磨并恰当翻译下划线。

Cannetella replied: 'That wicked man with the gold head and teeth treated me worse than a dog, and *many a time*, since I left you, have I <u>longed</u> to die. But I couldn't tell you all that I have suffered, for you would never believe me. It is enough that I am once more with you, and I shall never leave you again, for I would rather be <u>a slave in your house than queen in any other</u>.'

重点提示:替换斜体字部分并举例说明;第一处下划线还有哪些用法? 翻译第二处!

In the meantime Scioravante had returned to the stables, and one of the horses told him that Cannetella had been taken away by a cooper in a barrel.

When the wicked magician heard this he was beside himself with rage, and, hastening to the kingdom of Bello Puojo, he went straight to an old woman who lived exactly opposite the royal palace, and said to her: 'If you *will* let me see the king's daughter, I will give you whatever reward you like to ask for.'

The woman demanded a hundred ducats of gold, and Scioravante counted them out of his purse and gave them to her without a murmur. Then the old woman led him to the roof of the house, where he could see Cannetella combing out her long hair in a room in the top story of the palace.

重点提示：说说此处斜体字的用法；如何恰当再现下划线之意？

The princess happened to look out of the window, and when she saw her husband gazing at her, she got such a fright that she flew downstairs to the king, and said: 'My lord and father, unless you shut me up instantly in a room with seven iron doors, I am lost.'

重点提示：翻译两处下划线。

'If that's all,' said the king, 'it shall be done at once.' And he gave orders for the doors to be closed on the spot.

When Scioravante saw this he returned to the old woman, and said: 'I will give you whatever you like if you will go into the palace, hide under the princess's bed, and slip this little piece of paper beneath her pillow, saying, as you do so: "May everyone in the palace, except the princess, fall into a sound sleep."'

The old woman demanded another hundred golden ducats, and then *proceeded* to carry out the magician's wishes. No sooner had she slipped the piece of paper under Cannetella's pillow, than all the people in the palace fell fast asleep, and only the princess remained awake.

重点提示：替换斜体字，并举例说明。

Then Scioravante hurried to the seven doors and opened them one after the other. Cannetella screamed with terror when she saw her husband, but no one came to her help, for all in the palace lay as if they were dead. The magician seized her in the bed on which she lay, and was going to carry her off with him, when the little piece of paper which the old woman had placed under her pillow fell on the floor.

In an instant all the people in the palace woke up, and as Cannetella was still screaming for help, they rushed to her rescue. They seized Scioravante and put him to death; so he was caught in the trap which he had laid for the princess—and, as is so often the case in this world, the biter himself was bit.

重点提示：下划线颇有谚语意味，译文似应如此再现！

思考题：
人似乎不应过于固执，说说其中些许原因（用英文）。

47

11. The Daughter of Buk Ettemsuch

Once upon a time there lived a man who had seven daughters. For a long time they dwelt quite happily at home together, then one morning the father called them all before him and said: 'Your mother and I are going on a journey, and as we do not know how long we may be away, you will find enough provisions in the house to *last* you three years. But *see* you do not open the door to anyone till we come home again.'

重点提示:替换两处斜体字,并举例说明!

'Very well, dear father,' replied the girls.

For two years they never left the house or unlocked the door; but one day, when they had washed their clothes, and were spreading them out on the roof to dry, the girls looked down into the street where people were walking <u>to and fro</u>, and across to the market, with its stalls of fresh meat, vegetables, and other nice things.

重点提示:用恰当的词组替换下划线!

'Come here,' cried one. 'It makes me quite hungry! Why should not we have our share? Let one of us go to the market, and buy meat and vegetables.'

'Oh, we mustn't do that!' said <u>the youngest</u>. 'You know our father *forbade us to open* the door till he came home again.'

重点提示:如何处理下划线? 替换斜体字!

Then the eldest sister *sprang at* her and struck her, the second *spit at* her, the third abused her, the fourth pushed her, the fifth *flung her to the ground*, and the sixth tore her clothes. Then they *left her lying on the floor*, and went out with a basket.

重点提示:细思斜体字部分的几个动作,考虑怎么译更恰当!

In about an hour they came back with the basket full of meat and vegetables, which they put in a pot, and set on the fire, quite forgetting that the house door <u>stood wide open</u>. The youngest sister, however, <u>took no part in</u> all this, and when dinner was ready and the table *laid*, she stole *softly* out to the entrance hall, and hid herself behind a great cask which stood in one corner.

重点提示:思考第一处下划线的意思(包括第一个单词的词性和第二个单词的成分);替换第二处;第一、二处斜体字是过去式还是过去分词? 请给出带原级的词组,并举例说明;第二处斜体字需要译出来吗?

<u>Now</u>, while the other sisters were enjoying their feast, a <u>witch</u> passed by, and catching sight of the open door, she walked in. She went up to the eldest girl, and said: 'Where shall I begin on you, you <u>fat bolster</u>?'

重点提示:思考第一处下划线是何意? 一定得翻译吗? 第二处怎么翻更恰当? 如何处理最后一处?

'You must begin,' answered she, 'with the hand which struck my little sister.'

So the witch gobbled her up, and when the last scrap had disappeared, she came to the second and asked: 'Where shall I begin on you, my fat bolster?'

And the second answered, 'You must begin on my mouth, which spat on my sister.'

And so on to the rest; and very soon the whole six had disappeared. And as the witch was eating <u>the last mouthful of</u> the last sister, the youngest, who had been crouching, frozen with horror, behind the barrel, ran out through the open door into the street. Without looking behind her, she hastened *on and on*, as fast as <u>her feet would carry her</u>, till she saw an ogre's castle standing in front of her. In a corner near the door she *spied* a large pot, and she crept softly up to it and pulled the cover over it, and went to sleep.

重点提示: 第一处下划线该如何处置？替换第二处下划线和斜体字。

By-and-by the ogre came home. '*Fee, Fo, Fum,*' cried he, 'I smell the smell of <u>a man</u>. What ill fate has brought <u>him</u> here?' And he looked through all the rooms, and found nobody. 'Where are you?' he called. 'Do not be afraid, I will do you no harm.' But the girl was still silent.

重点提示: 斜体字中的三个词似乎没什么意义，但总得译吧；两处似乎让人觉得妖怪"猜错"了，是吗？

'Come out, I tell you,' repeated the ogre. 'Your life is quite safe. If you are an old man, you shall be my father. If you are a boy, you shall be my son. If *your years are as many as mine*, you shall be my brother. If you are an old woman, you shall be my mother. If you are a young <u>one</u>, you shall be my daughter. If you are middle-aged, you shall be my wife. So come out, and fear nothing.' Then the maiden came out of her hiding-place, and stood before him.

重点提示: 替换斜体字和下划线。

'Fear nothing,' said the ogre again; and when he went away to hunt he left her to look after the house. In the evening he returned, bringing with him hares, partridges, and gazelles, for the girl's supper; for himself he only cared for the flesh of men, which she cooked for him. He also <u>gave into her charge</u> *the keys of six rooms*, but the key of the seventh he kept himself.

重点提示: 用一个单词替换下划线！说说斜体字在句中的成分！

And time passed on, and the girl and the ogre still lived together. She called him 'Father,' and he called her 'Daughter,' and never once did he speak roughly to her.

One day the maiden said to him, 'Father, give me the key of the upper chamber.'

'No, my daughter,' replied the ogre. 'There is nothing there that is any use to you.'

'But I want the key,' she *repeated again*.

However the ogre took no notice, and pretended not to hear. The girl began to cry, and said to herself: 'Tonight, when he thinks I am asleep, I will watch and see where he hides it;' and after she and the ogre had <u>supped</u>, she bade him good-night, and left the room. In a few minutes she stole quietly back, and <u>watched</u> from behind a curtain. In a little while she saw the ogre take the key from his pocket, and hide it in a hole in the ground before he went to bed. And <u>when all was still</u> she took out the key, and went back to the house.

重点提示: 删除斜体字部分的最后一词会怎么样？替换、翻译第一、二处下划线；第三处该如何处理呢？

The next *morning* the ogre *awoke with the first ray of light*, and the first thing he did was *to look*

49

for the key. It was gone, and he guessed at once what had become of it. But instead of getting into a great rage, *as most ogres would have done*, he said to himself, 'If I wake the maiden up I shall only frighten her. For today she shall keep the key, and when I return tonight it will be time enough to take it from her.' So he went off to hunt.

重点提示：前两处斜体字怎么处理更好？第三处可删除吗？替换下划线！

The moment he was *safe* out of the way, the girl ran upstairs and opened the door of the room, which was quite bare. The one window was closed, and she threw back the lattice and looked out. Beneath lay a garden which belonged to the prince, and in the garden was an ox, who was drawing up water from the well all by himself —for there was nobody to be seen anywhere. The ox raised his head at the noise the girl made in opening the lattice, and said to her, 'Good morning, O daughter of Buk Ettemsuch! Your father is feeding you up till you are nice and fat, and then he will put you on a spit and *cook* you.'

重点提示：第一处下划线是什么意思，其中斜体字说明什么？第二处下划线该怎么理解呢？第三处似乎不难；第四处能单独翻译吗？第五、六处需查词典，以免犯不少译者曾出过的错！最后一处斜体字是"煮"的意思吗？

These words so frightened the maiden that she burst into tears and ran out of the room. All day she wept, and when the ogre came home at night, no supper was ready for him.

重点提示：替换下划线！

'What are you crying for?' said he. 'Where is my supper, and is it you who have opened the upper chamber?'

'Yes, I opened it,' answered she.

'And what did the ox say to you?'

'He said, "Good morning, O daughter of Buk Ettemsuch. Your father is feeding you up till you are nice and fat, and then he will put you on a spit and cook you."'

'Well, tomorrow you can go to the window and say, "My father is feeding me up till I am nice and fat, but he does not mean to eat me. If I had one of your eyes I would use it for a mirror, and look at myself *before and behind*; and your girths should be loosened, and you should be blind—seven days and seven nights."'

重点提示：如何理解斜体字部分？

'All right,' replied the girl, and the next morning, when the ox spoke to her, she answered him as she had been told, and he fell down straight upon the ground, and lay there seven days and seven nights. But the flowers in the garden withered, for there was no one to water them.

When the prince came into his garden he found nothing but yellow stalks; in the midst of them the ox was lying. With a blow from his sword he killed the animal, and, turning to his attendants, he said, 'Go and fetch another ox!' And they brought in a great beast, and he drew the water *out of* the well, and the flowers revived, and the grass grew green again. Then the prince called his attendants and went away. The next morning the girl heard the noise of the waterwheel, and she opened the lattice and looked out of the window.

重点提示：替换斜体字！品味下划线各单词的第一个字母，并给出类似例证！

'Good morning, O daughter of Buk Ettemsuch!' said the new ox. 'Your father is feeding you up till you are nice and fat, and then he will put you on a spit and cook you.'

And the maiden answered: 'My father is feeding me up till I am nice and fat, but he does not mean to eat me. If I had one of your eyes I would use it for a mirror, and look at myself before and behind; and your girths should be loosened, and you should be blind—seven days and seven nights.'

Directly she uttered these words the ox fell to the ground and lay there, seven days and seven nights.

Then he arose and began to draw the water from the well. He had only turned the wheel once or twice, when the prince took *it* into his head to visit his garden and see how the new ox was *getting on*. When he entered the ox was working busily; but in spite of that the flowers and grass were dried up. And the prince drew his sword, and rushed at the ox to slay him, as he had done the other. But the ox fell on his knees and said: 'My lord, only spare my life, and let me tell you how it happened.'

重点提示:如何处理第一处下划线(其中斜体字指什么)？替换第二处斜体字！猜一猜第二处下划线的意思！

'How what happened?' asked the prince.

重点提示:思考下划线为什么有两个疑问词？

'My lord, a girl looked out of that window and spoke a few words to me, and I fell to the ground. For seven days and seven nights I lay there, unable to move. But, O my lord, it is not given to us twice to behold beauty such as hers.'

重点提示:如何恰当处理下划线？

'It is a lie,' said the prince. 'An ogre dwells there. Is it li'ely that he keeps a maiden in his upper chamber?'

'Why not?' replied the ox. 'But if you come here at dawn tomorrow, and hide behind that tree, you will see for yourself.'

'So I will,' said the prince; 'and if I find that you have not spoken truth, I will kill you.' The prince left the garden, and the ox went on with his work. Next morning the prince came early to the garden, and found the ox busy with the waterwheel.

'Has the girl appeared yet?' he asked.

'Not yet; but she will not be long. Hide yourself in the branches of that tree, and you will soon see her.'

重点提示:如何处理、表达下划线更妥帖？

The prince did as he was told, and scarcely was he seated when the maiden threw open the lattice.

'Good morning, O daughter of Buk Ettemsuch!' said the ox. 'Your father is feeding you up till you are nice and fat, and then he will put you on a spit and cook you.'

'My father is feeding me up till I am nice and fat, but he does not mean to eat me. If I had one of your eyes I would use it for a mirror, and look at myself before and behind; and your girths should be loosened, and you should be blind—seven days and seven nights.'

And hardly had she spoken when the ox fell on the ground, and the maiden shut the lattice and

51

went away. But the prince knew that what the ox had said was true, and that she had not her <u>equal</u> in the whole world. And he came down from the tree, *his heart burning with love*.

重点提示： 下划线一词很常见，请说说该词此处的意思和别的用法（借助词典）！斜体字部分属于什么结构？

'Why has the ogre not eaten her?' thought he. 'This night I will invite him to supper in my palace and question him about the maiden, and find out if she is his wife.'

So the prince ordered a great ox to be slain and <u>roasted whole</u>, and two huge tanks to be made, one filled with water and the other with wine. And towards evening he called his attendants and went to the ogre's house to wait in the courtyard till he came back from hunting. The ogre was surprised to see so many people assembled in front of his house; but he bowed politely and said, '*Good morning*, dear neighbours! <u>To what do I owe the pleasure of this visit? I have not offended you, I hope?</u>'

重点提示： 如何处理第一处下划线？斜体字（所指时间与实际时间不吻合！）说明什么？怎么处理？第二处下划线的汉语措辞难把握，试试看！

'Oh, certainly not!' answered the prince.

'Then,' continued the ogre, 'What has brought you to my house today for the first time?'

'We should like to have supper with you,' said the prince.

'Well, supper is ready, and you are welcome,' replied the ogre, leading the way into the house, for he had <u>had a good day</u>, and there was plenty of *game* in the bag over his shoulder.

重点提示： 根据上下文猜下划线的意思；斜体字指的是什么？查阅词典！

A table was quickly prepared, and the prince had already <u>taken his place</u>, when he suddenly exclaimed, 'After all, Buk Ettemsuch, suppose you come to supper with me?'

重点提示： 怎么处理下划线更妥？

'Where?' asked the ogre.

'In my house. I know it is all ready.'

'But it is so far off—why not stay here?'

'Oh, I will come another day; but this evening I must be your host.'

So the ogre accompanied the prince and his attendants back to the palace.

After a while the prince turned to the ogre and said: '<u>It is as a *wooer* that I appear before you</u>. I seek a wife from an honourable family.'

重点提示： 如何处理下划线中的强调句为妥？其中的斜体字是什么意思？

'But I have no daughter,' replied the ogre.

'Oh, yes you have, I saw her at the window.'

'Well, you can marry her if you wish,' said he.

So the prince's heart was glad as he and his attendants rode back with the ogre to his house. And as they parted, the prince said to his guest, 'You will not forget the <u>bargain we have made</u>?'

重点提示： 将下划线还原成词组，并举例说明！

'I am not <u>a young man</u>, and never break my promises,' said the ogre, and went in and shut the door.

重点提示： 下划线该怎么处理才合原文口吻？

Upstairs he found the maiden, waiting till he returned to have her supper, for she did not like eating by herself.

'I have had my supper,' said the ogre, 'for I have been spending the evening with the prince.'

'Where did you meet him?' asked the girl.

'Oh, we are neighbours, and grew up together, and tonight I promised that you should be his wife.'

'I don't want to be any man's wife,' answered she; but this was only pretence, for <u>her heart too was glad</u>.

重点提示：如何处理下划线更恰当一点？能直译吗？

Next morning early came the prince, bringing with him bridal gifts, and splendid wedding garments, to carry the maiden back to his palace.

But before he let her go the ogre called her to him, and said, 'Be careful, girl, never to speak to the prince; and when he speaks to you, you must be dumb, unless he swears "by the head of Buk Ettemsuch." Then you may speak.'

'Very well,' answered the girl.

They set out; and when they reached the palace, the prince led his bride to the room he had prepared for her, and said 'Speak to me, my wife,' but she was silent; and by-and-by he left her, thinking that perhaps she was shy. The next day the same thing happened, and the next. At last he said, 'Well, if you won't speak, I shall go and get another wife who will.' And he did.

Now when the new wife was brought to the palace the daughter of Buk Ettemsuch rose, and spoke to the ladies who had come to attend on the second bride. 'Go and sit down. I will make ready the feast.' And the ladies sat down as they were told, and waited.

The maiden sat down too, and called out, 'Come here, firewood,' and the firewood came. 'Come here, fire,' and the fire came and kindled the wood. 'Come here, pot.' 'Come here, oil;' and the pot and the oil came. 'Get into the pot, oil!' said she, and the oil did it. When the oil was boiling, the maiden dipped all her fingers in it, and they became ten fried fishes. 'Come here, oven,' she cried next, and the oven came. 'Fire, heat the oven.' And the fire heated it. When it was hot enough, the maiden jumped in, just as she was, with her beautiful silver and gold dress, and all her jewels. In a minute or two she had turned into a snow-white loaf, that made your mouth water.

Said the loaf to the ladies, 'You can eat now; do not stand so far off;' but they only stared at each other, speechless with surprise.

'What are you staring at?' asked the new bride.

'At all these wonders,' replied the ladies.

'Do you call these wonders?' said she scornfully; 'I can do that too,' and she jumped straight into the oven, and was burnt up in a moment.

Then they ran to the prince and said: 'Come quickly, your wife is dead!'

'Bury her, then!' returned he. 'But why did she do it? I am sure I said nothing to make her throw herself into the oven.'

<u>Accordingly</u> the burnt woman was buried, but the prince would not go to the funeral as all his

53

thoughts were still with the wife who would not speak to him. The next night he said to her, 'Dear wife, are you afraid that something dreadful will happen if you speak to me? If you still persist in being dumb, I shall be forced to get another wife.'

重点提示:替换下划线。

The poor girl longed to speak, but dread of the ogre kept her silent, and the prince did as he had said, and brought a fresh bride into the palace. And when she and her ladies were seated in state, the maiden planted a sharp stake in the ground, and sat herself down comfortably on it, and began to spin.

重点提示:如何翻译两处下划线更像汉语?

'What are you staring at so?' said the new bride to her ladies. 'Do you think that is anything wonderful? Why, I can do as much myself!'

'I am sure you can't,' said they, much too surprised to be polite.

Then the maid sprang off the stake and left the room, and instantly the new wife took her place. But the sharp stake *ran through*, and she was dead in a moment. So they sent to the prince and said, 'Come quickly, and bury your wife.'

重点提示:请翻译两处下划线;注意斜体字的"非"寻常用法!

'Bury her yourselves,' he answered. 'What did she do it for? It was not by my orders that she *impaled* herself *on* the stake.'

重点提示:举例说明斜体字的用法!

So they buried her; and in the evening the prince came to the daughter of Buk Ettemsuch, and said to her, 'Speak to me, or I shall have to take another wife.' But she was afraid to speak to him.

The following day the prince hid himself in the room and watched. And soon the maiden woke, and said to the pitcher and to the water-jug, 'Quick! Go down to the spring and bring me some water; I am thirsty.'

And they went. But as they were filling themselves at the spring, the water-jug knocked against the pitcher and broke off its spout. And the pitcher burst into tears, and ran to the maiden, and said: 'Mistress, beat the water-jug, for he has broken my spout!'

'By the head of Buk Ettemsuch, I implore you not to beat me!'

'Ah,' she replied, 'if only my husband had sworn by that oath, I could have spoken to him from the beginning, and he need never have taken another wife. But now he will never say it, and he will have to go on marrying fresh ones.'

重点提示:用两个汉字处理下划线。

And the prince, from his hiding-place, heard her words, and he jumped up and ran to her and said, 'By the head of Buk Ettemsuch, speak to me.'

So she spoke to him, and they lived happily to the end of their days, because the girl kept the promise she had made to the ogre.

思考题:

简要说说"守诚信"的意义和所需付出的代价。

12. Laughing Eye and Weeping Eye, or the Limping Fox

Once upon a time there lived a man whose right eye always smiled, and whose left eye always cried; and this man had three sons, two of them very clever, and the third very stupid. Now these three sons were very curious about the *peculiarity* of their father's eyes, and as they could not <u>puzzle out</u> the reason for themselves, they determined to ask their father why he did not have eyes like other people.

重点提示:替换斜体字和下划线!

So the eldest of the three went one day into his father's room and <u>put the question straight out</u>; but, instead of answering, the man <u>flew into a fearful rage</u>, and sprang at him with a knife. The young fellow ran away in a terrible fright, and <u>took refuge *with*</u> his brothers, who were awaiting anxiously the result of the interview.

重点提示:请留心三处下划线的含义,尤其是后者中斜体字的用法!

'You had better go yourselves,' was all the reply they got, 'and see if you will *fare* any better.'

重点提示:查看词典对斜体字的解释!

Upon hearing this, the second son entered his father's room, <u>only to be treated in the same manner as his brother</u>; and back he came telling the youngest, the fool of the family, that it was his turn to try his luck.

重点提示:斜体字是什么意思?请举例说明;下划线在句中起什么作用?

Then the youngest son <u>marched boldly up to</u> his father and said to him, 'My brothers would not let me know what answer you had given to their question. But now, do tell me why your right eye always laughs and your left eye always weeps.'

重点提示:如何传达下划线之意?

As before, the father <u>grew purple with fury</u>, and rushed forwards with his knife. But the simpleton did not <u>stir a step</u>; he knew that he had really nothing to fear from his father.

重点提示:再现下划线之意!

'Ah, now I see who is my *true son*,' exclaimed the old man; 'the others are <u>mere cowards</u>. And as you have shown me that you are brave, I will <u>satisfy your curiosity</u>. My right eye laughs because I am glad to have a son like you; my left eye weeps because a precious treasure has been stolen from me. I had in my garden <u>a vine that yielded</u> a *tun* of wine every hour— someone has *<u>managed to steal it</u>*, so I weep its loss.'

重点提示:琢磨第一、二处斜体字的口气和意思!替换第三处;思考并翻译三处下划线!

The simpleton returned to his brothers and told them of their father's loss, and they all made up their minds to set out at once in search of the vine. They travelled together till they came to <u>some cross roads</u>, and there they parted, the two elder ones taking one road, and the simpleton the other.

重点提示：如何理解下划线？

'Thank goodness we have got rid of that idiot,' exclaimed <u>the two elders</u>. 'Now let us have some breakfast.' And they sat down by the roadside and began to eat.

重点提示：留意下划线的用法！

They had only half finished, when a lame fox came out of a wood and begged them to give him something to eat. But they jumped up and chased him off with their sticks, and the poor fox limped away <u>on</u> his three <u>pads</u>. As he ran he reached the spot where the youngest son was getting out the food he had brought with him, and the fox asked him for *a crust of bread*. The simpleton had not very much for himself, but he gladly gave half of his meal to the hungry fox.

重点提示：说说两处下划线（即 on 和 pads）的用法！如何处理斜体字部分？

'Where are you going, brother?' said the fox, when he had finished his share of the bread; and the young man told him the story of his father and the wonderful vine.

'Dear me, *how lucky*!' said the fox. 'I know what has become of it. Follow me!' So they went on till they came to the gate of a large garden.

重点提示：斜体字一定是"走运"之意吗？有无别的解释？

'You will find here the vine that you are seeking, but it will not be at all easy to get it. You must listen carefully to what I am going to say. Before you reach the vine you will have to pass twelve outposts, <u>each consisting of two guards</u>. If you see these guards looking straight at you, go on without fear, for they are asleep. But if their eyes are shut then beware, for they are wide awake. If you once get to the vine, you will find two shovels, one of wood and the other of iron. Be sure not to take the iron one; it will make a noise and rouse the guards, and then you are lost.'

重点提示：如何翻译两处下划线更恰当？

The young man got *safely* through the garden *without any adventures* till he came to the vine which yielded a tun of wine an hour. But he thought he should find it impossible to dig the hard earth with only a wooden shovel, so he picked up the iron one instead. The noise it made soon awakened the guards. They seized the poor simpleton and carried him to their master.

重点提示：如何理解两处斜体字？

'Why do you try to steal my vine?' demanded he; 'and <u>how did you manage to get past the guards?</u>'

重点提示：如何再现下划线的真实含义？

'The vine is not yours; it belongs to my father, and if you will not give it to me now, I will return and get it somehow.'

'You shall have the vine if you will <u>bring</u> me in exchange an apple off the golden apple-tree that flowers every twenty-four hours, and bears fruit of gold.' <u>So saying</u>, he gave orders that the simpleton should be released, and <u>this done</u>, the youth hurried off to consult the fox.

重点提示：第一处下划线的直接宾语是什么？替换第二处。说说第三处是什么结构，举例说明。

'Now you see,' observed the fox, 'this comes of not following my advice. However, I will help you to get the golden apple. It grows in a garden that you will easily recognize from my description. Near the apple-tree are two poles, one of gold, the other of wood. Take the wooden pole, and

56

you will be able to reach the apple.'

重点提示:斜体部分是什么意思？请 paraphrase 下划线,并译出说话人的口气。

Master Simpleton listened carefully to all that was told him, and after crossing the garden, and escaping as before from the men who were watching it, soon arrived at the apple-tree. But he was so dazzled by the sight of the beautiful golden fruit, that he quite forgot all that the fox had said. He seized the golden pole, and struck the branch a *sounding* blow. The guards at once awoke, and conducted him to their master. Then the simpleton had to tell his story.

重点提示:替换斜体部分如何反映第一处下划线的幽默口吻！第二处怎么译才合原意呢？

'I will give you the golden apple,' said the owner of the garden, 'if you will bring me in exchange a horse which can go round the world *in four-and-twenty hours*.' And the young man departed, and went to find the fox.

This time the fox was really angry, and *no wonder*. 'If you had listened to me, you would have been home with your father by this time. However I am willing to help you once more. Go into the forest, and you will find the horse with two halters round his neck. One is of gold, the other of hemp. Lead him by the hempen halter, or else the horse will begin to neigh, and will waken the guards. Then all is over with you.'

重点提示:仔细思考第一处斜体部分的表达法,再琢磨第二处的措词;替换并翻译下划线部分！

So Master Simpleton searched till he found the horse, and was struck dumb at its beauty.

重点提示:说说下划线的意思,并举例说明！

'What!' he said to himself, 'put the hempen halter on an animal like that? Not I, indeed!'

重点提示:下划线是什么意思？

Then the horse neighed loudly; the guards seized our young friend and conducted him before their master.

重点提示:如何理解此处的下划线？

'I will give you the golden horse,' said he, 'if you will bring me in exchange a golden maiden who has never yet seen either sun or moon.'

'But if I am to bring you the golden maiden you must lend me first the golden steed with which to seek for her.'

'Ah,' replied the owner of the golden horse, 'but who will undertake that you will ever come back?'

重点提示:猜一猜下划线之意！

'I swear on the head of my father,' answered the young man, 'that I will bring back either the maiden or the horse.' And he went away to consult the fox.

Now, the fox who was always patient and charitable to other people's faults, led him to the entrance of a deep grotto, where stood a maiden all of gold, and beautiful as the day. He placed her on his horse and prepared to mount.

重点提示:翻译两处下划线,其中后者恐难直译！

'Are you not sorry,' said the fox, 'to give such a lovely maiden in exchange for a horse? Yet you are bound to do it, for you have sworn by the head of your father. But perhaps I could manage *to take her place.*' So saying, the fox transformed himself into another golden maiden, so like the first that hardly anyone could tell the difference between them.

The simpleton took her straight to the owner of the horse, who was *enchanted with* her.

And the young man got back his father's vine and married the real golden maiden into the bargain.

重点提示：替换两处斜体字。

思考题：

"fox"通常给人的印象是什么？本故事说明什么？用英语谚语表达你的观点。

13. Donkey Skin

<u>There was once upon a time</u> a *king* who was so much beloved by his *subjects* that he thought himself the happiest monarch in the whole world, and he had everything *his heart could desire*. His palace was filled with the rarest of curiosities, and his gardens with the sweetest flowers, while in the marble stalls of his stables stood a row of milk-white Arabs, with big brown eyes.

重点提示:如何替换第一处下划线而不改变原义？两处斜体字(king/subjects)是什么关系？第二处下划线在句中作什么成分？请用一个单词替换其中斜体字！

Strangers who had heard of the marvels which the king had collected, and made long journeys to see them, were, however, surprised to find the most splendid stall of all occupied by a donkey, with particularly large and drooping ears. It was a very fine donkey; but still, as far as they could tell, nothing *so very* remarkable as to account for the care with which it was lodged; and they went away wondering, for they could not know that every night, when it was asleep, bushels of gold pieces <u>tumbled out</u> of its ears, which were picked up each morning by the attendants.

重点提示:如何删除斜体字中的一个单词并保留原义？如何翻译再现下划线之意？

After many years of prosperity a sudden blow *fell upon* the king *in the death of his wife*, whom he loved dearly. But before she died, the queen, who had always thought first of his happiness, gathered all her strength, and said to him: 'Promise me one thing: you must marry again, I know, *for the good of* your people, as well as of yourself. But do not set about it in a hurry. Wait until you have found a woman more beautiful and better formed than myself.'

重点提示:替换几处斜体字。

'Oh, do not speak to me of marrying,' sobbed the king; 'rather let me die with you!' But the queen only smiled faintly, and turned over on her pillow and died.

For some months the king's grief was great; then gradually he began to forget a little, and, besides, his counsellors were always urging him to seek another wife. At first he refused to listen to them, but *by-and-by* he allowed himself to be persuaded to think of it, only stipulating that the bride should be more beautiful and attractive than <u>the late queen</u>, according to the promise he had made her.

重点提示:替换斜体字;如何翻译下划线部分？

Overjoyed at having obtained what they wanted, the counsellors sent envoys far and wide to get portraits of all the most famous beauties of every country. The artists were very busy and did their best, but, alas! Nobody could even pretend that any of the ladies could *compare for a moment with* the late queen.

重点提示:能猜出斜体字的大意吗？

At length, one day, when he had turned away *discouraged from a fresh collection of pictures*, the king's eyes fell on his adopted daughter, who had lived in the palace since she was a baby, and he saw that, if a woman existed *on the whole earth* more lovely than the queen, *this was she*! He at once made known what his wishes were, but the young girl, who was not at all ambitious, and had not the faintest desire to marry him, was filled with dismay, and begged for time to think about it. That night, when everyone was asleep, she started in a little car drawn by a big sheep, and went to consult her fairy godmother.

重点提示：请思考并翻译本段中的三处斜体字！替换下划线。

'I know what you have come to tell me,' said the fairy, when the maiden stepped out of the car; 'and if you don't wish to marry him, I will show you how to avoid it. Ask him to give you <u>a dress that exactly matches the sky</u>. It will be impossible for him to get one, so you will be quite safe.' The girl thanked the fairy and returned home again.

重点提示：下划线部分怎么译（参见下一段第二行斜体字）？

The next morning, when her father (as she had always called him) came to see her, she told him that she could give him no answer until he had presented her with *a dress the colour of the sky*. The king, overjoyed at this answer, sent for all the choicest weavers and dressmakers in the kingdom, and commanded them to make a robe the colour of the sky without an instant's delay, or he would cut off their heads at once. Dreadfully frightened at this threat, they all began to dye and cut and sew, and in two days they brought back the dress, which looked as if it had been cut straight out of the heavens! The poor girl was thunderstruck, and did not know what to do; so in the night she harnessed her sheep again, and went in search of her godmother.

重点提示：翻译斜体部分，并说出其作用？请在本段找出 dress 的同义词！

'The king is cleverer than I thought,' said the fairy; 'but tell him you must have a dress of moonbeams.'

And the next day, when the king *summoned her into his presence*, the girl told him what she wanted.

重点提示：如何翻译斜体部分？（提示：两个汉字）

'*Madam, I can refuse you nothing*,' said he; and he ordered the dress to be ready in twenty-four hours, or every man should be hanged.

重点提示：翻译斜体字请注意其措辞（尤其是 Madam 的称呼）！

They set to work with all their might, and by dawn next day, the dress of moonbeams was laid across her bed. The girl, though she could not help admiring its beauty, began to cry, till the fairy, who heard her, came to her help.

'Well, <u>I could not have believed it of him</u>!' said she; 'but ask for a dress of sunshine, and I shall be surprised indeed if he manages that!'

重点提示：如何再现下划线之惊讶意味？

The goddaughter did not feel much faith in the fairy after her two previous failures; but not knowing what else to do, she told her father what she was bid.

The king made no difficulties about it, and even gave his finest rubies and diamonds to <u>ornament</u> the dress, which was so dazzling, when finished, that it could not be looked at <u>save</u> through smoked glasses!

重点提示：请 paraphrase 斜体部分！揣摩并替换两处下划线！

When the princess saw it, she pretended that the sight hurt her eyes, and *retired* to her room, where she found the fairy *awaiting* her, very much ashamed of herself.

重点提示:替换两处斜体部分,并说明下划线在句中的成分!

'There is only one thing to be done now,' cried she, 'you must demand the skin of the ass he *sets such store by*. It is from that donkey he obtains all his vast riches, and I am sure he will never give it to you.'

重点提示:查词典,找到斜体部分的确切意思(另请注意该部分中三个带s字母的单词)!

The princess was not so certain; however, she went to the king, and told him she could never marry him till he had given her the ass's skin. The king was both astonished and grieved at this new request, but did not hesitate an instant. The ass was *sacrificed*, and the skin *laid* at the feet of the princess.

重点提示:请替换两处斜体字!

The poor girl, seeing no escape from the fate she dreaded, wept *afresh*, and tore her hair; when, suddenly, the fairy stood before her.

重点提示:替换斜体部分。

'*Take heart*,' she said, 'all will now go well! Wrap yourself in this skin, and leave the palace and go as far as you can. I will look after you. Your dresses and your jewels shall follow you underground, and if you strike the earth whenever you need anything, you will have it at once. But go quickly: you have no time to lose.'

重点提示:斜体部分是什么意思?是正译好,还是反译好?

So the princess *clothed* herself in the ass's skin, and slipped from the palace *without being seen by anyone*.

重点提示:请各用一个单词替换两处斜体字!

Directly she was *missed* there was *a great hue and cry*, and every corner, possible and impossible, was searched. Then the king sent out parties along all the roads, but the fairy threw her invisible mantle over the girl when they approached, and none of them could see her.

重点提示:三处斜体部分的意思都能看明白吗?请举例说明!思考并处理下划线部分。

The princess walked on a long, long way, trying to find some one who would take her in, and let her work for them; but though the cottagers, whose houses she passed, gave her food from charity, the ass's skin was so dirty they would not allow her to enter their houses. For her flight had been so hurried she had had no time to clean it.

重点提示:斜体部分是什么意思(不妨借助全句内容琢磨)?请替换之!请仔细判别并翻译下划线。

Tired and disheartened at her ill fortune, she was wandering, one day, past the gate of a farmyard, situated just outside the walls of a large town, when she heard a voice calling to her. She turned and saw the farmer's wife standing among her turkeys, and making signs to her to come in.

重点提示:请用两个汉字代替下划线。

'I want a girl to wash the dishes and feed the turkeys, and clean out the pig-sty,' said the women, 'and, to judge by your dirty clothes, *you would not be too fine for the work.*'

重点提示:请找出本段中的一处拼写错误!同时翻译斜体部分。

The girl accepted her offer with joy, and she was at once set to work in a corner of the kitchen,

61

where all the farm servants came and made fun of her, and the ass's skin in which she was wrapped. But by-and-by they got so used to the sight of it that it ceased to amuse them, and she worked so hard and so well, that her mistress grew quite fond of her. And she was so clever at keeping sheep and herding turkeys that *you* would have thought she had done nothing else during her whole life!

重点提示:翻译时如何把握斜体字的处理?

One day she was sitting on the *banks* of a stream bewailing her wretched lot, when she suddenly caught sight of herself in the water. Her hair and part of her face was quite concealed by the ass's head, which was drawn right over like a hood, and the filthy matted skin covered her whole body. It was the first time she had seen herself as other people saw her, and she was filled with shame at the spectacle. Then she threw off her disguise and jumped into the water, plunging in again and again, till she shone like ivory. When it was time to go back to the farm, she was forced to put on the skin which disguised her, and now seemed more dirty than ever; but, as she did so, she comforted herself with the thought that tomorrow was a holiday, and that she would be able for a few hours to forget that she was a farm girl, and be a princess once more.

重点提示:按常规理解,斜体部分似乎不恰当,为什么? 替换下划线。

So, at break of day, she stamped on the ground, as the fairy had told her, and instantly the dress like the sky lay across her tiny bed. Her room was so small that there was no place for the *train* of her dress to spread itself out, but she pinned it up carefully when she combed her beautiful hair and piled it up on the top of her head, as she had always worn it. When she had done, she was so pleased with herself that she determined never to let a chance *pass* of putting on her splendid clothes, even if she had to wear them in the fields, with no one to admire her but the sheep and turkeys.

重点提示:斜体字 train 如何翻译? pass 是什么词性? 下划线在句中起什么作用?

Now the farm was a *royal farm*, and, one holiday, when 'Donkey Skin' (as they had nicknamed the princess) had locked the door of her room and clothed herself *in her dress of sunshine*, *the king's son* rode through the gate, and asked if he might come and rest himself a little after hunting. Some food and milk were set before him in the garden, and when he *felt rested* he got up, and began to explore the house, which was *famous throughout the whole kingdom for its age and beauty*. He opened one door after the other, admiring the old rooms, when he came to a handle that would not turn. He stooped and peeped through the keyhole to see what was inside, and was greatly astonished at beholding a beautiful girl, *clad* in a dress so dazzling that he could hardly look at it.

重点提示:尝试将各斜体部分处理成相应的汉语! 思考下划线部分的措词是否恰当。

The dark gallery seemed darker than ever as he turned away, but he went back to the kitchen and inquired who slept in the room at the end of the passage. *The scullery maid*, *they told him*, *whom everybody laughed at*, *and called* '*Donkey Skin*'; and though he perceived there was some strange mystery about this, he saw quite clearly there was nothing to be gained by asking any more questions. So he rode back to the palace, his head filled with the vision he had seen through the keyhole.

重点提示:理清斜体字部分的语法关系,并恰当翻译出来。

All night long he tossed about, and awoke the next morning in a high fever. The queen, who had no other child, and lived in a state of perpetual anxiety about this one, at once gave him up for lost, and indeed his sudden illness puzzled the greatest doctors, who tried the usual remedies in vain. At last they told the queen that some secret sorrow must be at the bottom of all this, and she threw herself on her knees beside her son's bed, and implored him to confide his trouble to her. If it was ambition to be king, his father would gladly resign the cares of the crown, and suffer him to reign in his stead; or, if it was love, everything should be sacrificed to get for him the wife he desired, even if she were daughter of a king with whom the country was at war at present!

重点提示：本段中值得留意的语言点（即下划线）较多，请用较为得体的汉语翻译之！

'Madam,' replied the prince, whose weakness would hardly allow him to speak, 'do not think me so unnatural as to wish to deprive my father of his crown. As long as he lives I shall remain the most faithful of his subjects! And as to the princesses you speak of, I have seen none that I should care for as a wife, though I would always obey your wishes, whatever it might cost me.'

重点提示：如何处理各处下划线更适合王子的身份？

'Ah! My son,' cried she, 'we will do anything in the world to save your life— and *ours too*, for if you die, we shall die also.'

重点提示：能理清斜体字的逻辑关系吗？

'Well, then,' replied the prince, 'I will tell you the only thing that will cure me — a cake made by the hand of "Donkey Skin."'

'Donkey Skin?' exclaimed the queen, who thought her son had gone mad; 'And who or what is that?'

'*Madam*,' answered one of the attendants present, who had been with the prince at the farm, '"Donkey Skin" is, *next to* the wolf, the most disgusting creature on the face of the earth. She is a girl who wears a black, greasy skin, and lives at your farmer's as hen-wife.'

重点提示：分别替换两处斜体字；翻译下划线！

'Never mind,' said the queen; 'my son seems to have eaten some of her pastry. It is the whim of a sick man, no doubt; but send at once and let her bake a cake.'

The attendant bowed and ordered a page to ride with the message.

Now it is by no means certain that 'Donkey Skin' had not caught a glimpse of the prince, either when his eyes looked through the keyhole, or else from her little window, which was over the road. But whether she had actually seen him or only heard him spoken of, directly she received the queen's command, she flung off the dirty skin, washed herself from head to foot, and put on a skirt and bodice of shining silver. Then, locking herself into her room, she took the richest cream, the finest flour, and the freshest eggs on the farm, and set about making her cake.

重点提示：用一个单词替换下划线处。

As she was stirring the mixture in the saucepan a ring that she sometimes wore in secret slipped from her finger and fell into the dough. Perhaps 'Donkey Skin' saw it, or perhaps she did not; but, any way, she went on stirring, and soon the cake was ready to be put in the oven. When it was nice and brown she took off her dress and put on her dirty skin, and gave the cake to the page, asking at the same time for news of the prince. But the page turned his head aside, and would not even *condescend* to answer.

重点提示:如何理解下划线词组？再举一例说明！斜体部分的真实意思是什么？

The page rode like the wind, and as soon as he arrived at the palace he snatched up a silver tray and hastened to present the cake to the prince. The sick man began to eat it so fast that the doctors thought he would choke; and, indeed, he very nearly *did*, for the ring was in one of the bits which he broke off, though he managed to extract it from his mouth without anyone seeing him.

重点提示:替换下划线！斜体字指的是什么？

The moment the prince was left alone he drew the ring from under his pillow and kissed it a thousand times. Then he set his mind to find how he was to see the owner— for even he did not dare to confess that he had only beheld 'Donkey Skin' through a keyhole, lest they should laugh at this sudden passion. All this worry brought back the fever, which the arrival of the cake had diminished for the time; and the doctors, not knowing what else to say, informed the queen that her son was simply *dying of love*. The queen, stricken with horror, rushed into the king's presence with the news, and together they hastened to their son's bedside.

'My boy, my dear boy!' cried the king, 'who is it you want to marry? We will give her to you for a bride; even if she is the humblest of our slaves. What is there in the whole world that we would not do for you?'

The prince, moved to tears at these words, drew the ring, which was an emerald of the purest water, from under his pillow.

重点提示:斜体部分的真实含义是什么？查词典以确定下划线的含义。

'Ah, dear father and mother, let this be a proof that she whom I love is no peasant girl. The finger which that ring fits has never been thickened by hard work. But be her condition what it may, I will marry no other.'

重点提示:斜体字和下划线分别是什么意思？请翻译。

The king and queen examined the tiny ring very closely, and agreed, with their son, that the wearer could be no mere farm girl. Then the king went out and ordered heralds and trumpeters to go through the town, summoning every maiden to the palace. And she whom the ring fitted would some day be queen.

重点提示:请恰当汉译下划线。

First came all the princesses, then all the duchesses' daughters, and so on, in proper order. But not one of them could slip the ring over the tip of her finger, to the great joy of the prince, whom excitement was fast curing. At last, when the high-born damsels had failed, the shopgirls and chambermaids took their turn, but with no better fortune.

重点提示:下划线部分在句中起什么作用？

'Call in the scullions and shepherdesses,' commanded the prince; but the sight of their fat, red fingers satisfied everybody.

重点提示:如何翻译下划线部分更妥帖？

'There is not a woman left, your Highness,' said the chamberlain; but the prince waved him aside.

'Have you sent for "Donkey Skin," who made me the cake?' asked he, and the courtiers began to laugh, and replied that they would not have dared to introduce so dirty a creature into the palace.

'Let someone go for her at once,' ordered the king. 'I commanded the presence of every maiden, high or low, and I meant it.'

重点提示:请查阅词典并恰当翻译下划线部分。

The princess had heard the trumpets and the proclamations, and knew quite well that her ring was at the bottom of it all. She, too, had fallen in love with the prince in the brief glimpse she had had of him, and trembled with fear lest someone else's finger might be as small as her own. When, therefore, the messenger from the palace rode up to the gate, she was nearly beside herself with delight. Hoping all the time for such a summons, she had dressed herself with great care, putting on the garment of moonlight, whose skirt was scattered over with emeralds. But when they began calling to her to come down, she hastily covered herself with her donkey-skin and announced she was ready to present herself before his Highness. She was taken straight into the hall, where the prince was awaiting her, but at the sight of the donkey-skin his heart sank. Had he been mistaken after all?

重点提示:请斟酌并翻译各下划线部分。

'Are you the girl,' he said, turning his eyes away as he spoke, 'are you the girl who has a room in the *furthest* corner of the inner court of the farmhouse?'

重点提示:替换斜体字!

'Hold out your hand then,' continued the prince, feeling that he must keep his word, whatever the cost, and, to the astonishment of every one present, a little hand, white and delicate, came from beneath the black and dirty skin. The ring slipped on with the *utmost* ease, and, as it did so, the skin fell to the ground, disclosing a figure of such beauty that the prince, *weak as he was*, fell on his knees before her, while the king and queen joined their prayers to his. Indeed, their welcome was so warm, and their caresses so bewildering, that the princess hardly knew how to find words to reply, when the ceiling of the hall opened, and the fairy godmother appeared, seated in a car made entirely of white lilac. In a few words she explained the history of the princess, and how she came to be there, and, without losing a moment, preparations of the most magnificent kind were made for the wedding.

The kings of every country in the earth were invited, including, of course, the princess's adopted father (who by this time had married a widow), and not one refused.

重点提示:替换下划线和斜体部分。

But what a strange assembly it was! Each monarch travelled in the way he thought most impressive; and some came borne in litters, others had carriages of every shape and kind, while the rest were *mounted* on elephants, tigers, and even upon eagles. So splendid a wedding had never been seen before; and when it was over the king announced that it was to be followed by a coronation, for he and the queen were tired of reigning, and the young couple must take their place.

重点提示:举例说明下划线的用法;替换斜体字。

The rejoicings lasted for three *whole* months, then the new sovereigns settled down to govern their kingdom, and made themselves so much beloved by their subjects, that when they died, a hundred years later, each man mourned them as his own father and mother.

重点提示：替换斜体字；下划线指谁？

思考题：
以本故事中的"Donkey Skin"的经历为例，表达你对"物质女"与"真爱女"的看法。

14. A Fairy's Blunder

Once upon a time there lived a fairy whose name was Dindonette. She was the best creature in the world, with the kindest heart; but she had not much sense, and was always doing things, to benefit people, which generally ended in causing pain and distress to everybody <u>concerned</u>. No one knew this better than the inhabitants of an island far off in the midst of the sea, which, according to the laws of fairyland, she had *taken under her special protection*, thinking day and night of what she could do to make the isle *the pleasantest place* in the whole world, as it was the most beautiful.

重点提示:说说第一处下划线与前面单词的关系;还原第一处斜体字的词组,并举例说明;替换第二处!

Now what happened was this: As the fairy went about, *unseen*, from house to house, she heard everywhere children longing for the time when they would be 'grown-up,' and able, they thought, to do as they liked; and old people talking about the past, and sighing to be young again.

重点提示:说明斜体字的成分!

'Is there no way of satisfying *these poor things*?' she thought. And then one night an idea occurred to her. 'Oh, yes, of course! It has been tried before; but I will manage better than the rest, <u>with</u> their old Fountain of Youth, which, after all, only <u>made people young again</u>. I will enchant the spring that bubbles up in the middle of the orchard, and the children that drink *of* it shall at once <u>become grown men and women</u>, and the old people return to the days of their childhood.'

重点提示:思考第一、二处下划线之间的关系;如何翻译第三处下划线更恰当? 说说两处斜体部分的真实意思。

And without stopping to consult one single other fairy, who might have given her good advice, <u>off rushed Dindonette</u>, to <u>cast her spell over the fountain</u>.

重点提示:留意两处下划线的用法。

It was the only spring of fresh water in the island, and at dawn was crowded with people of all ages, come to drink at its source. Delighted at her plan for making them all happy, the fairy hid herself behind <u>a thicket of roses</u>, and peeped out whenever footsteps came that way. It was not long before she had ample proof of the success of her enchantments. Almost before her eyes the children put on the size and strength of adults, while the old men and women instantly became helpless, <u>tiny babies</u>. Indeed, so pleased was she with the result of her work, that she could no longer remain hidden, and went about telling everybody what she had done, and <u>enjoying their gratitude and thanks</u>.

重点提示:如何翻译第一处下划线? 第二处能直译吗? 如何看待第三处?

But after the first outburst of delight at their wishes being granted, people began to be a little frightened at the rapid effects of the magic water. It was delicious to <u>feel yourself at the height of your power and beauty</u>, but you would wish to keep so always! Now this was exactly what the fairy had been in too much of a hurry to arrange, and no sooner had the children become grown up, and the men and women become babies, than they all rushed on to old age at an *appalling* rate! The fairy only found out her mistake when it was too late to set it right.

重点提示：如何理解第一处下划线？替换第二处下划线！替换斜体字。

When the inhabitants of the island saw what had befallen them, they were filled with despair, and did everything they could think of to escape from such a dreadful fate. They dug wells in their places, so that they should no longer need to drink from the magic spring; but the sandy soil yielded no water, and the rainy season was already past. They stored up the dew that fell, and the juice of fruits and of herbs, but all this was *as* a drop in the ocean of their wants. Some threw themselves into the sea, trusting that the current might carry them to other shores—they had no boats—and a few, still more impatient, put themselves to death on the spot. The rest submitted blindly to their destiny.

重点提示：替换斜体字！如何适当处理第一处下划线？用成语翻译第二处！

Perhaps the worst part of the enchantment was, that the change from one age to another was so rapid that the person had no time to prepare himself for it. It would not have mattered so much if the man who stood up in the assembly of the nation, to give his advice *as to* peace or war, had looked like a baby, as long as he spoke with the knowledge and sense of a full-grown man. But, alas! With the outward form of an infant, he had taken on its helplessness and foolishness, and there was no one who could train him to better things. The end of it all was, that before a month had passed the population had died out, and the fairy Dindonette, ashamed and grieved at the effects of her folly, had left the island for ever.

重点提示：替换斜体部分下划线是什么词性？当如何理解？

Many centuries after, the fairy Selnozoura, who had fallen into bad health, was ordered by her doctors to make the tour of the world twice a week for change of air, and in one of these journeys she found herself at Fountain Island. Selnozoura never made these trips alone, but always took with her two children, of whom she was very fond--Cornichon, a boy of fourteen, bought in his childhood at a slave-market, and Toupette, a few months younger, who had been entrusted to the care of the fairy by her guardian, the genius Kristopo. Cornichon and Toupette were intended by Selnozoura to become husband and wife, as soon as they were old enough. Meanwhile, they travelled with her in a little vessel, whose speed through the air was just a thousand nine hundred and fifty times greater than that of the swiftest of our ships.

重点提示：翻译第一处下划线！留意第二处的搭配？

Struck with the beauty of the island, Selnozoura ran the vessel to ground, and leaving it in the care of the dragon which lived in the hold during the voyage, stepped on shore with her two companions. Surprised at the sight of a large town whose streets and houses were absolutely desolate, the fairy resolved to *put her magic arts in practice to find out the cause*. While she was thus engaged, Cornichon and Toupette wandered away by themselves, and by-and-by arrived at the fountain, whose bubbling waters looked cool and delicious on such a hot day. Scarcely had they each drunk a deep draught, when the fairy, who by this time had discovered all she wished to know, hastened to the spot.

重点提示：替换第一、二处下划线；如何理解第三处？翻译第四处！替换斜体部分。

'Oh, beware! Beware!' she cried, the moment she saw them. 'If you drink that deadly poison you will be ruined for ever!'

'Poison?' answered Toupette. 'It is the most refreshing water I have ever tasted, and Cornichon will say so too!'

'<u>Unhappy</u> children, then I am too late! Why did you leave me? Listen, and I will tell you what has befallen the wretched inhabitants of this island, and what will befall you too. The power of fairies is *great*,' she added, when she had finished her story, 'but they cannot destroy the work of another fairy. Very shortly you will pass into the weakness and silliness of extreme old age, and all I can do for you is to make it as easy to you as possible, and to preserve you from the death that others have suffered, from having no one to look after them.

重点提示：替换下划线；如何理解斜体字？

But the charm is working already! Cornichon is taller and more manly than he was an hour ago, and Toupette no longer looks like a little girl.'

It was true; but this fact did not seem to render the young people as miserable as it did Selnozoura.

'Do not pity us,' said Cornichon. 'If we are fated to grow old so soon, let us no longer delay our marriage. What matter if we anticipate our decay, if we only anticipate our happiness too?'

The fairy felt that Cornichon had reason on his side, and seeing by a glance at Toupette's face that there was no opposition to be feared from her, she answered, 'Let it be so, then. But not in this dreadful place. We will return at once to Bagota, and the festivities shall be the most brilliant ever seen.'

They all returned to the vessel, and in a few hours the four thousand five hundred miles that lay between the island and Bagota were passed. Everyone was surprised to see the change which the short absence had made in the young people, but as the fairy had promised absolute silence about the adventure, <u>they were none the wiser</u>, and busied themselves in preparing their dresses for the marriage, which was fixed for the next night.

重点提示：如何理解并处理下划线？

Early on the following morning the genius Kristopo arrived at the Court, on one of the visits he was in the habit of <u>paying his ward</u> from time to time. Like the rest, he was astonished at the sudden improvement in the child. He had always been fond of her, and in a moment he fell violently in love. Hastily <u>demanding an audience of the fairy</u>, he laid his *proposals* before her, never doubting that she would give her consent to so brilliant a match. But Selnozoura refused to listen, and even hinted that <u>in his own interest Kristopo had better turn his thoughts elsewhere</u>. The genius pretended to agree, but, instead, he went straight to Toupette's room, and flew away with her through the window, at the very instant that the bridegroom was awaiting her below.

重点提示：如何理解第一处下划线？第二处的措辞用于什么氛围？斜体字似有不妥，请指出！第三处说得十分含蓄，不妨琢磨！

When the fairy discovered what had happened, she was furious, and sent *messenger after messenger* to the genius in his palace at Ratibouf, commanding him to restore Toupette without delay, and threatening to <u>make war in case of</u> refusal.

重点提示：替换斜体字，并举例说明！如何处理下划线？

Kristopo gave no direct answer to the fairy's envoys, but kept Toupette closely guarded in a tower, where the poor girl used all her powers of persuasion to induce him to put off their marriage. All would, however, have been quite vain if, in <u>the course of</u> a few days, sorrow, joined to the spell of the magic water, had not altered her appearance so completely that Kristopo was quite alarmed, and declared that she needed amusement and fresh air, and that, as his presence seemed to distress her, she should be <u>left her own mistress</u>. But <u>one thing he declined to do</u>, and that was to send her back to Bagota.

重点提示：第一处下划线可删除吗？如何理解第二处？举例说明！留心最后一处的结构！

In the meantime both sides had been busily <u>collecting armies</u>, and Kristopo had <u>given the command of his</u> to a famous general, while Selnozoura had <u>placed Cornichon at the head of</u> her forces. But before war was actually declared, Toupette's parents, who had been summoned by the genius, arrived at Ratibouf. They had never seen their daughter since they <u>parted from</u> her as a baby, but from time to time travellers to Bagota had brought back accounts of her beauty. <u>What was their amazement</u>, therefore, at finding, instead of a lovely girl, a middle-aged woman, handsome indeed, but quite <u>faded—looking</u>, in fact, older than themselves. Kristopo, hardly less astonished than they were at the sudden change, thought that it was a joke on the part of one of his courtiers, who had hidden Toupette away, and put this elderly lady in her place. Bursting with rage, he sent instantly for all the servants and guards of the town, and inquired who had the insolence to play him such a trick, and what had become of their prisoner. They replied that since Toupette had been in their charge she had never left her rooms unveiled, and that during her walks in the surrounding gardens, her food had been brought in and placed on her table; as she preferred to eat alone no one had ever seen her face, or knew what she was like.

重点提示：本段下划线较多，需逐一细心思考再翻译！

The servants were clearly speaking the truth, and Kristopo was obliged to believe them. 'But,' thought he, 'if they <u>have not had a hand in</u> this, it must be the work of the fairy,' and in his anger he ordered the army to be ready to march.

重点提示：如何理解下划线？举例说明！

On her side, Selnozoura of course knew what the genius had to expect, but was deeply offended when she heard of the base trick which she was believed to have invented. Her first desire was to give battle to Kristopo at once, but with great difficulty her ministers induced her to pause, and to send an ambassador to Kristopo to try to arrange matters.

So the Prince Zeprady departed for the court of Ratibouf, and on his way he met Cornichon, who was encamped with his army just outside the gates of Bagota. The prince showed him the fairy's <u>written order</u> that for the present peace must still be kept, and Cornichon, filled with longing to see Toupette once more, begged to be allowed to accompany Zeprady on his mission to Ratibouf.

重点提示：如何理解并处理下划线？

By this time the genius's passion for Toupette, which had caused all these troubles, had died out, and he willingly accepted the terms of peace offered by Zeprady, though he informed the prince that he still believed the fairy *to be guilty of* the dreadful change in the girl. To this the prince only replied that on that point he had a witness who could prove, better than anyone else, if it was Toupette or not, and desired that Cornichon should be sent for.

When Toupette was told that she was to see her old lover again, her heart leapt with joy; but soon the recollection came to her of all that had happened, and she remembered that Cornichon would be changed as well as she. The moment of their meeting was not all happiness, especially on the part of Toupette, who could not forget her lost beauty, and the genius, who was present, was at last convinced that he had not been deceived, and went out to sign the treaty of peace, followed by his attendants.

重点提示：替换斜体字部分。如何处理下划线？

'Ah, Toupette, my dear Toupette!' cried Cornichon, as soon as they were left alone, 'now that we are once more united, let our past troubles be forgotten.'

'Our past troubles!' answered she, 'and what do you call our lost beauty and the dreadful future before us? You are looking fifty years older than when I saw you last, and I know too well that fate has treated me no better!'

'Ah, do not say that,' replied Cornichon, clasping her hand. 'You are different, it is true; but every age has its graces, and surely no woman of sixty was ever handsomer than you! If your eyes had been as bright as of yore they would have matched badly with your faded skin. The wrinkles which I notice on your forehead explain the increased fullness of your cheeks, and your throat in withering is elegant in decay. Thus the harmony shown by your features, even as they grow old, is the best proof of their former beauty.'

重点提示：如何处置第一、二处下划线？第三、四处均带修辞，请分别说明。

'Oh, monster!' cried Toupette, bursting into tears, 'is that all the comfort you can give me?'

重点提示：如何处理下划线？

'But, Toupette,' answered Cornichon, 'you used to declare that you did not care for beauty, as long as you had my heart.'

'Yes, I know,' said she, 'but how can you go on caring for a person who is as old and plain as I?'

'Toupette, Toupette,' replied Cornichon, 'you are only talking nonsense. My heart is as much yours as ever it was, and nothing in the world can make any difference.'

At this point of the conversation the Prince Zeprady entered the room, with the news that the genius, full of regret for his behaviour, had given Cornichon full permission to depart for Bagota as soon as he liked, and to take Toupette with him, adding that, though he begged they would excuse his taking leave of them before they went, he hoped, before long, to visit them at Bagota.

Neither of the lovers slept that night—Cornichon from joy at returning home, Toupette from dread of the blow to her vanity which awaited her at Bagota. It was hopeless for Cornichon to try to console her during the journey with the reasons he had given the day before. She only grew worse and worse, and when they reached the palace went straight to her old apartments, entreating the fairy to allow both herself and Cornichon to remain concealed, and to see no one.

71

For some time after their arrival the fairy was *taken up with* the preparations for the rejoicings which were to celebrate the peace, and with the reception of the genius, who was determined to do all in his power to regain Selnozoura's lost friendship. Cornichon and Toupette were therefore <u>left entirely to themselves</u>, and though this was only what they wanted, still, they began to feel a little neglected.

重点提示：查实斜体部分的实意；还原下划线的词组,并举例说明!

At length, one morning, they saw from the windows that the fairy and the genius were approaching, in state, with all their courtiers in attendance. Toupette instantly hid herself in the darkest corner of the room, but Cornichon, forgetting that he was now no longer a boy of fourteen, ran to meet them. <u>In *so doing*</u> he tripped and fell, bruising one of his eyes severely. At the sight of her lover lying helpless on the floor, Toupette hastened to his side; but her feeble legs <u>gave way</u> under her, and she fell almost on top of him, knocking out three of her loosened teeth against his forehead. The fairy, who entered the room at this moment, burst into tears, and listened in silence to the genius, who hinted that by-and-by everything would be put *right*.

重点提示：解释第一处下划线,并说明斜体字替换的是什么！第二处下划线怎么理解？第二处斜体字作什么成分用？

'At the last assembly of the fairies,' he said, 'when the doings of each fairy were examined and discussed, a proposal was made to lessen, as far as possible, the mischief caused by Dindonette by enchanting the fountain. And it was decided that, as she had meant nothing but kindness, she should have the power of *undoing* one half of the spell. Of course she might always have destroyed the fatal fountain, which would have been best of all; but this she never thought of. Yet, in spite of this, her heart is so good, that I am sure that the moment she hears that she is wanted she will <u>fly to help</u>. Only, before she comes, it is for you, Madam, to make up your mind which of the two shall regain their former strength and beauty.'

重点提示：请琢磨并替换斜体部分如何理解和翻译下划线?

At these words the fairy's soul sank. Both Cornichon and Toupette were equally dear to her, and how could she favour one <u>at the cost of</u> the other? As to the courtiers, none of the men were able to understand why she hesitated a second to declare for Toupette, while the ladies were *equally strong on the side of Cornichon.*

重点提示：替换下划线！细心琢磨并翻译斜体部分。

But, however undecided the fairy might be, it was quite different with Cornichon and Toupette.

'Ah, my love,' exclaimed Cornichon, 'at length I shall be able to give you the best proof of my devotion by showing you how I *value* the beauties of your mind above those of your body! While the most charming women of the court will <u>fall victims to</u> my youth and strength, I shall think of nothing but how to <u>lay them at your feet</u>, and pay heart-felt homage to your age and wrinkles.'

重点提示：替换斜体字！请琢磨两处下划线的意思！

'Not so fast,' interrupted Toupette, 'I don't see why you should have it all. Why do you heap such humiliations upon me? But I will trust to the justice of the fairy, who will not treat me so.' Then she entered her own rooms, and refused to leave them, in spite of the prayers of Cornichon, who begged her to let him explain.

No one at the court thought or spoke of any other subject during the few days before the arrival of Dindonette, whom everybody expected to set things right in a moment. But, alas! She had no idea herself what was best to be done, and always adopted the opinion of the person she was talking to. At length a thought struck her, which seemed the only way of satisfying both parties, and she asked the fairy to call together all the court and the people to hear her decision.

重点提示:举例说明下划线的意思!

'Happy is he,' she began, 'who can repair the evil he has caused, but happier he who has never caused any.'

As nobody contradicted this remark, she continued: 'To me it is only allowed to *undo* one half of the mischief I have *wrought*. I could restore you your youth,' she said to Cornichon, 'or your beauty,' turning to Toupette. 'I will do both; and I will do neither.'

重点提示:替换两处斜体字,并举例说明!

A murmur of curiosity arose from the crowd, while Cornichon and Toupette trembled with astonishment.

'No,' went on Dindonette, 'never should I have the cruelty to leave one of you to decay, while the other enjoys the glory of youth. And as I cannot restore you both at once to what you were, one half of each of your bodies shall become young again, while the other half goes on its way to decay. I will leave it to you to choose which half it shall be—if I shall draw a line round the waist, or a line straight down the middle of the body.'

She looked about her proudly, expecting applause for her clever idea. But Cornichon and Toupette were shaking with rage and disappointment, and everyone else broke into shouts of laughter. In pity for the unhappy lovers, Selnozoura came forward.

'Do you not think,' she said, 'that instead of what you propose, it would be better to let them take it in turns to enjoy their former youth and beauty for a fixed time? I am sure you could easily manage that.'

'What an excellent notion!' cried Dindonette. 'Oh, yes, of course that is best! Which of you shall I touch first?'

'Touch her,' replied Cornichon, who was always ready to give way to Toupette. 'I know her heart too well to fear any change.'

重点提示:说说下划线的真实意思!

So the fairy bent forward and touched her with her magic ring, and in one instant the old woman was a girl again. The whole court wept with joy at the sight, and Toupette ran up to Cornichon, who had fallen down in his surprise, promising to pay him long visits, and tell him of all her balls and water parties.

The two fairies went to their own apartments, where the genius followed them to take his leave.

'Oh, dear!' suddenly cried Dindonette, breaking in to the farewell speech of the genius. 'I quite forgot to fix the time when Cornichon should in his turn grow young. How stupid of me! And now I fear it is too late, for I ought to have declared it before I touched Toupette with the ring. Oh, dear! Oh, dear! Why did nobody warn me?'

'You were so quick,' replied Selnozoura, who had long been aware of the mischief the fairy had again done, 'and we can only wait now till Cornichon shall have reached the utmost limits of his decay, when he will drink of the water, and become a baby once more, so that Toupette will have to spend her life as a nurse, a wife, and a caretaker.'

After the anxiety of mind and the weakness of body to which for so long Toupette had been a prey, it seemed as if she could not amuse herself enough, and it was seldom indeed that she found time to visit poor Cornichon, though she did not cease to be fond of him, or to be kind to him. Still, she was perfectly happy without him, and this the poor man did not fail to see, almost blind and deaf from age though he was.

But it was left to Kristopo to undo at last the work of Dindonette, and give Cornichon back the youth he had lost, and this the genius did all the more gladly, as he discovered, quite by accident, that Cornichon was in fact his son. It was on this plea that he attended the great yearly meeting of the fairies, and prayed that, in consideration of his services to so many of the members, this one *boon* might be granted him. Such a request had never before been heard in fairyland, and was objected to by some of the older fairies; but both Kristopo and Selnozoura were held in such high honour that the murmurs of disgust were *set aside*, and the latest victim to the enchanted fountain was pronounced to be free of the spell. All that the genius asked in return was that he might accompany the fairy back to Bagota, and be present when his son assumed his proper shape.

重点提示: 替换第一(见同一段)、二处斜体字！将第一、二处下划线还原成词组,并举例以证！

They made up their minds they would just tell Toupette that they had found a husband for her, and give her a pleasant surprise at her wedding, which was fixed for the following night. She heard the news with astonishment, and many pangs for the grief which Cornichon would certainly feel at his place being taken by another; but she did not dream of disobeying the fairy, and spent the whole day wondering who the bridegroom could be.

At the appointed hour, a large crowd assembled at the fairy's palace, which was decorated with the sweetest flowers, known only to fairyland. Toupette had taken her place, but where was the bridegroom?

'Fetch Cornichon!' said the fairy to her chamberlain.

But Toupette interposed: 'Oh, Madam, spare him, I entreat you, this bitter pain, and let him remain hidden and in peace.'

'It is necessary that he should be here,' answered the fairy, 'and he will not regret it.'

And, as she spoke, Cornichon was led in, smiling with the foolishness of extreme old age at the sight of the gay crowd.

'Bring him here,' commanded the fairy, waving her hand towards Toupette, who started back from surprise and horror.

Selnozoura then took the hand of the poor old man, and the genius came forward and touched him three times with his ring, when Cornichon was transformed into a handsome young man.

'May you live long,' the genius said, 'to enjoy happiness with your wife, and to love your father.'

And that was the end of the mischief wrought by the fairy Dindonette!

思考题：
借本故事说说"什么是真正的爱情"。

15. What Came of Picking Flowers

There was once a woman who had three daughters whom she loved very much. One day the eldest was walking in a water-meadow, when she saw a <u>pink</u> growing in the stream. She stooped to pick the flower, but her hand had scarcely touched it, when she vanished altogether. The next morning the second sister went out into the meadow, to see if she could find any traces of the lost girl, and as a branch of lovely roses lay trailing across her path, she bent down to move it away, and in so doing, could not resist plucking one of the roses. In a moment she too had disappeared. Wondering what could have become of her two sisters, the youngest followed in their footsteps, and <u>fell a victim to</u> a branch of delicious white jessamine. So the old woman was left without any daughters at all.

重点提示：查阅第一处下划线的真实意思，切勿猜测！请替换第二处！

She wept, and wept, and wept, all day and all night, and went on weeping so long, that her son, who had been a little boy when his sisters disappeared, grew up to be a tall youth. Then one night he asked his mother to tell him <u>what was the matter</u>.

重点提示：替换下划线！

When he had heard the whole story, he said, 'Give me your blessing, mother, and <u>I will go and search the world till I find them.</u>'

重点提示：怎么处理下划线更妥？

So he set forth, and after he had travelled several miles <u>without any adventures</u>, he came upon three big boys fighting in the road. He stopped and inquired what they were fighting about, and one of them answered: 'My lord! Our father left to us, when he died, a pair of boots, a key, and a cap. Whoever puts on the boots and wishes himself in any place, will find himself there. The key will open every door in the world, and with the cap on your head no one can see you. Now our eldest brother wants to *have* all three things *for himself*, and we wish to draw lots for them.'

重点提示：如何翻译下划线？能用两个汉字"概括"斜体字部分吗？

'Oh, that is easily settled,' said the youth. 'I will throw this stone as far as I can, and the one who picks it up first, shall have the three things.' So he took the stone and flung it, and while the three brothers were running after it, he drew hastily on the boots, and said, 'Boots, take me to the place where I shall find my eldest sister.'

<u>The next moment</u> the young man was standing on a steep mountain before the gates of a strong castle guarded by bolts and bars and iron chains. The key, which he had not forgotten to put in his pocket, opened the doors one by one, and he walked through a number of halls and corridors, till he met a beautiful and richly-dressed young lady who <u>started back in surprise</u> at the sight of him, and exclaimed, 'Oh, sir, how did you contrive to get in here?' The young man replied that he was her brother, and told her by *what means* he had been able to pass through the doors. <u>In return</u>, she told him how happy she was, except for one thing, and that was, her husband <u>lay under a spell</u>, and could never break it till there should be put to death a man who could not die.

重点提示：细心处理四处下划线，以确保译文言简意赅！用一个单词替换斜体部分。

They talked together for a long time, and then the lady said he had better leave her as she expected her husband back at any moment, and he might not like him to be there; but the young man assured her she need not be afraid, as he had with him a cap which would make him invisible. They were still deep in conversation when the door suddenly opened, and a bird flew in, but he saw nothing unusual, for, at the first noise, the youth had put on his cap. The lady jumped up and brought a large golden basin, into which the bird flew, reappearing directly after as a handsome man. Turning to his wife, he cried, 'I am sure someone is in the room!' She got frightened, and declared that she was quite alone, but her husband persisted, and in the end she had to confess the truth.

重点提示：思考三处下划线中的意思（其中第二处可能处理起来更费思量）！

'But if he is really your brother, why did you hide him?' asked he. 'I believe you are telling me a lie, and if he comes back I shall kill him!'

At this the youth took off his cap, and came forward. Then the husband saw that he was indeed so like his wife that he doubted her word no longer, and embraced his brother-in-law with delight. Drawing a feather from his bird's skin, he said, 'If you are in danger and cry, "Come and help me, King of the Birds," everything will go well with you.'

重点提示：下划线中的 like 是什么词性？

The young man thanked him and went away, and after he had left the castle he told the boots that they must take him to the place where his second sister was living.

As before, he found himself at the gates of a huge castle, and within was his second sister, very happy with her husband, who loved her dearly, but *longing for* the moment when he should be set free from the spell that kept him half his life a fish. When he arrived and had been introduced by his wife to her brother, he welcomed him warmly, and gave him a fish-scale, saying, 'If you are in danger, call to me, "Come and help me, King of the Fishes," and everything will go well with you.'

重点提示：琢磨下划线的句子结构，找出与斜体字平行的部分！

The young man thanked him and took his leave, and when he was outside the gates he told the boots to take him to the place where his youngest sister lived. The boots carried him to a dark cavern, with steps of iron leading up to it.

重点提示：见下划线的第一反应是什么？可否直译？

Inside she sat, weeping and sobbing, and as she had done nothing else the whole time she had been there, the poor girl had grown very thin. When she saw a man standing before her, she sprang to her feet and exclaimed, 'Oh, whoever you are, save me and take me from this horrible place!' Then he told her who he was, and how he had seen her sisters, whose happiness was spoilt by the spell under which both their husbands lay, and she, in turn, related her story. She had been carried off in the water-meadow by a horrible monster, who wanted to make her marry him by force, and had kept her a prisoner all these years because she would not submit to his will.

重点提示：四处下划线均值得琢磨：替换第一处、翻译第二处，第三、四处均可用两个汉字给予处理，不妨试试看！

Every day he came to beg her to consent to his wishes, and to remind her that there was no

77

hope of her being set free, as he was the <u>most constant man</u> in the world, and besides that he could never die. At these words the youth remembered his two enchanted *brothers-in-law*, and he advised his sister to promise to marry the old man, if he would tell her why he could never die. Suddenly everything began to tremble, as if it was shaken by a whirlwind, and the old man entered, and flinging himself at the feet of the girl, he said: 'Are you still determined never to marry me? If so you will have to sit there weeping *till the end of the world*, for I shall always be faithful to my wish to marry you!'

重点提示：第一处下划线可以不译吗？第二处怎么译？如何理解两处斜体部分？

'Well, I will marry you,' she said, 'if you will tell me why it is that you can never die.'

Then the old man burst into *peals* of laughter. 'Ah, ah, ah! You are thinking how you would be able to kill me? Well, to do that, you would have to find an iron casket which lies at the bottom of the sea, and has a white dove inside, and then you would have to find the egg which the dove laid, and bring it here, and dash it against my head.' And he laughed again *in his certainty that* no one had ever got down to the bottom of the sea, and that if they did, they would never find the casket, or be able to open it. When he could speak once more, he said, 'Now you will be obliged to marry me, as you know my secret.'

重点提示：替换两处斜体字！

But she begged <u>so hard</u> that the wedding might be put off for three days, that he consented, and went away <u>rejoicing at his victory</u>. When he had disappeared, the brother took off <u>the cap which had kept him invisible all this time</u>, and told his sister not to <u>lose heart</u> as he hoped in three days she would be free. Then he drew on his boots, and wished himself at the seashore, and there he was *directly*.

重点提示：第一处下划线为何意？如何简洁处理第二处？第三处与 lose one's heart 有何区别？斜体部分是什么词性？请替换！

Drawing out the fish-scale, he cried, 'Come and help me, King of the Fishes!' and his brother in-law swam up, and asked what he could do. The young man related the story, and when he had finished his listener <u>summoned all the fishes to his presence</u>.

重点提示：下划线出自什么人之口？

The last to arrive was a little sardine, who apologised for being so late, but said she had hurt herself by knocking her head against an iron casket that lay in the bottom of the sea. The king ordered several of the largest and strongest of his subjects to take the little sardine as a guide, and *bring* him the iron casket. They soon returned with the box <u>placed across their backs</u> and laid it down before him. Then the youth produced the key and said 'Key, open that box!' and the key opened it, and though they were all crowding round, ready to catch it, the white dove within flew away.

重点提示：用一个汉字翻译下划线！

It was useless to go after it, and for a moment the young man's heart sank. The next minute, however, he remembered that he had still his feather, and drew it out crying, 'Come to me, King of the Birds!' and a rushing noise was heard, and the King of the Birds perched on his shoulder, and asked what he could do to help him. His brother-in-law told him the whole story, and when he had finished the King of the Birds commanded all his subjects to hasten to his presence. In an instant the air was dark with birds of all sizes, and at the *very* last came the white dove, apologising for being so late by saying that an old friend had arrived at his nest, and he had been obliged to give him some dinner.

重点提示：下划线中的斜体字起什么作用？能删除吗？

The King of the Birds ordered some of them to show the young man the white dove's nest, and when they reached it, there lay the egg which was to break the spell and set them all free. When it was safely in his pocket, he told the boots to carry him straight to the cavern where his youngest sister *sat awaiting* him.

重点提示：下划线如何译？斜体字是先后动作，还是同时动作？

Now it was already far on into the third day, which the old man had fixed for the wedding, and when the youth reached the cavern with his cap on his head, he found the monster there, urging the girl to keep her word and let the marriage take place at once. At a sign from her brother she sat down and invited the old monster to lay his head on her lap. He did so with delight, and her brother standing behind her back passed her the egg unseen. She took it, and dashed it straight at the horrible head, and the monster started, and with a groan that people took for the rumblings of an earthquake, he turned over and died.

重点提示：第一处下划线作什么用，一定得译吗？第二处该怎么理解、翻译呢？替换三处。

As the breath went out of his body the husbands of the two eldest daughters resumed their proper shapes, and, sending for their mother-in-law, whose sorrow was so unexpectedly turned into joy, they had a great feast, and the youngest sister was rich to the end of her days with the treasures she found in the cave, collected by the monster.

思考题：

对于 brother 和 sister（包括 nephew 和 niece），你都知道些什么？不妨查查相关词条！

16. The Story of the Three Sons of Hali

Till his eighteenth birthday the young Neangir lived happily in a village about forty miles from Constantinople, believing that <u>Mohammed and Zinebi his wife</u>, who had brought him up, were his real parents.

重点提示: 如何将下划线的汉译"化繁为简"?

Neangir was quite <u>content with his lot</u>, though he was neither rich nor great, and unlike most young men of his age had no desire to leave his home. He was therefore completely taken by surprise when one day Mohammed told him with many sighs that the time had now come for him to go to Constantinople, and <u>fix on a profession</u> for himself. The choice would be left to him, but he would probably prefer either to be a soldier or <u>one of the doctors learned in the law</u>, who explain the Koran to the ignorant people. 'You *know* the holy book nearly *by heart*,' ended the old man, 'so that in a very short time you would be fitted to teach others. But write to us and tell us how you pass your life, and we, on our *side*, will promise never to forget you.' So saying, Mohammed gave Neangir four piastres to start him in the great city, and obtained leave for him to join a caravan which was about to set off for Constantinople.

重点提示: 如何处理第一处下划线?请翻译第二处;替换第三处?第一、二处斜体字(固定搭配)是什么意思?替换第三处斜体字!

The journey took some days, <u>as caravans go very slowly</u>, but at last the walls and towers of the capital appeared in the distance. When the caravan halted the travellers went their different ways, and Neangir was left, feeling very strange and rather lonely. <u>He had plenty of courage</u> and made friends very easily; still, not only was it the first time he had left the village where he had been brought up, but no one had ever spoken to him of Constantinople, and he did not *so much as* know the name of a single street or of a creature who lived in it.

重点提示: 第一处下划线说明什么?第二处该怎么译?斜体字是什么意思?请用一个单词替换。

Wondering what *he was to do next*, Neangir stood still for a moment to look about him, when suddenly a pleasant-looking man came up, and bowing politely, asked if the youth would do him the honour of staying in his house till he had made some plans for himself. Neangir, not seeing anything else he could do, accepted the stranger's offer and followed him home.

重点提示: 用较为恰当的英语 paraphrase 斜体字部分。

They entered a large room, where a girl of about twelve years old was <u>laying three places at the table</u>.

重点提示: 如何处理下划线的内容?

'Zelida,' said the <u>stranger</u>, 'was I not quite right when I told you that I should bring back a friend to *sup* with us?'

重点提示: 能直译下划线吗?替换斜体字!

'My father,' replied the girl, 'you are always right in what you say, and what is better still, you never mislead others.' As she spoke, an old slave placed on the table *a dish called pillau, made of rice and meat*, which is a great favourite among people in the East, and setting down glasses of sherbet before each person, left the room quietly.

重点提示：如何理解斜体字的含义？

During the meal the host talked a great deal upon all sorts of subjects; but Neangir did nothing but look at Zelida, as far as he could without being positively rude.

The girl blushed and grew uncomfortable, and at last turned to her father. 'The stranger's eyes never wander from me,' she said in a low and hesitating voice. 'If Hassan should hear of it, jealousy will make him mad.'

重点提示：怎么翻译下划线更合适？

'No, no,' replied the father, 'you are certainly not for this young man. Did I not tell you before that I intend him for your sister Argentine. I will at once take measures to fix his heart upon her,' and he rose and opened a cupboard, from which be took some fruits and a jug of wine, which he put on the table, together with a *small silver and mother-of-pearl box*.

重点提示：如何理解第一、二处下划线？第三处该怎么译？思考斜体字是怎么回事！

'Taste this wine,' he said to the young man, pouring some into a glass.

'Give me a little, too,' cried Zelida.

'Certainly not,' answered her father, '*you* and Hassan both had as much as was good for you the other day.'

重点提示：如何翻译斜体字？请替换下划线！

Then drink some yourself,' replied she, 'or this young man will think we mean to poison him.'

'Well, if you wish, I will do so,' said the father; 'this elixir is not dangerous at my age, as it is at yours.'

When Neangir had emptied his glass, his host opened the mother-of-pearl box and held it out to him. Neangir was beside himself with delight at the picture of a young maiden more beautiful than anything he had ever dreamed of. He stood *speechless* before it, while his breast swelled with a feeling *quite new to him*.

重点提示：如何处置下划线中的夸张表达？说出斜体字的成分！

His two companions watched him with amusement, until at last Neangir roused himself. 'Explain to me, I pray you,' he said, 'the meaning of these mysteries. Why did you ask me here? Why did you force me to drink this dangerous liquid which has *set fire to* my blood? Why have you shown me this picture which has almost deprived me of reason?'

重点提示：第一、二处下划线可直译吗？替换斜体字！

'I will answer some of your questions,' replied his host, 'but all, I may not. The picture that you hold in your hand is that of Zelida's sister. It has filled your heart with love for her; therefore, go and seek her. When you find her, you will find yourself.'

'But where shall I find her?' cried Neangir, kissing the charming miniature on which his eyes were fixed.

'I am unable to tell you more,' replied his host cautiously.

'But I can,' interrupted Zelida eagerly. 'Tomorrow you must go to the Jewish bazaar, and buy a watch from the second shop on the right hand. And at midnight—'

But what was to happen at midnight Neangir did not hear, for Zelida's father hastily laid his hand over her mouth, crying: 'Oh, be silent, child! Would you draw down on you by imprudence the fate of your unhappy sisters?' Hardly had he uttered the words, when a thick black vapour rose about him, *proceeding from the precious bottle*, which his rapid movement had overturned. The old slave rushed in and shrieked loudly, while Neangir, upset by this strange adventure, left the house.

重点提示：说说两处下划线之间的关系；斜体字在句中作什么成分？

He passed the rest of the night on the steps of a mosque, and with the first streaks of dawn he took his picture out of the folds of his turban. Then, remembering Zelida's words, he inquired the way to the bazaar, and went straight to the shop she had described.

重点提示：揣摩下划线的意思并翻译！

In answer to Neangir's request to be shown some watches, the merchant produced several and pointed out the one which he considered the best. The price was three gold pieces, which Neangir readily agreed to give him; but the man made a difficulty about handing over the watch unless he knew where his customer lived.

'That is more than I know myself,' replied Neangir. 'I only arrived in the town yesterday and cannot find the way to the house where I went first.'

'Well,' said the merchant, 'come with me, and I will take you to a good Mussulman, where you will have everything you desire at a small charge.'

重点提示：如何翻译两处下划线？

Neangir consented, and the two walked together through several streets till they reached the house recommended by the Jewish merchant. By his advice the young man paid in advance the last gold piece that remained to him for his food and lodging.

重点提示：替换下划线，并用两个汉字"概括"！

As soon as Neangir had dined he shut himself up in his room, and thrusting his hand into the folds of his turban, drew out his beloved portrait. As he did so, he touched a sealed letter which had apparently been hidden there without his knowledge, and seeing it was written by his foster-mother, Zinebi, he tore it eagerly open. *Judge of* his surprise when he read these words:

重点提示：下划线是什么意思？替换斜体字！

'My dearest child,—this letter, which you will some day find in your turban, is to inform you that you are not really our son. We believe your father to have been a great lord in some distant land, and inside this packet is a letter from him, threatening to be avenged on us if you are not restored to him at once. We shall always love you, but do not seek us or even write to us. It will be useless.'

重点提示：如何理解下划线？

In the same *wrapper* was a roll of paper with a few words as follows, traced in a hand unknown to Neangir:

重点提示：斜体字是什么意思？下划线与它有何关系？

'Traitors, you are no doubt in league with those magicians who have stolen the two daughters of the unfortunate Siroco, and have taken from them the talisman given them by their father. You have kept my son from me, but I have found out your hiding-place and swear by the Holy Prophet to punish your crime. The stroke of my scimitar is swifter than the lightning.'

重点提示:如何翻译下划线?

The unhappy Neangir on reading these two letters of which he understood absolutely nothing-felt sadder and more lonely than ever. It soon dawned on him that he must be the son of the man who had written to Mohammed and his wife, but he did not know where to look for him, and indeed thought much more about the people who had brought him up and whom he was never to see again.

重点提示:注意下划线的结构,并替换!

To shake off these gloomy feelings, so as to be able to make some plans for the future, Neangir left the house and walked briskly about the city till darkness had fallen. He then retraced his steps and was just crossing the threshold when he saw something at his feet sparkling in the moonlight. He picked it up, and discovered it to be a gold watch shining with precious stones. He gazed up and down the street to see if there was anyone about to whom it might belong, but there was not a creature visible. So he put it in his sash, by the side of a silver watch which he had bought from the Jew that morning.

重点提示:如何理解下划线? 可直译吗?

The possession of this piece of good fortune cheered Neangir up a little, 'for,' thought he, 'I can sell these jewels for at least a thousand sequins, and that will certainly last me till I have found my father.' And consoled by this reflection he laid both watches beside him and prepared to sleep.

重点提示:替换下划线!

In the middle of the night he awoke suddenly and heard a soft voice speaking, which seemed to come from one of the watches.

'Aurora, my sister,' it whispered gently. 'Did they remember to wind you up at midnight?'

'No, dear Argentine,' was the reply. 'And you?'

'They forgot me, too,' answered the first voice, 'and it is now one o'clock, so that we shall not be able to leave our prison till tomorrow—if we are not forgotten again—then.'

'We have nothing now to do here,' said Aurora. 'We must resign ourselves to our fate—let us go.'

Filled with astonishment Neangir sat up in bed, and beheld by the light of the moon the two watches slide to the ground and roll out of the room past the cats' quarters. He rushed towards the door and on to the staircase, but the watches slipped downstairs without his seeing them, and into the street. He tried to unlock the door and follow them, but the key refused to turn, so he gave up the chase and went back to bed.

重点提示:替换第一处下划线;注意第二处的用法!

The next day all his sorrows returned with tenfold force. He felt himself lonelier and poorer than ever, and in a fit of despair he thrust his turban on his head, stuck his sword in his belt, and left the house determined to seek an explanation from the merchant who had sold him the silver watch. When Neangir reached the *bazaar* he found the man he sought was absent from his shop, and his place filled by another Jew.

重点提示：思考下划线中的夸张手法！替换斜体字！

'It is my brother you want,' said he, 'we keep the shop in turn, and in turn go into the city to do our business.'

'Ah! What business?' cried Neangir in a fury. 'You are the brother of a scoundrel who sold me yesterday a watch that ran away in the night. But I will find it *somehow*, or else you shall pay for it, as you are his brother!'

重点提示：替换斜体字！

'What is that you say?' asked the Jew, around whom a crowd had rapidly gathered. 'A watch that ran away. If it had been a cask of wine, your story might be true, but a watch--! That is hardly possible!'

'The Cadi shall say whether it is possible or not,' replied Neangir, who at that moment perceived the other Jew enter the bazaar. Darting up, he seized him by the arm and dragged him to the Cadi's house; but not before the man whom he had found in the shop contrived to whisper to his brother, in a tone loud enough for Neangir to hear, 'Confess nothing, or we shall both be lost.'

重点提示：下划线该怎么译？

When the Cadi was informed of what had taken place he ordered the crowd to be dispersed by blows, after the Turkish manner, and then asked Neangir to state his complaint. After hearing the young man's story, which seemed to him most extraordinary, he turned to question the Jewish merchant, who instead of answering raised his eyes *to heaven* and fell down in a dead faint.

The judge *took no notice of* the swooning man, but told Neangir that his tale was so singular he really could not believe it, and that he should have the merchant carried back to his own house. This so enraged Neangir that he forgot the respect due to the Cadi, and exclaimed at the top of his voice, 'Recover this fellow from his fainting fit, and force him to confess the truth,' giving the Jew as he spoke a blow with his sword which caused him to utter a piercing scream.

重点提示：替换两处斜体字；判断下划线的成分！

'You see for yourself,' said the Jew to the Cadi, 'that this young man is out of his mind. I forgive him his blow, but do not, I pray you, leave me in his power.'

重点提示：分别替换两处下划线！

At that moment the Bassa chanced to pass the Cadi's house, and hearing a great noise, entered to inquire the cause. When the matter was explained he looked *attentively* at Neangir, and asked him gently how all these marvels could possibly have happened.

重点提示：替换斜体字！

'My lord,' replied Neangir, 'I swear I have spoken the truth, and perhaps you will believe me when I tell you that I myself have been the victim of spells wrought by people of this kind, who should be rooted out from the earth. For three years I was changed into a three-legged pot, and only returned to man's shape when one day a turban was laid upon my lid.'

重点提示：请翻译下划线！

At these words the Bassa rent his robe for joy, and embracing Neangir, he cried, 'Oh, my son, my son, have I found you at last? Do you not come from the house of Mohammed and Zinebi?'

84

重点提示：替换斜体字；如何处理下划线？

'Yes, my lord,' replied Neangir, 'it was they who *took care of* me during my misfortune, and taught me by their example to be less worthy of belonging to you.'

重点提示：替换斜体字；如何处置下划线？

'Blessed be the Prophet,' said the Bassa, 'who has restored one of my sons to me, at the time I least expected it! You know,' he continued, addressing the Cadi, 'that during the first years of my marriage I had three sons by the beautiful Zambac. When he was three years old a holy dervish gave the eldest a string of the finest coral, saying "Keep this treasure carefully, and be faithful to the Prophet, and you will be happy." To the second, who now stands before you, he presented a copper plate on which the name of Mahomet was engraved in seven languages, telling him never to part from his turban, which was the sign of a true believer, and he would taste the greatest of all joys; while on the right arm of the third the dervish clasped a bracelet with the prayer that his right hand should be pure and the left spotless, so that he might never know sorrow.

重点提示：思考下划线的意思！

'My eldest son neglected the *counsel* of the dervish and terrible troubles fell on him, as also on the youngest. To preserve the second from similar misfortunes I brought him up in a lonely place, under the care of a faithful servant named Gouloucou, while I was fighting the enemies of our Holy Faith. On my return from the wars I hastened to embrace my son, but both he and Gouloucou had vanished, and it is only a few months since that I learned that the boy was living with a man called Mohammed, whom I suspected of having stolen him. Tell me, my son, how *it* came about that you fell into his hands.'

重点提示：替换第一处斜体字；思考第二处（看与句子哪部分有关联？）

'My lord,' replied Neangir, 'I can remember little of the early years of my life, save that I dwelt in a castle by the seashore with an old servant. I must have been about twelve years old when one day as we were out walking we met a man whose face was like that of this Jew, coming dancing towards us. Suddenly I felt myself growing faint. I tried to raise my hands to my head, but they had become stiff and hard. In a word, I had been changed into a copper pot, and my arms formed the handle. What happened to my companion I know not, but I was conscious that someone had picked me up, and was carrying me quickly away.

'After some days, or so it seemed to me, I was placed on the ground near a thick hedge, and when I heard my captor snoring beside me I resolved to make my escape. So I pushed my way among the thorns as *well* as I could, and walked on steadily for about an hour.

重点提示：用三个单词替换下划线！斜体字是什么意思？用一个单词替换它！

'You cannot imagine, my lord, how awkward it is to walk with three legs, especially when your knees are as stiff as mine were. *At length* after much difficulty I reached a market-garden, and hid myself deep down among the cabbages, where I passed a quiet night.

重点提示：替换斜体字。

'The next morning, at sunrise, I felt some one stooping over me and examining me closely. "What have you got there, Zinebi?" said the voice of a man a little way off.

重点提示：如何翻译下划线？

'"The most beautiful pot in the whole world," answered the woman beside me, "and who would have dreamed of finding it among my cabbages!"

'Mohammed lifted me from the ground and looked at me with admiration. That pleased me, for everyone likes to be admired, even if he is only a pot! And I was taken into the house and filled with water, and put on the fire to boil.

'For three years I led a quiet and useful life, being scrubbed bright every day by Zinebi, then a young and beautiful woman.

'One morning Zinebi set me on the fire, with <u>a fine fillet of beef</u> inside me to cook for dinner. Being afraid that some of the steam would escape through the lid, and that the taste of her stew would be spoilt, she looked about for something to put over the cover, but could see nothing handy but her husband's turban. She tied it firmly round the lid, and then left the room. For the first time during three years I began to feel the fire burning the soles of my feet, and moved away a little—doing this with a great deal more ease than I had felt when making my escape to Mohammed's garden. I was somehow aware, too, that I was growing taller; in fact in a few minutes I was a man again.

重点提示:说说下划线之意!

'After the third hour of prayer Mohammed and Zinebi both returned, and you can guess their surprise at finding a young man in the kitchen instead of a copper pot! I told them my story, which at first they refused to believe, but in the end I succeeded in persuading them that I was speaking the truth. For two years more I lived with them, and was treated like their own son, till the day when they sent me to this city to seek my fortune. And now, my lords, here are the two letters which I found in my turban. Perhaps they may be another proof in favour of my story.'

Whilst Neangir was speaking, the blood from the Jew's wound had gradually ceased to flow; and at this moment there appeared in the doorway a lovely Jewess, about twenty-two years old, her hair and her dress all disordered, as if she had been *flying from some great danger*. In one hand she held two crutches of white wood, and was followed by two men. The first man Neangir knew to be the brother of the Jew he had struck with his sword, while in the second the young man thought he recognised the person who was standing by when he was changed into a pot. Both of these men had a wide linen band round their thighs and held <u>stout sticks</u>.

重点提示:替换斜体字;如何翻译下划线?

The Jewess approached the wounded man and laid the two crutches near him; then, fixing her eyes on him, she burst into tears.

'Unhappy Izouf,' she murmured, 'why do you suffer yourself to be led into such dangerous adventures? Look at the consequences, not only to yourself, but to your two brothers,' turning as she spoke to the men who had come in with her, and who had sunk down on the mat at the feet of the Jew.

The Bassa and his companions were struck both with the beauty of the Jewess and also with her words, and begged her to give them an explanation.

'My lords,' she said, 'my name is Sumi, and I am the daughter of Moizes, one of our most famous rabbis. <u>I am the victim of my love for Izaf</u>' pointing to the man who had entered last, 'and in spite of his ingratitude, I cannot tear him from my heart. <u>Cruel enemy of my life</u>,' she continued turning to Izaf, 'tell these gentlemen your story and that of your brothers, and try *to gain your pardon by repentance.*'

重点提示：如何处理第一、二处下划线才像汉语？替换斜体字！

'<u>We all three were born at the same time</u>,' said the Jew, obeying the command of Sumi at a sign from the Cadi, 'and are the sons of the famous Nathan Ben-Sadi, who gave us the names of Izif, Izouf, and Izaf. From our earliest years we were taught the secrets of magic, and as we were all born under the same stars we shared the <u>same happiness and the same troubles</u>.

重点提示：如何再现两处下划线的含义？

'Our mother died before I can remember, and when we were fifteen our father was <u>seized with</u> a dangerous illness which no spells could cure. Feeling death draw near, he called us to his bedside and took leave of us in these words：

重点提示：如何处理并替换下划线？

'"My sons, I have no riches to bequeath to you; my only wealth was those secrets of magic which you know. Some stones you already have, engraved with mystic signs, and long ago I taught you how to make others. But you still lack the most precious of all talismans—the three rings belonging to the daughters of Siroco. Try to get possession of them, but take heed on beholding these young girls that you do not <u>fall under the power of their beauty</u>. Their religion is different from yours, and *further*, they are the betrothed brides of the sons of the Bassa of the Sea. And to preserve you from a love which can bring you nothing but sorrow, I counsel you <u>in time of peril</u> to seek out the daughter of Moizes the Rabbi, who cherishes a hidden passion for Izaf, and possesses the Book of Spells, which her father himself wrote with the sacred ink that was used for the Talmud." So saying, our father fell back on his cushions and died, leaving us burning with desire for the three rings of the daughters of Siroco.

重点提示：替换斜体字！妥善处置两处下划线！

'No sooner were our <u>sad duties</u> finished than we began to make inquiries where these young ladies were to be found, and we learned after much trouble that Siroco, their father, had fought in many wars, and that his daughters, whose beauty was famous throughout all the land, were named Aurora, Argentine, and Zelida.'

重点提示：下划线能直译吗？

At the second of these names, both the Bassa and his son gave a start of surprise, but they said nothing and Izaf went on with his story.

'The first thing to be done was to put on a disguise, and it was in the dress of foreign merchants that we at length approached the young ladies, taking care to carry with us a collection of fine stones which we had hired for the occasion. But alas! It was <u>to no purpose</u> that Nathan Ben-Sadi had warned us to <u>close our hearts against their charms</u>! The peerless Aurora was clothed in a garment of golden hue, studded all over with flashing jewels; the fair-haired Argentine wore a dress of silver, and the young Zelida, <u>loveliest of them all</u>, the costume of a Persian lady.

重点提示：替换第一处下划线；如何再现第二处的暗含意思？第三处是什么成分？

'Among other curiosities that we had brought with us, was a flask containing an elixir which had the quality of exciting love in the breasts of any man or woman who drank of it. This had been given me by the fair Sumi, who had used it herself and was full of wrath because I refused to drink it likewise, and so return her passion. I showed this liquid to the three maidens who were engaged in examining the precious stones, and choosing those that pleased them best; and I was in the act of pouring some in a crystal cup, when Zelida's <u>eyes fell on</u> a paper wrapped round the flask containing these words. "Beware lest you drink this water with any other man than him who will one day be <u>your husband.</u>" "Ah, traitor!" she exclaimed, "what <u>snare have you laid for</u> me?" and glancing where her finger pointed I recognised the writing of Sumi.

重点提示:直译第一处下划线;如何翻译第二处? 举例说明其用法;还原第三处的词组,并举例说明。

'By this time my two brothers had already <u>got possession of</u> the rings of Aurora and Argentine in exchange for some merchandise which they coveted, and no sooner had the magic circles left their hands than the two sisters vanished completely, and in their place nothing was to be seen but a watch of gold and one of silver. At this instant the old slave whom we had bribed to let us enter the house, rushed into the room announcing the return of Zelida's father. My brothers, trembling with fright, hid the watches in their turbans, and while the slave was <u>attending to</u> Zelida, who had <u>sunk fainting to the ground</u>, we managed to make our escape.

重点提示:替换第一处下划线;第二处是什么意思? 恰当处理第三处!

'Fearing to be traced by the enraged Siroco, we did not dare to go back to the house where we lodged, but took refuge with Sumi.

'"Unhappy wretches!" cried she, "is it thus that you have followed the counsels of your father? This very morning I consulted my magic books, and saw you in the act of abandoning your hearts to the fatal passion which will one day be your ruin. No, do not think I will tamely bear this insult! It was I who wrote the letter which stopped Zelida in the act of drinking the elixir of love! As for you," she went on, turning to my brothers, "you do not yet know what those two watches will cost you! But you can learn it now, and the knowledge of the truth will only serve to render your lives still more miserable."

'As she spoke she held out the sacred book written by Moizes, and pointed to the following lines:

'"If at midnight the watches are wound with the key of gold and the key of silver, they will resume their proper shapes during the first hour of the day. They will always remain under the care of a woman, and will come back to her wherever they may be. And the woman appointed to guard them is the daughter of Moizes."

'My brothers were full of rage when they saw themselves outwitted, <u>but there was no help for it</u>. The watches were delivered up to Sumi and they went their way, while I remained behind curious to see what would happen.

重点提示:如何理解并翻译下划线?

'<u>As night wore on</u> Sumi wound up both watches, and when midnight struck Aurora and her sister made their appearance. They knew nothing of what had occurred and supposed they had just awakened from sleep, but when Sumi's story made them understand their terrible fate, they both sobbed with despair and were only consoled when Sumi promised never to forsake them. Then one o'clock sounded, and they became watches again.

重点提示：翻译并替换下划线！

'All night long I was a prey to vague fears, and I felt as if something unseen was pushing me on—in what direction I did not know. At dawn I rose and went out, meeting Izif in the street suffering from the same dread as myself. We agreed that Constantinople was no place for us any longer, and calling to Izouf to accompany us, we left the city together, but soon determined to travel separately, so that we might not be so easily recognised by the spies of Siroco.

重点提示：如何理解并再现两处下划线？

'A few days later I found myself at the door of an old castle near the sea, before which a tall slave was pacing to and fro. The gift of one or two worthless jewels loosened his tongue, and he informed me that he was in the service of the son of the Bassa of the Sea, at that time making war in distant countries. The youth, he told me, had been destined from his boyhood to marry the daughter of Siroco, whose sisters were to be the brides of his brothers, and went on to speak of the talisman that his charge possessed. But I could think of nothing but the beautiful Zelida, and my passion, which I thought I had conquered, awoke in full force.

重点提示：琢磨第一处下划线，并适当措辞；第二处当如何理解？厘清第三、四处的关系！第五处指什么？请查词典并举例说明！

'In order to remove this dangerous rival from my path, I resolved to kidnap him, and to this end I began to act a madman, and to sing and dance loudly, crying to the slave to fetch the boy and let him see my tricks. He consented, and both were so diverted with my antics that they laughed till the tears ran down their *cheeks*, and even tried to *imitate* me. Then I declared I felt thirsty and begged the slave to fetch me some water, and while he was absent I advised the youth to take off his turban, so as to cool his head. He complied gladly, and in the twinkling of an eye was changed into a pot. A cry from the slave warned me that I had no time to lose if I would save my life, so I snatched up the pot and fled with it like the wind.

重点提示：思考第一处下划线的意思,并举例说明;替换第二处;替换第一处斜体字;恰当处理第二处！

'You have heard, my lords, what became of the pot, so I will only say now that when I awoke it had disappeared; but I was partly consoled for its loss by finding my two brothers fast asleep not far from me. "How did you get here?" I inquired, "and what has happened to you since we parted?"

'"Alas!" replied Izouf, "we were passing a wayside inn from which came sounds of songs and laughter, and fools that we were--we entered and sat down. Circassian girls of great beauty were dancing for the amusement of several men, who not only received us politely, but placed us near the two loveliest maidens. Our happiness was complete, and time flew unknown to us, when one of the Circassians leaned forward and said to her sister, 'Their brother danced, and they must dance too.' What they meant by these words I know not, but perhaps you can tell us?"

重点提示：第一处下划线似可直译；如何理解并翻译第二处？第三处是什么成分？最后一处是固定搭配,请举例说明。

'"I understand quite well," I replied. "They were thinking of the day that I stole the son of the Bassa, and had danced before him."

重点提示：下划线可替换吗？

'"Perhaps you are right," continued Izouf, "for the two ladies took our hands and danced with us till we were quite exhausted, and when at last we sat down a second time to table we drank <u>more wine than was good for us</u>. Indeed, our heads grew so confused, that when the men jumped up and threatened to kill us, we could make no resistance and suffered ourselves to be robbed of everything we had about us, including the most precious possession of all, the two talismans of the daughters of Siroco."

重点提示：下划线带有隐含意味，如何再现之？

'Not knowing what else to do, we all three returned to Constantinople to ask the advice of Sumi, and found that she was already aware of our misfortunes, having read about them in the book of Moizes. The kind-hearted creature wept bitterly at our story, but, being poor herself, could give us little help. At last I proposed that every morning we should sell the silver watch into which Argentine was changed, as it would return to Sumi every evening unless it was wound up with the silver key--which was not at all likely. Sumi consented, but only on the condition that we would never sell the watch without ascertaining the house where it was to be found, so that she might also take Aurora thither, and thus Argentine would not be alone if by any chance she was wound up at the mystic hour. For some weeks now we have <u>lived by this means</u>, and the two daughters of Siroco have never failed to return to Sumi each night. Yesterday Izouf sold the silver watch to this young man, and in the evening placed the gold watch on the steps by order of Sumi, just before his customer entered the house, from which both watches came back early this morning.'

重点提示：思考并翻译下划线，且举例加以说明！

'*If I had only known*!' cried Neangir. 'If I had had more <u>presence of mind</u>, I should have seen the lovely Argentine, and if her portrait is so fair, what must <u>the original</u> be!'

重点提示：特别留心斜体字的句式，再举例说明该用法；思考并给出第一处下划线的反义词；如何再现第二处下划线之意？

'It was not your fault,' replied the Cadi, 'you are no magician; and who could guess that the watch must be wound at such an hour? But I shall give orders that the merchant is to hand it over to you, and this evening you will certainly not forget.'

'It is impossible to let you have it today,' answered Izouf, 'for it is already sold.'

'If that is so,' said the Cadi, 'you must return the three gold pieces which the young man paid.'

The Jew, delighted to get off so easily, put his hand in his pocket, when Neangir stopped him.

'No, no,' he exclaimed, 'it is not money I want, but the adorable Argentine; without her everything is valueless.'

'My dear Cadi,' said the Bassa, 'he is right. The treasure that my son has lost is absolutely priceless.'

'My lord,' replied the Cadi, 'your wisdom is greater than mine. Give judgment I pray you in the matter.'

So the Bassa desired them all to accompany him to his house, and commanded his slaves not to lose sight of the three Jewish brothers.

When they arrived at the door of his dwelling, he noticed two women sitting on a bench close by, thickly veiled and beautifully dressed. Their wide satin trousers were embroidered in silver, and their muslin robes were of the finest texture. In the hand of one was a bag of pink silk tied with green ribbons, containing something that seemed to move.

At the approach of the Bassa both ladies rose, and came towards him. Then the one who held the bag addressed him saying, 'Noble lord, buy, *I pray you*, this bag, without asking to see what it contains.'

重点提示：用一个单词替换斜体字！

'How much do you want for it?' asked the Bassa.

重点提示：分别替换两处下划线！

'Three hundred sequins,' replied the unknown.

At these words the Bassa laughed contemptuously, and passed on without speaking.

'You will not repent of your bargain,' went on the woman. 'Perhaps if we come back tomorrow you will be glad to give us the four hundred sequins we shall then ask. And the next day the price will be five hundred.'

重点提示：留意该用法，并举例说明。

'Come away,' said her companion, taking hold of her sleeve. 'Do not let us stay here any longer. It may cry, and then our secret will be discovered.' And so saying, the two young women disappeared.

The Jews were left in the front hall under the care of the slaves, and Neangir and Sumi followed the Bassa inside the house, which was magnificently furnished.

At one end of a large, brilliantly-lighted room a lady of about thirty-five years old reclined on a couch, still beautiful in spite of the sad expression of her face.

'Incomparable Zambac,' said the Bassa, going up to her, 'give me your thanks, for here is the lost son for whom you have shed so many tears,' but before his mother could clasp him in her arms Neangir had flung himself at her feet.

'Let the whole house rejoice with me,' continued the Bassa, 'and let my two sons Ibrahim and Hassan be told, that they may embrace their brother.'

'Alas! My lord!' said Zambac, 'do you forget that this is the hour when Hassan weeps on his hand, and Ibrahim gathers up his coral beads?'

'Let the command of the Prophet be obeyed,' replied the Bassa; 'then we will wait till the evening.'

'Forgive me, noble lord,' interrupted Sumi, 'but what is this mystery? With the help of the Book of Spells perhaps I may be of some use in the matter.'

'Sumi,' answered the Bassa, 'I owe you already the happiness of my life; come with me then, and the sight of my unhappy sons will tell you of our trouble better than any words of mine.'

The Bassa rose from his divan and drew aside the hangings leading to a large hall, closely followed by Neangir and Sumi. There they saw two young men, one about seventeen, and the other nineteen years of age. The younger was seated before a table, his forehead resting on his right hand, which he was watering with his tears. He raised his head for a moment when his father entered, and Neangir and Sumi both saw that this hand was of ebony.

The other young man was <u>occupied busily in</u> collecting coral beads which were scattered all over the floor of the room, and as he picked them up he placed them on the same table where his brother was sitting. He had already gathered together ninety-eight beads, and thought they were all there, when they suddenly rolled off the table and he had to begin his work over again.

重点提示：用 busy 的恰当用法替换下划线！

'Do you see,' whispered the Bassa, 'for three hours daily one collects these coral beads, and for the same space of time the other laments over his hand which has become black, and I am wholly ignorant what is the cause of either misfortune.'

'Do not let us stay here,' said Sumi, 'our presence must add to their grief. But permit me to fetch the Book of Spells, which I feel sure will tell us not only the cause of their *malady* but also its *cure*.'

重点提示：替换两处斜体字！

The Bassa readily agreed to Sumi's proposal, but Neangir objected strongly. 'If Sumi leaves us,' he said to his father, 'I shall not see my beloved Argentine when she returns tonight with the fair Aurora. And life is *an eternity* till I behold her.'

重点提示：替换斜体字！

'Be comforted,' replied Sumi. 'I will be back before sunset; and I leave you my adored Izaf as a pledge.'

Scarcely had the Jewess left Neangir, when the old female slave entered the hall where the three Jews still remained carefully guarded, followed by a man whose splendid dress prevented Neangir from recognising at first as the person in whose house he had dined two days before. But the woman he knew at once to be the nurse of Zelida.

He started eagerly forward, but before he had time to speak the slave turned to the soldier she was conducting. 'My lord,' she said, 'those are the men; I have tracked them from the house of the Cadi to this palace. They are the same; I am not mistaken, strike and avenge yourself.'

As he listened the face of the stranger <u>grew scarlet with anger</u>. He drew his sword and in another moment would have rushed on the Jews, when Neangir and the slaves of the Bassa seized hold of him.

重点提示：如何理解下划线？

'What are you doing?' cried Neangir. 'How dare you attack those whom the Bassa has taken under his protection?'

'Ah, my son,' replied the soldier, 'the Bassa would withdraw his protection if he knew that these wretches have robbed me of all I have dearest in the world. He knows them as little as he knows you.'

'But he knows me very well,' replied Neangir, 'for he has recognised me as his son. Come with me now into his presence.'

The stranger bowed and passed through the curtain held back by Neangir, whose surprise was great at seeing his father spring forward and clasp the soldier in his arms.

'What! Is it you, my dear Siroco?' cried he. 'I believed you had been slain in that awful battle when the followers of the Prophet were *put to flight*. But why do your eyes kindle with the flames they shot forth on that fearful day? Calm yourself and tell me what I can do to help you. See, I have found my son, let that be a good omen for your happiness also.'

重点提示:斜体字是什么意思?

'I did not guess,' answered Siroco, 'that the son you have so long mourned had come back to you. Some days since the Prophet appeared to me in a dream, floating in a circle of light, and he said to me, "Go tomorrow at sunset to the Galata Gate, and there you will find a young man whom you must bring home with you. He is the second son of your old friend the Bassa of the Sea, and that you may make no mistake, put your fingers in his turban and you will feel the plaque on which my name is engraved in seven different languages."

'I did as I was bid,' went on Siroco, 'and so charmed was I with his face and manner that I caused him to fall in love with Argentine, whose portrait I gave him. But at the moment when I was rejoicing in the happiness before me, and looking forward to the pleasure of restoring you your son, some drops of the elixir of love were spilt on the table, and caused a thick vapour to arise, which hid everything. When it had cleared away he was gone. This morning my old slave informed me that she had discovered the traitors who had stolen my daughters from me, and I hastened hither to avenge them. But I place myself in your hands, and will follow your counsel.'

'Fate will favour us, I am sure,' said the Bassa, 'for this very night I expect to secure both the silver and the gold watch. So send at once and pray Zelida to join us.'

A rustling of silken stuffs drew their eyes to the door, and Ibrahim and Hassan, whose daily penance had by this time been performed, entered to embrace their brother. Neangir and Hassan, who had also drunk of *the elixir of love*, could think of nothing but the beautiful ladies who had *captured their hearts*, while the spirits of Ibrahim had been cheered by the news that the daughter of Moizes hoped to find in the Book of Spells some charm to *deliver* him from collecting the magic beads.

重点提示:如何再现三处斜体字的含义?

It was some hours later that Sumi returned, bringing with her the sacred book.

'See,' she said, beckoning to Hassan, 'your destiny is written here.' And Hassan stooped and read these words in Hebrew. 'His right hand has become black as ebony from touching the fat of an impure animal, and will remain so till the last of its race is drowned in the sea.'

'Alas!' sighed the unfortunate youth. '*It now comes back to my memory*. One day the slave of Zambac was making a cake. She warned me not to touch, as the cake was mixed with lard, but I did not heed her, and in an instant my hand became the ebony that it now is.'

重点提示:替换斜体字!

'Holy dervish!' exclaimed the Bassa, 'how true were your words! My son has neglected the advice you gave him on presenting him the bracelet, and he has been severely punished. But tell me, O wise Sumi, where I can find the last of the accursed race who has brought this doom on my son?'

重点提示:如何理解下划线?

93

'It is written here,' replied Sumi, turning over some leaves. 'The little black pig is in the pink bag carried by the two Circassians.'

When he read this the Bassa sank on his cushions in despair.

'Ah,' he said, 'that is the bag that was offered me this morning for three hundred sequins. Those must be the women who caused Izif and Izouf to dance, and took from them the two talismans of the daughters of Siroco. They only can break the spell that has been <u>cast on</u> us. Let them be found and I will gladly give them the half of my possessions. <u>Idiot that I was to send them away</u>!'

重点提示：请思考并恰当处置两处下划线！

While the Bassa was bewailing his folly, Ibrahim in his turn had opened the book, and blushed deeply as he read the words: 'The chaplet of beads has been defiled by the game of "Odd and Even." Its owner has tried to cheat by concealing one of the numbers. Let the faithless Moslem seek for ever the missing bead.'

'O heaven,' cried Ibrahim, 'that unhappy day rises up before me. I had cut the thread of the chaplet, while playing with Aurora. Holding the ninety-nine beads in my hand she guessed "Odd," and in order that she might lose I let one bead fall from my hand. Since then I have sought it daily, but it never has been found.'

'Holy dervish!' cried the Bassa, 'how true were your words! From the time that the sacred chaplet was no longer complete, my son has borne the penalty. But may not the Book of Spells teach us how to deliver Ibrahim also?'

'Listen,' said Sumi, 'this is what I find: "The coral bead lies in the fifth fold of the dress of yellow brocade."'

'Ah, what good fortune!' exclaimed the Bassa; 'we shall shortly see the beautiful Aurora, and Ibrahim shall at once search in the fifth fold of her yellow brocade. For it is she no doubt of whom the book speaks.'

As the Jewess closed the Book of Moizes, Zelida appeared, accompanied by a whole *train* of slaves and her old nurse. <u>At her entrance</u> Hassan, beside himself with joy, flung himself on his knees and kissed her hand.

重点提示：替换斜体字；说明下划线在句中的成分。

'My lord,' he said to the Bassa, 'pardon me these transports. No elixir of love was needed to inflame my heart! Let the marriage rite make us speedily one.'

'My son, are you mad?' asked the Bassa. 'As long as the misfortunes of your brothers last, shall you alone be happy? And whoever heard of a bridegroom with a black hand? Wait yet a little longer, till the black pig is drowned in the sea.'

'Yes! Dear Hassan,' said Zelida, 'our happiness will be <u>increased tenfold</u> when my sisters have regained their proper shapes. And here is the elixir which I have brought with me, so that their joy may equal ours.' And she held out the flask to the Bassa, who had it closed in his presence.

重点提示：如何翻译下划线？

Zambac was filled with joy at the sight of Zelida, and embraced her with delight. Then she led the way into the garden, and invited all her friends to seat themselves under the thick overhanging branches of a splendid jessamine tree. No sooner, however, were they comfortably settled, than they were astonished to hear a man's voice, speaking angrily on the other side of the wall.

'Ungrateful girls!' it said, 'is this the way you treat me? Let me hide myself for ever! This cave is no longer dark enough or deep enough for me.'

A burst of laughter was the only answer, and the voice continued, 'What have I done to earn such contempt? Was this what you promised me when I managed to get for you the talismans of beauty? Is this *the reward I have a right to expect* when I have bestowed on you the little black pig, who is certain to bring you good luck?'

重点提示:如何理解这看似正面意思的斜体字？下划线用作什么成分？

At these words the curiosity of the listeners passed all bounds, and the Bassa commanded his slaves instantly to tear down the wall. It was done, but the man was nowhere to be seen, and there were only two girls of extraordinary beauty, who seemed quite at their ease, and came dancing gaily on to the terrace. With them was an old slave in whom the Bassa recognised Gouloucou, the former guardian of Neangir.

重点提示:将两处下划线联系起来思考,其意思似乎更明朗！

Gouloucou shrank with fear when he saw the Bassa, as he expected nothing less than death at his hands for allowing Neangir to be snatched away. But the Bassa made him signs of forgiveness, and asked him how he had escaped death when he had thrown himself from the cliff. Gouloucou explained that he had been picked up by a dervish who had cured his wounds, and had then given him as slave to the two young ladies now before the company, and in their service he had remained ever since.

'But,' said the Bassa, 'where is the little black pig of which the voice spoke just now?'

'My lord,' answered one of the ladies, 'when at your command the wall was thrown down, the man whom you heard speaking was so frightened at the noise that he caught up the pig and ran away.'

重点提示:如何理解下划线？

'Let him be pursued instantly,' cried the Bassa; but the ladies smiled.

重点提示:替换下划线！

'Do not be alarmed, my lord,' said one, 'he is sure to return. Only give orders that the entrance to the cave shall be guarded, so that when he is once in he shall not get out again.'

By this time night was falling and they all went back to the palace, where coffee and fruits were served in a splendid gallery, near the women's apartments. The Bassa then ordered the three Jews to be brought before him, so that he might see whether these were the two *damsels* who had forced them to dance at the inn, but to his great vexation it was found that when their guards had gone to knock down the wall the Jews had escaped.

重点提示:替换斜体字！下划线在句中起什么作用？举例说明。

At this news the Jewess Sumi turned pale, but glancing at the Book of Spells her face brightened, and she said half aloud, 'There is no cause for disquiet; they will capture the dervish,' while Hassan lamented loudly that as soon as fortune appeared on one side she fled on the other!

On hearing this reflection one of the Bassa's pages broke into a laugh. 'This fortune comes to us dancing my lord,' said he, 'and the other leaves us on crutches. Do not be afraid. She will not go very far.'

The Bassa, shocked at his impertinent interference, desired him to leave the room and not to come back till he was sent for.

'<u>My lord shall be obeyed</u>,' said the page, 'but when I return, it shall be in such good company that you will welcome me gladly.' So saying, he went out.

重点提示：如何恰当处理下划线？

When they were alone, Neangir turned to the fair strangers and implored their help. 'My brothers and I,' he cried, 'are filled with love for three peerless maidens, two of whom are under a cruel spell. If their fate happened to be in your hands, would you not do all in your power to restore them to happiness and liberty?'

But the young man's appeal only stirred the two ladies to anger. 'What,' exclaimed one, 'are the sorrows of lovers to us? Fate has deprived us of our lovers, and if it depends on us the whole world shall suffer as much as we do!'

This unexpected reply was heard with amazement by all present, and the Bassa entreated the speaker to tell them her story. Having obtained permission of her sister, she began:

思考题：
试着理清故事的线索！

17. The Story of the Fair Circassians

'We were <u>born</u> in Circassia <u>of poor people</u>, and my *sister's* name is Tezila and mine Dely. Having nothing but our beauty to help us in life, we were carefully trained in all the accomplishments that give pleasure. We were both quick to learn, and from our childhood could play all sorts of instruments, could sing, and above all could dance. We were besides, lively and merry, as in spite of our misfortunes we are to this day.

重点提示:留心两处下划线的用法(与当代英语略有不同,是吗?)!斜体字是"姐姐"还是"妹妹"?

'We were easily pleased and quite content with our lives at home, when one morning the officials who had been sent to find wives for the Sultan saw us, and were <u>struck with our beauty</u>. We had always expected something of the sort, and were <u>resigned to our lot</u>, when we chanced to see two young men enter our house. The elder, who was about twenty years of age, had black hair and very bright eyes. The other could not have been more than fifteen, and was so fair that he might easily have <u>passed for a girl</u>.

重点提示:琢磨三处下划线,尤其是最后一处!

'They knocked at the door with *a timid air* and begged our parents to give them shelter, as they had lost their way. After some hesitation their request was granted, and they were invited into the room in which we were. And if our parents' hearts were touched by their beauty, our own were *not any harder*, so that our departure for the palace, which had been arranged for the next day, suddenly became intolerable to us.

重点提示:用一个单词替换第一处斜体字;恰当翻译第二处斜体字(留意此处的低调措辞)!

'Night came, and I awoke from my sleep to find the younger of the two strangers sitting at my bedside and felt him take my hand.

'"Fear nothing, lovely Dely," he whispered, "from one who never knew love till he saw you. My name," he went on, "is Prince Delicate, and I am the son of the king of the Isle of Black Marble. My friend, who travels with me, is one of the richest nobles of my country, and the secrets which he knows are the envy of the Sultan himself. And we left our native country because my father wished me to marry a lady of great beauty, but <u>with one eye a trifle smaller than the other</u>."

重点提示:如何处理下划线?

'My vanity was flattered at so *speedy* a conquest, and I was charmed with the way the young man had declared his passion. I *turned my eyes slowly* on him, and the look I gave him caused him almost to lose his senses. He fell fainting forward, and I was unable to move till Tezila, who had hastily put on a dress, ran to my assistance together with Thelamis, the young noble of whom the Prince had spoken.

重点提示:思考并替换三处斜体字!

'As soon as <u>we were all ourselves again</u> we began to bewail our fate, and the journey that we were to take that very day to Constantinople. But we felt a little comforted when Thelamis assured us that he and the prince would follow *in our steps*, and would somehow contrive to speak to us. Then they kissed our hands, and left the house by a side way.

重点提示：两处下划线当如何处理更妥？用一个单词替换斜体字！

'A few moments later our parents came to tell us that the escort had arrived, and having *taken farewell of* them we mounted the camels, and took our seats in a kind of box that was fixed to the side of the animal. These boxes were large enough for us to sleep in comfortably, and as there was a window in the upper part, we were able to see the country through which we passed.

重点提示：下划线是何意（指人,还是指事）？替换斜体字！

'For several days we journeyed on, feeling sad and anxious as to what might become of us, when one day as I was looking out of the window of our room, I heard my name called, and beheld a beautifully dressed girl jumping out of the box on the other side of our camel. One glance told me that it was the prince, and my heart bounded with joy. It was, he said, Thelamis's idea to disguise him like this, and that he himself had assumed the character of a slave-dealer who was taking this peerless maiden as a present to the Sultan. Thelamis had also persuaded the officer in charge of the caravan to let him hire the vacant box, so it was easy for the prince to scramble out of his own window and approach ours.

重点提示：请翻译两处下划线！

'This ingenious trick enchanted us, but our agreeable conversation was soon interrupted by the attendants, who perceived that the camel was walking in a crooked manner and came to find out what was wrong. Luckily they were slow in their movements, and the prince had just time to get back to his own box and restore the balance, before the trick was discovered.

重点提示：用两个汉字翻译下划线！

'But neither the prince nor his friend had any intention of allowing us to enter the Sultan's palace, though it was difficult to know how we were to escape, and what was to become of us when once we had escaped. At length, one day as we were drawing near Constantinople, we learned from the prince that Thelamis had made acquaintance with a holy dervish whom he had met on the road, and had informed him that we were his sisters, who were being sold as slaves against his will. The good man was interested in the story, and readily agreed to find us shelter if we could manage to elude the watchfulness of our guards. The risk was great, but it was our only chance.

'That night, when the whole caravan was fast asleep, we raised the upper part of our boxes and by the help of Thelamis climbed silently out. We next went back some distance along the way we had come, then, striking into another road, reached at last the retreat prepared for us by the dervish. Here we found food and rest, and I need not say what happiness it was to be free once more.

'The dervish soon became a slave to our beauty, and the day after our escape he proposed that we should allow him to conduct us to an inn situated at a short distance, where we should find two Jews, owners of precious talismans which did not really belong to them. "Try," said the dervish, "by some means to get possession of them."

重点提示：如何处理下划线？

'The inn, though not on the direct road to Constantinople, was a favourite one with merchants, owing to the excellence of the food, and on our arrival we discovered at least six or eight other people who had stopped for refreshment. They greeted us politely, and we sat down to table together.

'In a short time the two men described by the dervish entered the room, and at a sign from him my sister made room at her side for one, while I did the same for the other.

'Now the dervish had happened to mention that "their brother had danced." At the moment we paid no attention to this remark, but it *came back to our minds* now, and we determined that they should dance also. To accomplish this we used all our arts and very soon bent them to our wills, so that they could refuse us nothing. At the end of the day we remained possessors of the talismans and had left them *to their fate*, while the prince and Thelamis fell more in love with us than ever, and declared that we were more lovely than any women in the world.

重点提示:如何理解第一处斜体字? 替换第二处! 下划线是什么意思?

'The sun had set before we *quitted* the inn, and we had made no plans as to where we should go next, so we readily consented to the prince's proposal that we should embark without delay for the Isle of Black Marble. What a place it was! Rocks blacker than jet towered above its shores and shed thick darkness over the country. Our sailors had not been there before and were nearly as frightened as ourselves, but *thanks to* Thelamis, who undertook to be our pilot, we landed safely on the beach.

重点提示:思考并替换两处斜体字!

'When we had left the coast behind us, with its walls of jet, we entered a lovely country where the fields were greener, the streams clearer, and the sun brighter than anywhere else. The people crowded round to welcome their prince, whom they loved dearly, but they told him that the king was still full of rage at his son's refusal to marry his cousin the Princess Okimpare, and also at his flight. Indeed, they all begged him not to visit the capital, as his life would hardly be safe. So, much as I should have enjoyed seeing the home of my beloved prince, I implored him to listen to this wise advice and to let us all go to Thelamis's palace in the middle of a vast forest.

'To my sister and myself, who had been brought up in a cottage, this house of Thelamis's seemed like fairyland. It was built of pink marble, so highly polished that the flowers and streams surrounding it were reflected as in a mirror. One set of rooms was furnished especially for me in yellow silk and silver, to suit my black hair. Fresh dresses were provided for us every day, and we had slaves to wait on us. Ah, why could not this happiness have lasted for ever!

'The peace of our lives was troubled by Thelamis's jealousy of my sister, as he could not endure to see her on *friendly* terms with the prince, though knowing full well that his heart was mine. Every day we had scenes of tender reproaches and of explanations, but Tezila's tears never failed to bring Thelamis to his knees, with prayers for forgiveness.

重点提示:替换斜体字;如何理解下划线的含义?

'We had been living in this way for some months when one day the news came that the king had fallen *dangerously* ill. I begged the prince to hurry at once to the Court, both to see his father and also to show himself to the senators and nobles, but as his love for me was greater than his desire of a crown, he hesitated as if foreseeing all that afterwards happened. At last Tezila spoke to him so seriously in Thelamis's presence, that he determined to go, but promised that he would return before night.

重点提示：替换斜体字！

'Night came but no prince, and Tezila, who had been the cause of his departure, showed such signs of uneasiness that Thelamis's jealousy was at once awakened. As for me, I cannot tell what I suffered. Not being able to sleep I rose from my bed and wandered into the forest, along the road which he had taken so many hours before. Suddenly I heard in the distance the sound of a horse's hoofs, and in a few moments the prince had flung himself down and was by my side. "Ah, how I adore you!" he exclaimed; "Thelamis's love will never equal mine." The words were hardly out of his mouth when I heard a slight noise behind, and before we could turn round both our heads were rolling in front of us, while the voice of Thelamis cried:

'"Perjured wretches, answer me; and you, faithless Tezila, tell me why you have betrayed me like this?"

'Then I understood what had happened, and that, in his rage, he had mistaken me for my sister.

'"Alas," replied my head in weak tones, "I am not Tezila, but Dely, whose life you have destroyed, as well as that of your friend." At this Thelamis paused and seemed to reflect for an instant.

'"Be not frightened," he said more quietly, "*I can make you whole again*," and laying a magic powder on our tongues he placed our heads on our necks. *In the twinkling of an eye* our heads were joined to our bodies without leaving so much as a scar; only that, blinded with rage as he still was, Thelamis had placed my head on the prince's body, and his on mine!

重点提示：思考、替换并翻译两处斜体字！

'I cannot describe to you how *odd* we both felt at this strange transformation. We both instinctively put up our hands—he to feel his hair, which was, of course, dressed like a woman's, and I to raise the turban which pressed heavily on my forehead. But we did not know what had happened to us, for the night was still dark.

'At this point Tezila appeared, followed by a troop of slaves bearing flowers. It was only by the light of their torches that we understood what had occurred. Indeed the first thought of both of us was that we must have changed clothes.

'Now in spite of what we may say, we all prefer our own bodies to those of anybody else, so *notwithstanding* our love for each other, at first we could not help feeling a little cross with Thelamis. However, so deep was the prince's passion for me, that very soon he began to congratulate himself on the change. "My happiness is perfect," he said; "my heart, beautiful Dely, has always been yours, and now I have your head also."

重点提示：替换两处斜体字！

'But though the prince made the best of it, Thelamis was much ashamed of his stupidity. "I have," he said hesitatingly, "two other pastilles which have the same magic properties as those I used before. Let me cut off your heads again, and that will put matters *straight*." The proposal sounded tempting, but was a little risky, and after consulting together we decided to let things remain as they were. "Do not blame me then," continued Thelamis, "if you will not accept my offer.

But take the two pastilles, and if it ever happens that you are decapitated a second time, make use of them in the way I have shown you, and each will get back his own head." So saying he presented us with the pastilles, and we all returned to the castle.

重点提示：请恰当理解并处置下划线！替换斜体字。

'However, the troubles caused by the unfortunate exchange were only just beginning. My head, without thinking what it was doing, led the prince's body to my apartments. But my women, only looking at the dress, declared I had mistaken the corridor, and called some slaves to conduct me to his highness's rooms. This was bad enough, but when--as it was still night my servants began to undress me, I nearly fainted from surprise and confusion, and no doubt the prince's head was suffering in the same manner at the other end of the castle!

'By the next morning--you will easily guess that we slept but little—we had grown partly accustomed to our strange situation, and when we looked in the mirror, the prince had become brown-skinned and black-haired, while my head was covered with his curly golden locks. And after that first day, everyone in the palace had become so accustomed to the change that they thought no more about it.

'Some weeks after this, we heard that the king of the Isle of Black Marble was dead. The prince's head, which once was mine, was full of ambitious desires, and he longed to ride straight to the capital and proclaim himself king. But then came the question as to whether the nobles would recognise the prince with a girl's body, and indeed, when we came to think of it, which was prince and which was girl?

'At last, after much argument, my head carried the day and we set out; but only to find that the king had declared the Princess Okimpare his successor. The greater part of the senators and nobles openly professed that they would much have preferred the rightful heir, but as they could not recognise him either in the prince or me, they chose to consider us as impostors and threw us into prison.

'A few days later Tezila and Thelamis, who had followed us to the capital, came to tell us that the new queen had accused us of high treason, and had herself been present at our trial—which was conducted without us. They had been in mortal terror as to what would be our sentence, but by a piece of extraordinary luck we had been condemned to be beheaded.

重点提示：如何理解两处下划线？

'I told my sister that I did not see exactly where the luck came in, but Thelamis interrupted me rudely:

'"What!" he cried, "of course I shall make use of the pastilles, and—" but here the officers arrived to lead us to the great square where the execution was to take place--for Okimpare was determined there should be no delay.

'The square was crowded with people of all ages and all ranks, and in the middle a platform had been erected on which was the scaffold, with the executioner, in a black mask, standing by. At a sign from him I mounted first, and in a moment my head was rolling at his feet. With a bound my sister and Thelamis were beside me, and like lightning Thelamis seized the sabre from the headsman, and cut off the head of the prince. And before the multitude had recovered from their astonishment at these strange proceedings, our bodies were joined to our right heads, and the pastilles placed on our tongues. Then Thelamis led the prince to the edge of the platform and presented him to the people, saying, "Behold your lawful king."

'Shouts of joy <u>rent the air</u> at the sound of Thelamis's words, and the noise reached Okimpare in the palace. Smitten with despair at the news, she fell down unconscious on her balcony, and was lifted up by the slaves and taken back to her own house.

重点提示:如何翻译下划线?

'Meanwhile our happiness was all turned to sorrow. I had rushed up to the prince to embrace him fondly, when he suddenly grew pale and staggered.

'"<u>I die faithful to you</u>," he murmured, turning his eyes towards me, "and I die *a king*!" and leaning his head on my shoulder he expired quietly, for one of the arteries in his neck had been cut through.

重点提示:请翻译下划线,并说出斜体字的成分!

'Not knowing what I did I staggered towards the sabre which was lying near me, with the intention of following my beloved prince as speedily as possible. And when Thelamis seized my hand (but only just in time), in my madness I turned the sabre upon him, and he fell struck through the heart at my feet.'

The *whole company* were listening to the story *with breathless attention*, when it became plain that Dely could go no further, while Tezila had flung herself on a heap of cushions and hidden her face. Zambac ordered her women to give them all the attention possible, and desired they should be carried into her own rooms.

重点提示:第一处斜体字指谁? 如何翻译第二处斜体字?

When the two sisters were in this condition, Ibrahim, who was a very prudent young man, suggested to his parents that, as the two Circassians were both unconscious, it would be an excellent opportunity to search them and see if the talismans belonging to the daughters of Siroco were concealed about their persons. But the Bassa, shocked at the notion of treating his guests in so inhospitable a manner, refused to do anything of the kind, adding that the next day he hoped to persuade them to give the talismans up of their own free will.

By this time it was nearly midnight and Neangir, who was standing near the Jewess Sumi, drew out the portrait of Argentine, and heard with delight that she was even more beautiful than her picture. Everyone was <u>waiting on tip-toe</u> for the appearance of the two watches, who were expected when the clock struck twelve to come in search of Sumi, and that there might be no delay the Bassa ordered all the doors to be flung wide open. It was done, and there entered not the longed-for watches, but the page who had been sent away in disgrace.

重点提示:请恰当处理下划线!

Then the Bassa arose in wrath. 'Azemi,' he said, 'did I not order you to stand no more in my presence?'

'My lord,' replied Azemi, modestly, 'I was hidden outside the door, listening to the tale of the two Circassians. And as I know you are fond of stories, <u>give me also leave to tell you one</u>. I promise you it shall not be long.'

重点提示：查词典，看下划线如何翻译更恰当？

'Speak on,' replied the Bassa, 'but take heed what you say.'

'My lord,' began Azemi, 'this morning I was walking in the town when I noticed a man going in the same direction followed by a slave. He entered a baker's shop, where he bought some bread which he gave to the slave to carry. I watched him and saw that he purchased many other kinds of provisions at other places, and when the slave could carry no more his master commanded him to return home and have supper ready at midnight.

'When left alone the man went up the street, and turning into a jeweller's shop, brought out a watch that as far as I could see was made of silver. He walked on a few steps, then stooped and picked up a gold watch which lay at his feet. At this point I ran up and told him that if he did not give me half its price I would report him to the Cadi; he agreed, and conducting me to his house produced four hundred sequins, which he said was my share, and having got what I wanted I went away.

'As it was the hour for attending on my lord I returned home and accompanied you to the Cadi, where I heard the story of the three Jews and learned the importance of the two watches I had left at the stranger's. I hastened to his house, but he had gone out, and I could only find the slave, whom I told that I was the bearer of important news for his master. Believing me to be one of his friends, he begged me to wait, and showed me into a room where I saw the two watches lying on the table. I put them in my pocket, leaving the four hundred sequins <u>in place of</u> the gold watch and three gold pieces which I knew to be the price of the other. As you know the watches never remain with the person who buys them, this man may think himself very lucky to get back his money. I have wound them both up, and at this instant Aurora and Argentine are locked safely into my own room.'

重点提示：如何理解下划线？

Everybody was so delighted to hear this news that Azemi was nearly stifled with their embraces, and Neangir could hardly be prevented from running to break in the door, though he did not even know where the page slept.

But the page begged to have the honour of fetching the ladies himself, and soon returned leading them by the hand.

For some minutes all was <u>a happy confusion</u>, and Ibrahim took advantage of it to fall on his knees before Aurora, and search in the fifth fold of her dress for the missing coral bead. The Book of Spells had told the truth; there it was, and as the chaplet was now complete the young man's days of seeking were over.

重点提示：下划线属于什么修辞？如何理解、翻译更好？

In the midst of the general rejoicing Hassan alone bore a gloomy face.

'Alas!' he said, 'everyone is happy but the miserable being you see before you. I have lost the only consolation in my grief, which was to feel that I had a brother in misfortune!'

'Be comforted,' replied the Bassa; 'sooner or later the dervish who stole the pink bag is sure to be found.'

Supper was then served, and after they had all eaten of rare fruits which seemed to them the most delicious in the whole world, the Bassa ordered the flask containing the elixir of love to be

103

brought and the young people to drink of it. Then their eyes shone with a new fire, and they swore to be true to each other till death.

This ceremony was scarcely over when the clock struck one, and in an instant Aurora and Argentine had vanished, and in the place where they stood lay two watches. Silence fell upon all the company--they had forgotten the enchantment; then the voice of Azemi was heard asking if he might be allowed to take charge of the watches till the next day, pledging his head to end their enchantment. With the consent of Sumi, this was granted, and the Bassa gave Azemi a purse containing a thousand sequins, as a reward for the services he had already rendered to them. After this everybody went to his own apartment.

Azemi had never possessed so much money before, and never closed his eyes for joy the whole night long. Very early he got up and went into the garden, thinking how he could break the enchantment of the daughters of Siroco. Suddenly the soft tones of a woman fell on his ear, and peeping through the bushes he saw Tezila, who was arranging flowers in her sister's hair. The rustling of the leaves caused Dely to start; she jumped up as if to fly, but Azemi implored her to remain and begged her to tell him what happened to them after the death of their lovers, and how they had come to find the dervish.

'The punishment decreed to us by the Queen Okimpare,' answered Dely, 'was that we were to dance and sing in the midst of our sorrow, at a great fete which was to be held that very day for all her people. This cruel command nearly turned our brains, and we swore a solemn oath to make all lovers as wretched as we were ourselves. *In* this design *we succeeded* so well that in a short time the ladies of the capital came in a body to Okimpare, and prayed her to banish us from the kingdom, before their lives were made miserable for ever. She consented, and commanded us to be placed on board a ship, with our slave Gouloucou.

重点提示：请留意此处的斜体字是固定搭配。

'On the shore we saw an old man who was busily engaged in drowning some little black pigs, talking to them all the while, as if they could understand him.

' "Accursed race," said he, "it is you who have caused all the misfortunes of him to whom I gave the magic bracelet. Perish all of you!"

'We drew near <u>from curiosity</u>, and recognised in him the dervish who had sheltered us on our first escape from the caravan.

重点提示：说说下划线的大意并替换之！

'When the old man discovered who we were he was beside himself with pleasure, and offered us a refuge in the cave where he lived. We gladly accepted his offer, and to the cave we all went, taking with us the last little pig, which he gave us as a present.

' "The Bassa of the Sea," he added, "will pay you anything you like to ask for <u>it</u>."

重点提示：下划线可删除吗？

'Without asking why it was so precious I took the pig and placed it in my work bag, where it has been ever since. Only yesterday we offered it to the Bassa, who laughed at us, and this so enraged us against the dervish that we cut off his beard when he was asleep, and now he dare not show himself.'

'Ah,' exclaimed the page, 'it is not fitting that such beauty should waste itself in making other people miserable. Forget the unhappy past and think only of the future. And accept, I pray you, this watch, to mark the brighter hours in store.' So saying he laid the watch upon her knee. Then he turned to Tezila. 'And you fair maiden, permit me to offer you this other watch. True it is only of silver, but it is all I have left to give. And I feel quite sure that you must have somewhere a silver seal, that will be exactly the thing to go with it.'

'Why, so you have,' cried Dely; 'fasten your silver seal to your watch, and I will hang my gold one on to mine.'

The seals were produced, and, as Azemi had guessed, they were the talismans which the two Circassians had taken from Izif and Izouf, mounted in gold and silver. *As quick as lightning* the watches slid from the hands of Tezila and her sister, and Aurora and Argentine stood before them, each with her talisman on her finger.

重点提示:如何理解斜体字?

At first they seemed rather confused themselves at the change which had taken place, and the sunlight which they had not seen for so long, but when gradually they understood that their enchantment had come to an end, they could find no words to express their happiness.

The Circassians could with difficulty be comforted for the loss of the talismans, but Aurora and Argentine entreated them to dry their tears, as their father, Siroco, who was governor of Alexandria, would not fail to reward them in any manner they wished. This promise was soon confirmed by Siroco himself, who came into the garden with the Bassa and his two sons, and was speedily joined by the ladies of the family. Only Hassan was absent. It was the hour in which he was condemned to bewail his ebony hand.

<u>To the surprise of all</u> a noise was at this moment heard in a corner of the terrace, and Hassan himself appeared *surrounded by slaves*, clapping his hands and shouting with joy. 'I was weeping as usual,' cried he, 'when all at once the tears refused to come to my eyes, and on looking down at my hand I saw that its blackness had vanished. And now, lovely Zelida, nothing prevents me any longer from offering you the hand, when the heart has been yours always.'

重点提示:下划线和斜体字在句子中分别作什么成分用?

But though Hassan never thought of asking or caring what had caused his cure, the others were by no means so indifferent. It was quite clear that the little black pig must be dead--but how, and when? To this the slaves answered that they had seen that morning a man pursued by three others, and that he had taken refuge in the cavern which they had been left to guard. Then, <u>in obedience to orders</u>, they had rolled a stone over the entrance.

重点提示:替换下划线!

Piercing shrieks interrupted their story, and a man, whom the Circassians saw to be the old dervish, rushed round the corner of the terrace with the three Jews behind him. When the fugitive beheld so many people collected together, he turned down another path, but the slaves captured all four and brought them before their master.

What was the surprise of the Bassa when he beheld in the old dervish the man who had given the chaplet, the copper plaque, and the bracelet to his three sons. 'Fear nothing, holy father,' he said, 'you are safe with me. But tell us, how came you here?'

'My lord,' explained the dervish, 'when my beard was cut off during my sleep by the two Circassians, I was ashamed to appear before *the eyes of* men, and fled, bearing with me the pink silk bag. In the night these three men fell in with me, and we passed some time in conversation, but at dawn, when it was light enough to see each other's faces, one of them exclaimed that I was the dervish travelling with the two Circassians who had stolen the talismans from the Jews. I jumped up and tried to fly to my cave, but they were too quick for me, and just as we reached your garden they snatched the bag which contained the little black pig and *flung* it into the sea. By this act, which delivers your son, I would pray you to forgive them for any wrongs they may have done you—*nay more*, that you will recompense them for it.'

重点提示：第一处斜体字一定得保留吗？替换第二处！第三处起什么作用？

The Bassa granted the holy man's request, and seeing that the two Jews had *fallen victims to the charms of* the Circassian ladies, gave his consent to their *union*, which was fixed to take place at the same time as that of Izaf with the wise Sumi. The Cadi was sent for, and the Jews exchanged the hats of their race for the turbans of the followers of the Prophet. Then, after so many misfortunes, the Bassa's three sons entreated their father to delay their happiness no longer, and the six marriages were performed by the Cadi at the hour of noon.

重点提示：替换第一处斜体字；第二处能直译吗？

思考题：
读完这则"故事中的故事"，你从中学到了什么？

Chinese Translation for Reference

1. 妖　　驹

"今晚就待在壁炉这儿,"佩吉老奶奶警告道,"风刮得房子直摇晃;况且是万圣节前夕,巫婆出没,手下的妖仆乔装打扮,四处游荡,专害小孩。"

"我干吗待在这儿?"大孙子说道,"就不,我得去看制绳匠雅各布大叔的女儿在干吗。我要不去看她爸,她那双蓝眼睛会一晚睁着。"

"我得去抓龙虾、螃蟹,"二孙子说道,"就算遍地都是巫婆、小妖,也甭想阻拦我。"

孙子们执意自行其是或找乐子,对佩吉老奶奶的话不屑一顾。见小孙子犹豫了一下她说道:"你待着,理查德小乖乖,我给你讲些好听的故事。"

可他想借月光采摘些百里香叶和黑草莓,于是跟着哥哥们跑了出去。孩子们刚出门就嘀咕:"老婆子说啥风呀雨的,可今晚天气再好没有,晴空万里。瞧,月亮穿过透明云彩那神气劲儿!"

突然,他们看到旁边有匹黑驹。

"啊!哇!"哥几个叫道,"老瓦伦丁家的马驹,肯定是从马厩里逃出来,要去饮马池喝水。"

"我的乖马驹,"老大边拍边说,"可别跑太远啰。我这就带你去饮马池。"说完,他跃身上马,二弟紧跟而上,接着是老三、老四,直到不喜欢被落下的小理查德也跨骑了上去。

路上,他们遇到几个伙伴,还邀他们一同骑上去。他们上了,马驹似乎并不在乎这额外的重量,依然欢快地慢跑着。

马驹跑得越快,小家伙们越开心。他们双脚紧夹马肚,还高叫道:"奔腾吧,小马,你何曾见过更勇猛的骑手!"

这时,海浪迎风咆哮。马驹似乎便不在意,欢快地奔向海边,而不是饮马池。

理查德开始后悔没去采摘百里香叶和黑草莓,老大想起了制绳商雅各布女儿那双蓝眼睛,抓住马鬃,想让它转向。他拉啊拽啊,全白搭。马驹径直奔大海而去,前蹄随后触到了海浪。一触碰到水,马驹发出畅快的嘶声,兴奋地蹦跶起来,继而没入翻飞的巨浪中。见波浪淹过大腿,孩子们开始后悔自己的草率行为,纷纷嚷道:"这该死的黑驹中邪了。当初要听佩吉奶奶的忠告,我们岂会落此下场!"

小驹越前行,海浪越高。海浪最后盖过孩子们头顶,个个因此丧命。

佩吉老奶奶挂念着孙子们,天不亮就出了门。她四处找他们无果,问遍邻居,却无人知其下落,大孙子也没去看制绳匠雅各布家的蓝眼女儿。

悲痛的她躬身往回走,一匹黑驹蹦跶而来,在靠近她时巨声嘶鸣,接着擦身而过,旋即踪影全无。

2. 黄 金 搭 档

从前,有个小偷在海边闲逛,路见一人纹丝不动地望着波浪。

"不知您见过石头游泳没?"小偷问陌生人。

"那还用说,"对方答道,"我甚至见过同一块石头跃出水面、穿空而行呢!"

"答得妙,"小偷答道,"咱俩合伙,准能发大财。咱俩去邻国王宫,之后我单独参见国王,给他编个耸人听闻的故事,你随后替我续谎。"

说定后,两人出发了。几天后,他俩来到(王宫所在的)都城。分手数小时后,小偷独自拜见国王后,恳请陛下赐他一杯啤酒。

"没有,"国王说道,"今年庄稼、酒花、葡萄均歉收,王国上下既无葡萄酒,也无啤酒。"

"不可思议!"小偷答道,"我刚从某国来,那儿庄稼长势良好,我见到一枝酒花酿出 12 桶啤酒。"

"我赌 300 弗罗林没那回事儿,"国王说。

"我赌 300 弗罗林有那回事儿,"小偷答。

双方随即各押 300 弗罗林。国王说他派仆人打探虚实后再定输赢。

仆人遂策马上路,途遇一人,便问他来自何处,对方说来他来自仆人要去的地方。

"既是如此,"仆人问,"那你可知贵国酒花长多高,一枝酒花可酿多少桶啤酒吗?"

"这我说不准,"那人答道,"不过我路过酒花收割现场,见三人用斧头砍了三天才砍倒一枝酒花。"

仆人心想这可省他长途跋涉,于是奉上 10 弗罗林,要求对方把话给国王重述一遍。两人随后一起返回参见国王。

国王问:"酒花之事是否属实?"

"是的,陛下,"仆人答道,"这里,我从该国带回的证人可以作证。"

于是,国王给了小偷 300 弗罗林。搭档俩又踏上寻奇之途。小偷途中对同伴说道:"我要再去见个国王,告诉他更离奇的故事,你随后帮我续谎,不信从他那儿弄不到钱。"

一到那儿,拜见国王的小偷求赐给一颗花菜。国王说道:"蔬菜闹虫害,没有花菜。"

"怪事,"小偷说道,"我刚从某国来,那里花菜长势良好,一颗装满 12 桶。"

"胡说,"国王反驳道。

"我赌 600 弗罗林有那回事儿,"小偷说道。

"我赌 600 弗罗林没那回事儿,"国王答道。他叫来仆人,令他即去小偷来的国家,查看花菜一说是否属实。仆人途遇一人,下马问他从何而来。对方说来自仆人要去的地方。

"既是如此,"仆人问道,"可知贵国花菜长多大?能大到一颗装满 12 桶吗?"

"那倒没见过,"对方答道,"不过我见到过 12 匹马拉 12 辆车,运一颗花菜去集市。"

仆人说:"伙计,收下这 10 弗罗林,酬谢你省我远途奔波。你跟我走,把刚才的话告诉国王。"

"好吧,"那人答应了,俩人一同去王宫。国王问仆人是否查清花菜的真相,仆人答道:"陛下,您所听到的完全属实。此人来自该国,他可以作证。"

国王只得给小偷 600 弗罗林。搭档俩带着钱上路了。

他俩来到邻国,参见国王的小偷说邻国某城有座高耸的教堂尖塔,塔上曾栖息过啄掉不少星星的一只长嘴鸟,问陛下是否听说过。

"鬼才信,"国王说道。

"我愿赌1200弗罗林真有其事,"小偷说道。

"我赌1200弗罗林那是谎言,"国王说道,随即派仆人去邻国查明真相。

仆人驱马前往,遇一人迎面而来,问对方来自何方。那人说来自仆人要去的地方。仆人问起长嘴鸟一事。

"不清楚,"对方答道,"我从未见过那鸟,不过见到过12人拿扫帚使劲往地窖里推一只硕大的蛋。"

"太好了,"仆人边说边奉上10弗罗林。"快把这话告诉国王,这可省了我旅途劳顿。"

听过这事,国王只好给小偷1200弗罗林。

搭档俩带着黑心钱离去,可负责分赃的小偷却少给了撒谎者3弗罗林。不久后两人各自结婚,安顿下来。一天,撒谎者发现被搭档骗了3弗罗林,便去他家索要。

"下周六来,我如数奉还,"小偷承诺道。由于他无心还钱,便在周六早上直挺挺地躺在床上,嘱咐老婆说自己死了。妻子拿洋葱抹了抹眼睛。骗子一到,她泪汪汪地迎了过去,说丈夫已死,还不了他那3弗罗林。

骗子知道搭档的把戏,立刻怀疑其中蹊跷,说:"他不还钱,那我就狠抽他三鞭了结吧。"

小偷一听,跳将起来,出现在门口,保证撒谎者下周六来,一定还他钱。得此承诺,撒谎者满意而去。

周六一早,小偷起床藏进阁楼干草堆中。

撒谎者来索要那3弗罗林,小偷的老婆又眼泪汪汪地迎上去,说丈夫死了。

撒谎者问:"你把他埋哪儿了?"

"草堆里,"小偷老婆答道。

"我这就去那儿,拿干草抵债,"撒谎者说道。撒谎者一到干草阁楼,就用草叉往干草里一通乱戳。小偷害怕丢了小命,从里面爬出来,向撒谎者保证下周六还钱。

那天太阳刚升起,小偷就起床,躲进了附近教堂的密室,直挺挺地躺在一口陈旧的石棺里。

可同样聪明的搭档很快想到了密室,于是去了教堂,自信能找到朋友的藏身地。他刚进去,还没适应里面的黑暗,就听到格子窗传来窃窃私语声。细听之后,撒谎者获取了一伙劫匪的密谋。他们打算把带来的财宝藏进密室,再寻财路。

他们边议论边拔开窗销,一进密室就会发现撒谎者。撒谎者迅速裹起斗篷,直立壁龛中,昏暗灯光下的他俨然一尊古石像。这伙劫匪一进去,就开始分赃。

劫匪共12个,匪首却错分成了13堆。发现弄错后,他说没功夫再分,还说谁能一剑削掉那石像的脑袋,那一份就归谁。说完,他举斧逼近撒谎者站立的壁龛。他刚把斧子举过头顶,石棺里便传来阵阵恐怖声:"快跑啊,不然死人会跳出棺材,墙上雕像也会脱落,你等将落个半死不活。"

小偷"砰"地一下跳出棺材,撒谎者也跳出壁龛,那些强盗吓得撇下财宝,慌忙逃出密室,发誓不再踏进这闹鬼之地半步。搭档俩带着瓜分的财宝各自回家。他俩后事如何,唯老天知道。

3. 羊 脸 女

从前,农夫马沙尼罗家有十二个女儿,年龄呈梯状,依次相差一岁。这位不幸之人能做的就是尽力将这群孩子拉扯成人。为养活她们,他整天挖地。他的辛苦劳作仅够糊口,可怜的姑娘们常饿着肚子上床睡觉。

一天,马沙尼罗正在高山脚下干活儿,偶遇一个洞口。洞穴昏暗阴沉,连阳光也害怕射入。突然,从洞里爬出一只绿色的大蜥蜴,站立在他面前。一见此状,马沙尼罗吓得六神无主,因为这只野兽大如鳄鱼,样子也同样凶残。

不过,蜥蜴很友善地坐在他身边,说道:"别怕,先生,我不会伤害你,相反还急于想帮你一把。"

一听这话,农夫跪在蜥蜴面前,哀求道:"尊敬的夫人,我不知怎么称呼您。我听您的,但求您行行好,因为家里还有十二个苦命幼小的女儿靠我养活。"

"我正为此事而来,"蜥蜴答道,"明早带上你的幺女,我会如同己出抚养她,当她是我的心肝宝贝。"

一听此言,马沙尼罗非常难过,他认定蜥蜴要他那娇小的幺女,无非想把她当作晚餐的甜心吃掉。他自忖道:"我若拒绝这一要求,蜥蜴就会当场把我吃掉。我若答应,她只夺走我一部分,我若不答应,那它就会夺走我的一切。我该怎么办才能摆脱这一困境呢?"

他正嘀咕着,蜥蜴却说:"下决心照我说的去做。我要定了你家的幺女,若不照办,我只能说你会倒霉透顶。"

见别无选择,马沙尼罗起身,带着一脸苍白、悲惨样儿回到家中。妻子见状便问:"老公,怎么啦?是跟人吵架,还是那可怜的驴死了?"

"都不是,"丈夫答道,"但比这更糟糕。一只可怕的蜥蜴差点没吓死我,它恐吓说我若不把幺女送给她,就会让我追悔莫及。我脑子晕得就像转磨轮似的,不知道怎么办,真是进退两难啊。你知道我多爱仁卓拉。可如果明早不把她交给蜥蜴,我就没命了。你看我怎么办?"

听完丈夫那番话,妻子说道:"老公,你怎么知那蜥蜴一定是咱们的仇家呢?她没准是朋友呢,你跟她不期而遇,也许是好运到、霉运了呢!所以把孩子带去,直觉告诉我,你绝不会后悔的。"

妻子的话让他大为宽慰。第二天一亮,他带着幺女来到洞穴。

正等农夫到来的蜥蜴迎上前去,牵过姑娘的手,随即给他满袋金子,说道:"把这金子拿回去,给其他女儿置办嫁妆,把她们都嫁出去吧。高兴一点,我会像爹妈一样对待仁卓拉的。遇上我,也算她命好啊!"

感激涕零的农夫谢过蜥蜴,回到妻子身边。

得知农夫这么富裕,几个女儿的求婚者络绎不绝。他很快把女儿都嫁了出去。尽管花销很大,但是剩下的金子还是足够夫妇俩一生过得舒服、充实。

农夫刚走,蜥蜴把洞穴变成了一座华丽的宫殿,然后把仁卓拉领了进去,把她当小公主抚养着,要啥有啥,丰盛的饭菜、华丽的衣服以及 1000 个仆人。

话说国王某天在蜥蜴宫殿附近的林中打猎,赶上天色渐晚。见宫中有灯光,国王派侍从前去打听,问可否借宿那儿。

侍从一敲门,蜥蜴变成一位漂亮的女人,亲自开门。得知国王请求,她让侍从捎信说她非常乐意见到陛下,且愿听其吩咐。

接到盛情邀请,国王立刻前往宫中,受到了最为热情的款待。100个侍从举着火把前来迎接,另100个伺候用餐,还有100个挥舞大蒲扇为国王驱赶蚊虫。仁卓拉亲自为国王斟酒,那优雅的举止让陛下看得直出神。

用过膳且收拾停当后,国王准备就寝。仁卓拉脱掉了国王的鞋,也脱掉了他的魂。国王迷恋着她,叫来蜥蜴仙子,请求对方答应他向仁卓拉求婚。善良的仙子一心想着姑娘的幸福,欣然答应,外加7000金币的嫁妆。

仁卓拉对仙子的苦心竟毫无半点感恩之意,陪着欣喜的国王准备启程。

一见姑娘如此薄情,蜥蜴决意要惩罚她。她一声诅咒,顷刻间让姑娘的脸变成了羊面。

刹那间,仁卓拉漂亮的小嘴凸显出来,胡须一码长,双颊凹陷,两条亮丽的辫子成了一对犀利的触角。

国王回头一看,还以为自己昏了头,一边痛哭,一边嚷嚷:"让我迷恋的长发在哪儿?让我心驰神往的双眼在哪儿?我吻过的双唇在哪儿?我今生注定得跟一只山羊结合吗?不,绝不!我绝不能因为羊面女而招致臣民的嘲笑!"

回去后,国王把仁卓拉和一个侍女关在宫中塔楼的一间小屋里,要求她俩一周内各纺好十捆亚麻布。

侍女尊圣旨立刻动手,她先理好亚麻,后绕上纺锤,继而坐在纺轮前辛勤劳作,到周六晚上几近干完了自己分内之事。

娇生惯养在仙宫的仁卓拉,丝毫不察自己容颜已改,竟把亚麻扔出窗外,还抱怨道:"国王怎么想到让我干这种活儿?要穿衬衫他自己可以买呀。他当我是从污水沟捡来的,他该记得我可给他带来了7000金币的嫁妆,再说我是王后,不是奴隶。这样对我,他分明是疯了。"

说归说,到周六晚上,仁卓拉见侍女已干完了活儿,害怕自己的懒惰会招致惩罚,于是赶回仙宫,诉说了自己的不幸。仙子温情地拥抱她,给她满满一袋亚麻布成品,好让国王看到她灵巧的一面。仁卓拉接过袋子,没说声"谢谢"便转身回宫去了。善良的仙子为此薄情大为生气。

见亚麻布都已纺成,国王又让仁卓拉和侍女各养一只小狗,令其好好照看、细心调教。侍女精心养狗,跟带自家的儿子一样,仁卓拉却抱怨道:"我真不明白。我是到了疯人院吗?国王还想我亲自给狗梳头喂食吗?"说完,她开窗把可怜的小动物往外一扔,小东西掉地后当即毙命。

数月后,国王传信说想看狗长得怎么样了。仁卓拉闻讯后非常忐忑,再次赶到仙宫。

这次,她在仙宫门前见到一个老头。这老头问道:"你是谁?想干吗?"

听此发问,仁卓拉没好气地反问道:"连我都不认识?竟敢这样跟我说话?老山羊头!"

"罐儿别嫌壶儿黑,"老人答道,"我不是山羊头,你才是。等着,不知感恩的东西。我让你知道忘恩负义是什么结果。"

说完,老人匆匆离去,回来时手持一面镜子举在仁卓拉面前。见那张丑陋、毛茸茸的脸,姑娘吓得几乎晕倒,继而大哭起来。

老人随后说道:"你得记住自己出生农家,仁卓拉,仰仗仙子才成为王后,可你忘恩负义,对她所做的一切连个'谢'都没说过。她决定惩罚你。你若想让你那长长的白胡须消失,那就去给她跪下,求她原谅。她为人心软,想来会怜悯你的。"

仁卓拉深感愧疚,接受了老人的建议。仙子不仅恢复了她的原貌,还让她穿上金边连衣裙,送她一驾漂亮的马车,由一群仆人护送着回到了丈夫的身边。

国王见她貌美如初,再次爱上了她,还为让她吃苦受罪悔恨不已。仁卓拉钟爱丈夫、尊敬蜥蜴仙子、感激老人指点迷津,此后一生幸福无比。

4. 本叔达图的故事

从前有三位绝色公主。国王夫妇从早到晚一心想着怎样让她们过得开心。

一天,公主们禀告国王:"亲爱的父王,我们很想去乡下野炊。"

"行啊,孩子们。那就去野炊吧!"国王答道,同时下令一切准备就绪。

一辆马车载着熟食,另一辆载着王室一家直奔乡下,最后来到数英里外一处王属花园别墅,离别墅不远处便是他们喜爱的野炊之地。一路颠簸后,他们胃口大开,结果吃得所剩无几。

差不多吃饱后,她们禀告父王、母后:"我们逛一会花园,回宫时叫我们一声,"之后有说有笑地沿花园绿地方向跑去。

她们刚穿过篱笆,一片乌云劈头罩下,让她们辨不清方向。国王夫妇此时惬意地坐在石楠丛中。一两小时转眼即逝。见夕阳西下,他们觉得是回宫的时候了,于是一遍遍地呼唤公主们,却不见回应。

见此,国王、王后吓坏了,他们搜遍花园、别墅及邻近树林的每个角落,踪影全无,公主们好似被大地吞没似的。可怜的父母绝望之极,母后一路哭着回到宫中,之后数日依然伤心不已。国王颁布圣旨:谁能找回走失的公主,可娶其中一位为妻并适时继任王位。

话说宫中住着两位年轻的将军,一听圣旨便相互嘀咕道:"咱俩去找公主!说不定会走运呢!"之后,他俩各带衣物、钱财,跨上高头大马而去。

两人过村便问,却未见公主们的音讯,钱也渐渐花光,只能卖马或者放弃寻找。可卖马的钱没撑多久。让两人不挨饿的只有随身携带的衣物了。他们卖掉了绑在马鞍上的衣服。他们饿极了,就着一身衣服走进路边馆子讨饭吃。等吃饱喝足付账后,他们对店家说道:"我们没钱,除这身衣服外别无他物。这些衣服归您,给我们几件破衣服就行,请留下我俩干活吧!"这桩生意让店家很满意,两位将军就此成了佣人。

宫中的国王、王后一直思念着公主们,却没盼来她们的消息,连两位将军也杳无音信。

宫中有位多年的忠实侍从,名叫本叔达图。见国王那悲伤样儿,他高声说道:"陛下,让我去找公主们吧!"

"不,不,本叔达图,"国王答道,"我失去了三个女儿、两位将军,我怎能再失去你呢?"

本叔达图再三恳求:"陛下,让我去吧!相信我,我一定把她们带回来!"

国王同意了。本叔达图策马而去,最后来到那家饭馆、下马、点菜。上菜的正是那两位将军。尽管两人破衣烂衫,本叔达图还是一眼认出了他们。吃惊的本叔达图问他俩怎么到了这儿。

他们原原本本讲了经历,本叔达图叫来店家说道:"把衣服还给他们,欠多少由我还。"

店家照做了。两位将军换上自己的衣物,起誓随本叔达图寻找公主们。

三人骑马走了很久,来到一片荒无人烟的旷野。夜幕降临,他们唯恐迷失在荒郊野外,于是策马前行,最后见到了一小屋窗户透出的光亮。

他们敲门,里面传来问话:"谁呀?"

"噢,三个疲乏的迷路人,可怜可怜我们,让我们借住一宿吧!"本叔达图答道。

一老妇人开门,往后一退,示意几位进屋。她问:"诸位何处来,又将去何处?"

"老人家,我们肩负重任,"本叔达图答道,"来找几位公主,并带她们回宫!"

"噢,真可怜啊,"老妇人叹道,"几位可知在干吗!她们曾被一团乌云罩住。谁知道她们这会儿在哪儿。"

"老人家,您若知道,烦请告诉我们!"本叔达图哀求道,"我们的幸福全仰仗她们了。"

老妇人说道:"就算我告诉你们,你们也救不了她们。要救她们,你们得下到河底深处。你们在那儿能找到她们,但两个巨人看守着两位大公主,一条七头毒蛇监视着小公主。"

听过老妇人那番话,站在一旁的两位将军吓破了胆,恨不得立马返回,本叔达图则坚定地说道:"事已至此,我们必须坚持到底。请告诉我们那条河的位置,我们好赶过去。"老妇人告诉了他们,还给了他们奶酪、酒、面包,以免他们路上饿着。他们吃饱喝足后,躺下睡去。

等第二天太阳上山,他们才醒来。告别好心的老妇人,他们骑马奔向那条大河。

"我最年长,"一位将军说道,"我有权先下。"

另两位给他系好绳子,给他系好小铃铛,把他放进河里。水刚没过头顶,他就听到四周"唰唰"声响和阵阵雷声。他吓坏了,赶紧摇铃,生怕这些噪音让河岸上的人听不见铃声。见绳子慢慢上升,他这才如释重负。

另一位将军随后下水,可不比第一位强,很快就回到了岸上。

"嗨,瞧你这对勇士!"本叔达图边在腰间系绳边说道,"我倒要看会出什么事!"他听到四周的雷声和嘈杂声时,心想:"哦,再大声响又奈我何哉!"双脚触到河底时,他发现自己来到一个宽敞而明亮的大厅,大公主坐在大厅中央,面前有个巨人正在酣睡。一见本叔达图,大公主朝他点头,那眼神是问他怎么来这儿。

作为回应,他拔剑准备朝巨人的脑袋砍去。大公主赶忙制止,示意他躲好,因为巨人正要醒来。"我闻到了人的味道!"巨人边伸懒腰边嘟哝。

"唉,怎么会有人来这河底呢?"她答道,"还是继续睡吧!"

巨人翻身睡了过去。公主暗示本叔达图动手。他一剑挥去,巨人的脑袋滚到了墙角。公主怦然心跳,给本叔达图戴上金色王冠,称他为救命恩人。"告诉我你的妹妹们在哪儿,我一并救走!"本叔达图说道。

公主打开一扇门,带他走进另一个大厅。二公主坐在里面,由一个沉睡的巨人把守着。一见两人到来,二公主示意藏好,因为巨人就要醒来。

"我怎么闻着生人的味道?"巨人睡眼惺忪地嘟哝道。

"怎么会有生人来这河底呀?"二公主说道,"你继续睡吧!"

巨人一闭眼,本叔达图从墙角溜出来,朝巨人头上一剑挥去,脑袋滚得老远。二公主的感激之情无以言表,也把金色王冠放在本叔达图的手中。

"告诉我你们的小妹在哪儿,我一并救走!"本叔达图说道。

"唉,怕是你救不了!"公主俩叹气道,"她被一条七头毒蛇监视着呢!"

"带我去吧,"本叔达图答道,"你们就等着瞧好吧!"

二公主打开一扇门,本叔达图走进去,发现那大厅比前两个还大。墙上铁链牢牢拴着的小公主站着,面前有一条恐怖的七头毒蛇。本叔达图一上前,毒蛇就扭动着七个脑袋朝他扑来。本叔达图拔剑一阵挥舞,直到七个脑袋滚落一地。本叔达图扔下剑,奔向公主,砸断了铁链。小公主喜极而泣、拥抱过他后,取下头上的金色王冠放在他的手中。

"我们得返回地面,"本叔达图边说边带着小公主来到河底。两位大公主已等在那儿。本叔达图给大公主系好绳子,摇摇铃。地面上的两位将军听见后,便轻轻将她拉了上去。他们随后解开绳子,扔回到河底。二公主很快到了姐姐的身边。

这下只剩下本叔达图和小公主。"亲爱的本叔达图,"小公主央求道,"求你啦,让他们先把你拉上去!我怕两位将军会使诈的。"

"万万不可,"本叔达图答道,"我绝不会把你留在这儿!自己人没啥可怕的。"

"你执意我先上,那我发誓终身不嫁,除非你随后来娶我!"他给她系好绳,将军俩把她拉了上去。

他的勇敢和成功,让两位将军满心妒忌,他俩不仅没把绳子抛入河底,反倒转身离去,让他自生自灭。此外,他俩还威胁公主,逼她们承诺回去告诉国王、王后,说是被他们救回去的。他俩还说:"要是他们问起本叔达图,你们就说从没见着他!"三位公主怕他俩起杀心,全都答应了,于是一同骑马回到宫中。

见到亲爱的女儿们,国王、王后乐不可支。两位将军讲述了经历和种种危险。国王当即宣布了给予他们的回报,即分别娶两位公主为妻。

可怜的本叔达图在干吗?

他耐心地等了很久,却不见绳子下来,知道小公主说的没错,那两位家伙背叛了自己。"唉,我是回不去了,"他喃喃自语道。但作为勇敢者,他深知自哀自弃无济于事。他起身寻遍了三个大厅,希望能找到可用之物。在最后一个大厅里,他见到一个盛着食物的盘子,这下才想起自己饿了,于是坐下吃喝起来。

几个月过去了。一天早上,他正在几个大厅里来回走动时,忽见墙上挂着一个之前不曾见过的袋子!他取下打量起来。"有何吩咐?"一听袋子发出声音,他惊讶得差点儿把它扔到了地上。

"啊!快带我离开这鬼地方,回到地面上!"他紧握袋子很快站在了河岸上。

"我这就要一艘最漂亮的船,配足人手,随时出海!"船出现在眼前,桅杆上飘着一面"三冠之王"的旗帜。

本叔达图随后上船,朝公主们的都城驶去。进港后,他又敲鼓来又吹号,引得人人倚立在门窗前观望。

国王既听说也目睹了那艘漂亮的船,心想:"他有三顶王冠,我只有一顶,一定是位了不起的君王。"他急忙前去将客人迎回城堡,心想:"让他做小公主的夫君挺不错!"可待嫁的小公主对任何求婚者概不理会。

本叔达图离宫太久,国王丝毫没料到这位衣着光鲜的客人正是自己深深悼念之人。"尊贵的君王,"国王说道,"咱俩欢庆、享受一番!之后,您若愿意,可娶小女为妻!"

本叔达图很是高兴,大家都坐下来享受丰盛的美食和娱乐活动。唯有小公主闷闷不乐,因为她一门心思想着本叔达图。众人餐毕起身,国王这才对小公主说:"乖孩子,这位尊贵的君王向你求婚。"

"哦,父王,"小公主答道,"别呀,我终身不嫁!"

本叔达图转身对她说道:"我若是本叔达图,你也这样回答吗?"

就在她默默端详时,对方补充道:"瞧,我就是本叔达图。且听我道来。"

听完本叔达图的历险经历,国王、王后心中五味杂陈。他刚说完,国王拉着他的手说道:"亲爱的本叔达图,小女就许配与你。此外,我去世后,王位由你继承。那两个背叛你的家伙,将被赶出国门,永不返回。"之后他下令为本叔达图和小公主举行婚宴以及为期三天的庆祝活动。

5. 花岛女王的故事

从前,有位女王统治着花岛。令她悲痛不已的是,丈夫婚后几年就去世了。寡居的女王几乎全身心投入两位公主的教育。见可爱的大公主逐渐长大,女王害怕她会引起诸岛王后的嫉妒。该王后以世上第一美人自居,坚持要所有对手为其美貌折服。

为充分满足自己的虚荣心,诸岛王后敦促国王向邻国开战。而国王最大的心愿就是取悦于王后,每征服一个国家,只提出一个条件:该国的公主一满15岁就得去他的王宫,向王后的绝世美貌表示敬意。

花岛女王清楚这条法令,决定在大女儿满十五岁后就去参拜那位骄傲的王后。

王后早已耳闻公主的惊世之美,于是忐忑地等待着她前来觐见。她那忐忑不安之心很快变成了妒忌,因为在公主参拜期间,众人都被她那无限的魅力征服,连王后也承认从没见过这般标致的人儿。

当然,王后自忖"我除外",她自信其美貌无与伦比。

王宫上下流露出的惊羡使她很快警醒,非常不悦的她装病回到寝宫,以免看见公主获胜的样儿。她捎话给花岛女王,为身体欠佳不能再见她而抱歉,劝女王带公主回国。

捎话的那位贵妇人碰巧是花岛女王的老朋友。她劝花岛女王别做什么正式告别,尽快返回。

女王随即悟出这一暗示,立马接受建议。女王深知醋意十足的王后拥有高强的法力,因此告诫女儿,在随后半年里,无论她因何种理由离开王宫都有危险。

公主答应听命,并想方设法打发时间。

半年时间即将过去。就在最后一天,一场盛会将在王宫旁边美丽的草坪上举行。公主从窗口能够看见众人忙碌的身影,于是央求女王让她去草坪。女王想应该没什么危险,答应亲自带她去。

见可爱的公主重获自由,王宫上下非常开心,于是兴高采烈地前去参加这场盛会。

公主很高兴又来到户外。她正在众人前面走着,脚下突然裂开,公主一下就掉了进去,地面随即合上!

受惊吓的花岛女王当即昏了过去;小公主嚎啕大哭,好不容易才被带离危险地;灭顶之灾让整个王宫惊愕不已。

王宫下令掘地三尺,却一无所获。消失的公主不见任何踪迹。

再说公主不住地往下落,最后来到一个荒漠之地,除石头、树木外不见人影。公主见到的唯一生灵是一只漂亮的小狗。小狗跑向公主,开始亲近她。公主抱起小狗玩了一会儿,之后把它放下。它在前面带路,不时回头看,好似哀求她跟上。

公主让小狗带路,很快来到一座小山前,山谷里遍布着可爱的果树,既开花又挂果,连地上都满是花儿和果子。山谷中那柔软草坪中央冒出一眼喷泉。

公主快步跑向那迷人的地方,刚坐在草地上,便思忖起自己的不幸来。一想到此时的处境,她不禁恸哭起来。

她知道,果子和清水能解饥渴,可一旦野兽要吃她,那她该怎么办呢?

公主想到了可能出现的各种厄运,最后试着用逗小狗来分散自己的注意力。她整天都待在喷泉边。夜幕降临,就在她不知所措时,她发现小狗正在扯她的裙子。

她起初并没理会,可小狗还是不停地拽她,接着朝某个方向跑几步。公主最后决定跟着它。小狗停在一块巨石前,石头中间有个巨大的豁口。小狗显然是想让她进去。

公主进去后,发现是个漂亮的大洞穴,在四周的石头映照下闪闪发光。洞子一角有张小床,上面铺着柔软的苔藓。公主躺下来,小狗依偎在她的脚边。公主劳碌一天累坏了,很快就熟睡了过去。

第二天,群鸟的叫声将她早早吵醒。小狗也醒来,在她身边非常亲昵地蹦来跳去。公主起身走到洞外,小狗一如既往在前面跑着带路,不时扯她裙子,拉她向前走。

公主让小狗带路,很快回到头一天逗留过的那个漂亮果园。她吃了些水果,喝了点泉水,仿佛吃了顿大餐。她在花丛中漫步,逗小狗玩,晚上又回到山洞睡觉。

公主就这样过了几个月,随着起初恐惧逐渐消失,她也听天由命起来。小狗也成了她的慰藉物和忠实伴侣。

一天,公主留意到小狗似乎很难过,不像平时那样亲近她。公主担心它生病了,于是抱着它去见它吃过特殊草药的地方,希望这能让它好起来,可它碰也不碰。小狗整夜哼叫叹息不停,一副痛苦样儿。

公主后来睡着了,醒来时首先想到的就是那小宠物。一见小狗不像往常那样睡在脚边。她跑到洞外寻找。她一出洞就瞧见一位老人。不等公主看清,对方拔腿跑得无影无踪。

这让公主既新奇也震惊,跟小狗失踪一样。从第一天邂逅起,小狗就一直跟着她。公主不知它是迷失了,还是被老人偷走了。

带着种种古怪念头和恐惧,公主游来荡去。这时,她忽觉被一团乌云裹着,在空中穿行。她没作任何抵抗,很快吃惊地发现来到一条通往她出生的王宫大路。乌云也随即不见了踪影。

临近王宫时,公主见人人身披黑纱,不免满心恐惧。她赶紧前行,很快被人认出,继而是一阵欢迎的呼叫声。妹妹听见欢呼声,跑出来拥抱这位归来者。带着幸福泪水,小公主告诉她,母后——花岛女王——因她失踪而饱受打击,没几天就去世了。之后,小公主戴上了王冠,现在打算归还给法定的继承人。

但是,大公主想拒绝,说只有妹妹答应和她分享王权才肯接受王冠。

女王继位后,先是哀悼尊敬的母后,后对妹妹尽显怜爱之情。可她仍未走出丢失小狗的阴影,于是派人各国寻找,但音信全无。新任女王伤心不已,承诺找回小狗者获赠半个王国。

受巨额赏赐的诱惑,宫廷不少贵族八方寻找小狗,终究空手而归。绝望的女王觉得没有小狗,生活难以为继,于是又宣布,谁找回小狗,她就嫁给谁。

如此诱人的奖赏,所有朝臣纷纷寻狗而去,王宫一时向门可罗雀。人们出走后的一天,女王得到禀报,说一面目可憎之人求见。女王示意将他带向一间仅有她和妹妹在场的屋子。

见面后,那人说,女王若信守诺言,他就归还小狗。

小公主先发话。她说,女王未经国民同意无权结婚,还说如此重大之事,须召开国民议会。女王对此不便反驳,不过下令在王宫给此人安排一个套间,并授意次日召集国民议会。

次日,议会如期隆重召开。经公主提议,最后决定为赏给寻找小狗的人一大笔钱,如果此人不领情,便将其逐出王国,不得再见女王。对方没接受开价,离开了大厅。

公主如实禀报了决定,女王悉数认同,同时补充道,自己的事自己做主,决定放弃王位,周游各国,直到找回小狗为止。这一决定让公主非常吃惊,便恳请女王改变想法。

她俩正议此事,一名侍从前来禀报,说海湾满是船只。姐妹俩跑到阳台,见一支船队浩浩荡荡驶进港口。由于每艘船上挂着鲜艳彩旗、彩条、三角旗,领航的是一艘小型船,上面挂着象征和平的大白旗,她俩很快断定船队一定来自友邦。

女王派特使前去港口,很快得知是绿宝石岛国王子的船队,来者恳请停靠该国,并向她致意。女王立刻派几位显要大臣前往迎接王子。女王端坐王座以待。王子一露面,她起身上前几步相迎,然后邀他入座,还跟他亲切交谈了约一个时辰。

王子被领进豪华套房。次日,他提出私下会晤女王,并获准前往女王的私人会客厅,与女王及妹妹就坐。

一番寒暄后,王子跟女王说有些蹊跷事相告,她会相信是真的。

"陛下,"他说道,"我跟诸岛王后隔一块小地峡相邻。我有一天猎鹿时不幸遇上她,可没认出她,于是没止步向她致意。您比谁都知道她有多强的报复心和高深的魔法。这两点我吃尽苦头才见识到了。我脚下土地突然裂开,接着掉了进去,很快发现自己在遥远的荒漠之地变成一只小狗。身为小狗的我有幸遇到了陛下您。六个月后,花岛王后的怨气还没出够,于是又把我变成了一个丑陋的老头。我怕这样子吓着你,于是藏身在林子深处长达三月之久。最后,我有幸遇上一位仁慈的仙女,她让我脱离了傲慢王后的魔法,还告诉我陛下您的遭遇,叫我到此找您。我今天来向您表达我的心意,那颗自我俩邂逅时就属于陛下的心。"

几天后,花岛女王和年轻王子宣布联姻的喜讯传遍了王国。他俩在国泰民安中幸福生活了许多年。那坏心眼的诸岛王后,因虚荣和妒忌作祟而被仙女们剥夺魔法以示惩处。

6. 白　狼

　　从前,某国王有三位漂亮的女儿,不过老幺最显眼。
　　话说父王一天决定巡游偏远之地。临行时,小公主要他带花环回来。准备回宫时,国王想起了女儿们的礼物,于是到珠宝店给大公主买了一串漂亮的项链,又去豪华商铺给二公主买了件金丝银线连衣裙。国王走遍花店和市场,却没能找到小公主心仪的花环,只好踏上归程。国王穿过一片密林,在离王宫约四英里之地,忽见一只白狼蹲在路边,瞧! 它头上就戴着花环。
　　国王叫车夫停车,命他下车去取回白狼头上的花环。听见国王命令的白狼说道:"陛下,我可以把花环给您,不过我得有所回报。"
　　"你要啥?"国王问道,"朕愿拿厚物相换。"
　　"我不要什么厚物,"狼说道,"我就要您回宫路上最新见到的东西,三天后便来取走。"
　　国王心想:"我离宫还远着呢,一路定会碰到野兽、小鸟什么的。答应它没啥问题。"国王同意了,带着花环离去。可他一路未见任何活物,直到通向王宫大门的拐角处,小公主正在此迎驾。
　　当晚,一想到自己承诺,国王就伤心不已。得知原委的王后也落泪不少。小女儿见状问他们为何悲伤、流泪。国王说出了事情的原委:他为带回那花环得付出巨大的代价,因为三天后,有只白狼要来带走她,从此就再也见不着她了。王后左思右想,最后想出个办法。
　　宫里有个女佣,个头和年龄与公主相当。王后给她穿上小公主的漂亮裙子,决定把她嫁给不辨彼此的白狼。
　　第三天,白狼大步迈进王宫大院,登上气派的楼梯,来到国王夫妇就坐的房间。
　　"我是来索取您的承诺的,"狼说道,"请把小公主交给我吧!"
　　他们把女佣带到面前。白狼说道:"骑到我背上,我带你回城堡。"说完,它一把将她扯到背上离宫而去。
　　来到上次遇国王、献上花环的地方,白狼停下来,让女佣下来歇口气。他俩在路边坐下。
　　"我在想,"狼说道,"你父亲要是有这片树林,他会做什么用?"
　　"我父亲很穷,所以会砍掉所有的树,锯成木板卖掉,从此不受穷、不愁吃。"
　　白狼明白没有得到真公主,于是把女佣扯在背上,驮回到王宫,气冲冲地走进国王的寝宫,说道:"快交出真公主! 再骗我,我就掀起风暴,推倒所有墙壁,把你们全埋在废墟下!"
　　眼看毫无退路可言,国王夫妇抹着泪,叫人请来小公主。国王对她说道:"好孩子,委屈你跟白狼去吧。父王答应过它,不能食言啊!"
　　公主准备离宫。动身前,她回闺房取下花环,戴到头上。白狼一把将公主扯到背上走了。在跟女佣休息的地方,白狼放下公主在路边歇脚。白狼转身问公主:"你父亲要是有这片树林,他会做什么用?"
　　公主答道:"父王会砍下这些树,把它建成美丽的花园,以便夏天带大臣来散步。"
　　"这是真公主!"白狼心想,接着高声说道:"骑在我背上,我带你去城堡。"她刚骑上去,白狼开始穿越那片森林,跑呀、跑呀,最后停在一个气派庭院的大门前。
　　大门一道道打开,公主迈步而入,"城堡真漂亮!"她叹道:"要离父王母后近点多好哇!"
　　白狼答道:"我们年末回去拜望他们。"说完,白皮毛从身上滑落。公主发现站在面前的不是狼,而是个高大、气派的英俊小生。它牵着公主,拾阶而上。

半年后的某一天,它走进公主房间说道:"亲爱的,快准备参加一场婚礼!大姐要出嫁了,我带你回宫去。婚礼结束后,我接你回来。我在门外吹口哨,你听见后立刻出来,别管父王和王后说什么,别留恋舞会和美餐。因为我不接你,你一人无法穿过森林找到家。"

公主准备出发时,发现白狼又披上狼皮,变回原来的样儿。白狼把公主扯到背上,直奔王宫而去。一到那儿,它留下公主独自回了家,黄昏时又返回接公主。它在宫门外吹了声又长又响的口哨,正在跳舞的公主听见后,立刻走了出来。白狼又把她扯到背上,驮回了城堡。

半年后的某一天,白狼装扮的王子走进公主房间,说道:"心肝,准备参加二姐的婚礼吧。我今天就送你去父王的宫殿,我们待到明天一早。"

他俩参加婚礼去了。到晚上只剩他俩时,它脱下狼皮,变成了王子,岂知母后躲在这屋子里。一见落到地上的白狼皮,母后悄悄离去,让仆人偷走狼皮,扔进厨房火里烧掉。火焰一碰狼皮,惊雷炸起,王子如旋风般冲出宫门,独自逃了回去。

小公主伤心不已,整晚哭泣不止,次日清晨离开,试图找到回去的路,她在树林中走来绕去,找不到方向。整整十四天,她毫无目标地在林子里乱转,困了就在树下睡一会儿,饿了就吃点野果和草根。最后,她来到一间小屋,推开门,走进去,见风神独坐其中,于是打听道:"风神,您可曾见过白狼?"

风神答道:"我在全世界昼夜不停地刮,这才回家,没看见它。"风神拿出一双鞋,告诉她穿上这鞋,一步能走100英里。

公主穿过空气,来到星星跟前:"星星,请告诉我,您可曾见到过白狼?"

星星答道:"我整晚都在眨眼睛,没看见它!"星星拿出一双鞋,告诉公主,说穿上这双鞋,一大步可迈出200英里。

公主穿上鞋,来到月亮面前,问道:"尊贵的月亮,您可曾见过白狼?"

月亮答道:"我整晚都忙着穿过天空,刚回家,没看见他!"它也拿出一双鞋,说穿上这鞋,一大步可迈出400英里。

公主去了太阳那儿,问道:"尊敬的太阳,您可曾见到白狼?"

太阳答道:"见到了。它以为你抛弃了它,于是又挑了一位新娘,正准备婚礼呢!不过,我会帮你。这儿有双鞋,穿上后,你能踩玻璃、冰雪,还能攀爬最陡峭的地方。这儿有架纺车,能把青苔织成丝绸。从这儿出发,你会到一座玻璃山,穿上我给你的鞋,就能轻松爬上去。白狼的宫殿就在山顶上。"

公主随即出发,很快来到了玻璃山,看见了山顶上太阳所指的白狼宫殿。

公主扮成一个裹着头巾的老太婆,没有人认得出来。宫里正为次日婚礼忙碌着。公主拿太阳送的纺车将青苔纺成丝绸。见此,经过公主身边的白狼新娘问道:"啊妈,纺车送我行吗?"

公主答道:"你若让我今晚睡在王子门外的席子上,我就送给你。"

新娘答道:"好,你就睡在门外的席子上吧。"

公主把纺车送给了她。为免被人认出,公主当晚裹着头巾,躺在白狼门外的席子上。当宫中人人入睡后,她讲起了自己的遭遇。她说自己在三姐妹中最年幼、最漂亮,说父亲怎样让她嫁给白狼,说自己如何独自参加大姐的婚礼,后来又和丈夫一起参加二姐的婚礼,说母亲如何派人把白色的狼皮扔进火堆,说自己如何林中迷路,如何含泪寻找白狼,还有风神、星星、月亮和太阳是如何善待自己,如何帮助自己来到白狼的宫殿。

听完公主的讲述,白狼知道门外正是自己的原配夫人:她历尽艰辛寻找,这才找到他。他没说话,只等参加第二天婚礼的众宾客,即远道而来的君王及王子的到来。宾客齐聚盛宴厅时,白狼说道:"诸位国王、王子,且听我言。我曾弄丢了宝盒的钥匙,便命人配了把新的,我这下找着了那把旧的。请问,哪一把更好呢?"

贵宾众口一词:"当然是旧的好!"

"如此说来,"白狼说道,"那还是前任新娘更好。"

他请来新娘,把她许给在场的一位王子,转身对嘉宾说道:"我的新娘在此。"美丽的公主被引领入场,坐到白狼王位旁边。他还说道:"我以为她忘了我,不再回来,可她到处寻找我。我俩现在团聚了,就绝不会再分离!"

7. 傻　　子

从前,有个人富得出奇。诚如世无完全幸福一样,他仅有一个儿子傻得连二加二是多少都不知道。最后,父亲无法再忍受其愚蠢,想到了"傻子出门游,强过待家头"一说,于是给他满满一袋金币,打发他出国闯荡去了。

这位名为莫赛贤的小伙骑上马,前往威尼斯,希望从那儿搭船去开罗。他骑了一段路,见一棵白杨树下站着一个人,于是问道:"朋友贵姓？从哪里来？都会些啥？"

对方答道:"快如思,舰队镇人,行动如闪电。"

"那我倒要瞧瞧。"莫赛贤回道。

"那你等着,"快如思说道,"我这就证明自己的诚实。"

话音刚落,一只小雌鹿从他俩站的地方一窜而过。

快如思先让它先跑上一段距离,然后猛追过去,那轻快劲儿,就算地上撒满上面粉,也见不着他的足印。他几个蹦跶就赶过了雌鹿。深感那敏捷步伐,莫赛贤请求快如思跟他同行,还承诺给他丰厚的报酬。

快如思认可了这一提议,两人继续行进,不出一英里,又遇上一个小伙,莫赛贤止步问道:"朋友贵姓？从哪里来？都会些啥？"

小伙立即答道:"兔耳朵,好奇谷人,就地贴耳一听,便知世间事,如王宫、农舍的种种阴谋以及老鼠、人类的每个计划。"

"既是如此,"莫赛贤问道:"那说说我家正发生啥事。"

小伙耳朵贴地,随即报告:"老头正在对老伴说:'谢天谢地,我俩总算打发掉了莫赛贤,因为他闯荡后,兴许能学些见识,回来时不像出门那么傻。'"

"打住,打住,"莫赛贤叫道:"你说得没错,我信了。跟咱走,不会亏待你的。"

小伙答应了。他们前行约十英里,遇到第三个人。莫赛贤又问道:"壮士贵姓？从哪里来？都会些啥？"

男子答道:"我叫箭如神,来自全中城。我箭射得准,能射中石头上的豌豆。"

"若不介意,我想见识一下！"莫赛贤说道。

男子立即在石头上放上豌豆,拉动弓箭,轻松射中。

莫赛贤见他所言不虚,立即邀他入伙。走了数日后,他们见不少人正顶着烈日挖沟渠。

莫赛贤顿生同情,于是问道:"朋友们,这天气一分钟就能烤熟鸡蛋,你们咋干得这么欢呢？"

有人答道:"背后有个小伙在鼓风,我们如沐西风,清新得像雏菊。"

"让我见见他,"莫赛贤说道。

人们叫来小伙,莫赛贤问道:"贵姓？从哪里来？都会些啥？"

"随君吹,风镇人,能吹出你想要的风。你要西风,我立马就给;你要北风,我着你的当面吹倒这些房子。"

莫赛贤谨慎地答道:"眼见为实！"

随君吹开始用事实折服莫赛贤。他先轻轻吹,恰如晚风徐来,随后转过身去,刮起暴风,一排橡树随即倒地。

见此，莫赛贤高兴不已，恳求随君吹入伙。途中他们又碰到一名男子，莫赛贤一如既往地招呼道："贵姓？从哪里来？都会些啥？"

"背坚挺，大力镇人，力气大到扛山如持鸿毛。"

"果如此，"莫赛贤说道："准是能人，拿你的力气让我开开眼！"

背坚挺往背上放的巨石和树桩，连100架马车也载不走。

见此，莫赛贤鼓动背坚挺入伙。一行上路，最后来到名曰鲜花谷的国家。

该国之君有位独生女，行动快如风，过燕麦地身轻似燕。有皇榜称有赛过公主者可娶其为妻，败北者人头落地。

听闻皇榜，莫赛贤即刻拜见国王，意在挑战公主。可比赛日早上，莫赛贤给国王带信，说身体不适，将派人替他参赛。

"我无所谓，"卡内特拉公主说道："有胆的就来，我随时恭候。"

赛时一到，场上满是期待的人群。快如思和身着短裙、便鞋的卡内特拉公主准时出现在起跑线上。

银喇叭一响，对手俩起跑，俨然如猎犬追野兔一般。果如其名的快如思胜了公主，观众边鼓掌边欢呼："异乡人万岁！"

卡内特拉为失利而万分沮丧，好在比赛分两次举行，她暗下决心不能再输，回宫后便给快如思送去一条魔法项链——带它别说奔跑，连走路也困难，求他为她而戴上。

次日清晨，观众重聚赛场，公主和快如思开始了新一轮的较量。公主依旧健步如飞，可怜的快如思却如重载之驴，寸步难行。

兔耳朵一听说公主在作弊，剑如神意识到朋友的险境，搭弓射掉快如思项链上的宝石。小伙的两腿重获自由，五个跳跃就超过了卡内特拉，继而赢得了比赛。

见只得认莫赛贤作驸马，国王厌恶之极，于是召来大臣以求摆脱困境。他们觉得，对于一个流浪汉而言，公主无异于是天鹅肉，建议国王赏给他些金子，像他这样的乞丐准会要钱不要老婆。

国王欣喜地接受了该建议，便招来莫赛贤，问他要多少金子才肯放弃新娘。

和同伴商量后，莫赛贤答道："几个跟班能扛走多少黄金珠宝，我就要多少。"

国王心想捡了个大便宜，于是搬出无数金箱、银袋和宝石柜，可背坚挺越扛站得越直。

国库搬空了，国王于只得让臣子向臣民征集金银，结果无济于事，背坚挺要求再加。

不料建议竟带来这等后果，大臣们便说让几个毛贼从本国带走这么多财宝太愚蠢了，纷纷恳请国王派兵追回金银珠宝。

国王派出一队武装步兵和骑兵去追背坚挺扛走的财宝。

不等地平线出现扬起尘土的追兵，兔耳朵早闻讯大臣给国王的献计，并如实相告同伴。

风随君获知他们的危险处境，马上卷起一股强风，国王的军队就像九柱戏的木柱，纷纷倒下，再也爬不起来。于是，莫赛贤和朋友们丝毫无阻，一路行进。

一到家，莫赛贤跟同伴们高兴地瓜分了战利品。随他生活的父亲最后只得承认，儿子并不像看上去那么傻。

8. 街 头 乐 师

　　从前有头忠心劳作多年的驴,可怜的它后来年迈体弱,工作渐成一种负担。由于没太多利用价值,主人决定一枪结果它。得知厄运来临,驴却不甘心,遂决定逃到临近城里作街头乐师。
　　小跑一阵后,驴遇到一只灵缇犬,躺在路边直喘粗气。"喂,兄弟,"驴问道,"怎么的啦?瞧你累的。"
　　灵缇犬答道:"真累。我日渐衰老,无法再捕猎,主人准备毒死我。可生活这么好,我逃出来了,却不知如何谋生为好。"
　　"哦,"驴说道,"我去附近的大城市,打算作个街头乐师。咋不跟我去搞音乐?我吹笛,你敲定音鼓嘛。"
　　灵缇犬喜欢这主意,就一起去了。走了一会儿,它俩遇到一只猫,脸长得像见了连下三天雨似的。驴问道:"猫友,遇到什么事不高兴呀?"
　　"沮丧的心咋高兴得起来啊,"猫答道,"我现在年事已高,牙齿快掉完了,因此喜欢烤火胜过抓鼠。我那年迈的女主人想溺死我。我还不想死,就从她那儿逃走了,现在不知该去哪儿、做什么。千金难买好建议啊!"
　　"咱们去附近的大城市,"驴说道,"尝试街头卖艺。我知道你晚上发出的美妙音乐,肯定能走红的。"
　　驴的建议让猫很是高兴。朋友仨一起赶路。它们很快走进一家旅馆院内,见一只公鸡没命地叫。"你到底咋啦?"驴问公鸡,"你叫得都快震破我们的耳膜了。"
　　"我在预报好天气呢,"公鸡答道,"明天有盛宴。因为节日一到,旅馆会来不少人。老板娘下令今晚抹我脖子,为明日之宴作汤。"
　　"听我说,红冠,"驴说道,"你最好跟我们去附近的城镇。你有副好嗓子,可加入我们正在组建的街头乐队。"公鸡很高兴听到这主意。一行四个继续前行。
　　临近的城镇路太远,要一天多时间才能到。晚上,它们来到一片树林,决定就此过夜。驴和灵缇犬躺在一棵大树下,猫和公鸡上了树枝,公鸡还直飞到树梢,觉得那儿最安全。睡觉前,公鸡环顾四周,见远处闪烁着光亮,确信不远处有人家,于是朝同伴喊道。
　　一听到这个,驴立刻说道:"那我们得起身去找那屋子,因为这地儿歇脚太差劲了。"灵缇犬补充道:"没错,我觉得最好能找到几根骨头和一两块肉。"
　　他们走向那泛着微光的远处之地,越靠近,光越亮,最后来到亮堂堂的屋前。一行中驴的个头最大,它走到窗前往里瞧。
　　公鸡问道:"喂,灰头,你看到怎么啦?"
　　"满满一桌,"驴答道,"好吃、好喝的全都有。几个盗贼围坐着起劲吃喝呢。"
　　公鸡说道:"真希望我也那样。"
　　"我也是,"驴答道,"咱们干吗不想法赶走这伙盗贼,然后住进去?"
　　他们于是商量采取怎样的行动。最后,大伙决定由驴站窗边,把前脚放在窗台上,灵缇犬站在驴的背上,猫站到灵缇犬的肩上,公鸡站在猫的头上。它们这样一组合,按照既定信号,一起发不同的乐声:驴叫声、犬吠声、猫喵声、鸡鸣声。它们接着爬进窗户,弄得窗玻碎成一片。
　　这可怕的噪声惊动了盗贼,吓得他们毛发直竖,至少以为是一群鬼怪闯了进来,于是匆匆跑进树林。四个同伴为得计而兴奋，坐在桌边享用着伙盗贼留下的食物和美酒。

吃完饭，它们熄灯，各自选个舒适地儿睡觉。驴躺在屋外院子里，狗睡门后，猫睡火旁，公鸡飞到搁板上。一天旅途劳顿后，个个很快睡着了。

午夜刚过，那伙盗贼见到屋里灯火全灭，万籁俱寂，匪首说道："我们真蠢，这么轻易被吓跑。"他转向一个手下，命令他去打探一下是否一切安全。

这家伙发现一切宁静，漆黑一片，于是走进厨房，觉得最好点一盏灯。他误把一双凶狠的猫眼当成两块烧炭。他试图拿火柴去点燃。猫可不认为这有啥好玩，朝他脸上扑去，可劲儿地又啐又挠。盗贼吓个半死，从后门夺路而逃，结果被灵缇犬绊倒，腿上挨了一口。盗贼惨叫着穿过院子，不料在经过那头驴时，又被它后腿踹了一脚。公鸡这时从睡梦中惊醒，一时兴起，从栖息的搁板上叫了声："几个一起。"

盗贼慌忙回去报告匪首："老大，屋里有个可怕的巫婆，她朝我脸上又啐又挠。门前站个长刀客，使劲砍了我大腿。院里有个黑魔，拿大棒偷袭我。这还没完，屋顶还坐个法官，高喊：'几个一起。'我就逃走了"。

这伙盗贼之后再也没敢擅闯这屋，也再没去过那儿。四个街头乐师对住所很满意，决定将盗贼的屋子据为己有，也许现在还住着，谁知道呢。

9. 孪生兄弟

从前有个渔夫,家境富有,但却膝下无子。一天,有个老妇人对他的妻子说道:"你没孩子,那么多的财富又有何用?"

"那都是命啊,"渔妇答道。

"不,孩子,这不能怪命的,要怪你的丈夫。只要他能抓到那条小金鱼,你们就会有孩子的。他今晚一回家,你就告诉他务必抓到那条小鱼,之后把它切成六块——你俩各吃一块,你们不久会有两个孩子,第三块喂狗,狗会产下两只幼崽,第四块喂马,马会产下两头小驹,第五、六块埋在家门的左右两边,就会长出两棵柏树来。"

渔夫晚上回来,妻子讲了老妇人的建议。渔夫答应捕回那条小金鱼。第二天一早,渔夫去河里,抓到了那条小鱼,然后按老妇人吩咐,把小金鱼切成六块。渔妇如期生下两个一模一样的对男孩,狗也下了两只极相像的小崽,马也产下了两头小驹,门前两边也长出两棵极相似的柏树。

男孩俩长大后,尽管家产不少,都不愿意待在家里,而是想出门去扬名立万。父亲就这两个儿子,因此不让他俩同时离开。他说道:"先去一个,回来后,另一个再走。"

其中一位带着马和狗出门,同时嘱托兄弟:"门前两棵柏树苍翠如旧,就表明我活着,身体健康;但如有一棵开始枯萎,请速来找我。"说完,他就闯荡江湖去了。

一天,他借宿一老妇人家。他晚上坐在门前时,见对面山上有个城堡,便向老妇人打听其主人。老妇人答道:"孩子,那是'国色天香'的城堡。"

"我为求婚而来!"

"孩子,很多人都试过,结果都送了命。她砍下求婚者的头,挂在那根柱子上,你看那儿。"

"要么让她砍头,要么我成功,因为我明天就去向她求婚。"

他随后抄起齐特拉琴,弹得棒极了,举国上下没人听过如此美妙的音乐,连公主本人都倚窗倾听。

第二天一早,国色天香请去老妇人,问道:"谁住在你那儿?好个齐特拉琴手!"

"回公主,昨晚才到的陌生人,"老妇人答道。

公主随即下令请陌生人去见她。

陌生人一到,公主问了他一些诸如来自何方、家庭之类的事,最后还承认他弹奏的齐特拉琴带给她极大的快乐,并希望跟他结为夫妇。陌生人说他正是为此事而来。

公主接着说道:"你这就去见我的父王,告诉他你想娶我为妻。他给你出完三个难题后,你就来告诉我。"陌生人直接拜见国王,说想娶公主为妻。

国王答道:"你若能满足我提出的要求,我将非常乐意,否则可是要掉脑袋的。听着,那地上有根圆木,直径两英尺多。你若用剑一劈为二,我就把女儿嫁给你,否则你就没命了。"

陌生人退下,灰心丧气地回到了老妇人的住处,因为他知道第二天只得拿自己的人头向国王谢罪。他满脑子想的就是如何劈开那木头,全忘了弹琴的事。

晚上,公主到窗前听琴,不料寂静一片,随即朝他喊道:"你为何今晚这么沮丧,连琴都不弹了呢?"他如实相告。

公主对此一笑置之,朝他喊道:"就为这点事伤心吗?快拿出琴来,给我助助兴。明天一早来找我。"

听此,陌生人抄琴为公主弹了一夜。

第二天一早,公主从发绺中拔出一根给他,说道:"用它绕在你的剑上,定能把木头一劈为二。"

陌生人走上前去,一剑劈开了木头。

国王却说:"在你娶我女儿之前,我还要交给你一个任务。"

"陛下请讲,"陌生人说道。

"听着,"国王说道:"你得双手各端一满杯水,骑马全速跑完三英里路。如果滴水不洒,我就把女儿嫁给你,否则我就要你的命。"

陌生人随后回到老妇人家,又因烦恼而忘了弹琴。

晚上,公主依旧来到窗前听他弹琴,但不见如何响动。公主朝他喊道:"你咋不弹琴呢?"

他讲了国王的吩咐。公主答道:"不用烦恼,现在只管弹琴,明天一早来找我。"

第二天一早,他去了。公主给他一枚戒指,说道:"把它扔到水里,水会立刻冻结,一滴都不会洒。"按照公主的吩咐,陌生人一路稳稳当当地把水端了过去。

国王又说:"现在我给你第三个任务,也是最后一个。我有个黑人明天跟你角斗,你若赢了,就可以娶我女儿。"

陌生人满心欢喜地回到老妇人家。冲他那晚的高兴劲儿,公主朝他喊道:"今晚你好像很开心,父王跟你说了什么,让你如此高兴?"

他答道:"您父王告诉我,明天我跟他的黑人角斗,这黑人和我一样是人,我有希望征服他,赢得比赛。"

公主却说:"这个最难。我就是那个黑人,因为我一喝酒,就会变成一个力大无比的黑人。明天早上到集市去,买上十二张牛皮,裹好你的马,拿这块布裹好你自己。我明天被放出来进攻你,就拿这布朝我一亮,就会阻止我,不会伤着你。跟我角斗时,你得尽量刺我那匹马的两眼中间。你杀死了这匹马就等于赢了我。"

因此,他第二天一早去集市上买了十二张牛皮,裹好了他的马,然后与黑人角斗。他俩打斗多时,十一张牛皮都被戳破,陌生人终于刺中黑人那匹马的两眼中间部位,马倒地毙命,黑人告输。

国王随后说道:"你已解开了我的三道难题,我认你做我的驸马。"

陌生人却说:"我还有事需要了结。十四天后,我回来迎娶新娘。"

他随后去了别国的一个大城镇,投宿于一老妇人家中。吃过晚饭后,他向老妇人要水喝,可对方却说:"孩子,我没有水给你,有个巨人霸占着井泉,我们每年给他送去一个少女,才只让取水一次。他先把少女吃掉,然后再让我们取水;这次刚好轮到国王的女儿,明天就要被送去那儿。"

第二天,公主如期带到,用一根金链绑在那儿。之后人们纷纷离去。

众人离开后,陌生人来到少女身边,问她为何那么伤心。少女说有巨人要来吃掉她。陌生人说,如果她答应做他的妻子,就救她。公主愉快地同意了。

巨人一出现,陌生人就放狗上去,咬住他的喉咙,直到他窒息死亡,公主因此获救。

国王得知这事,欣然同意了这桩婚事,并举行了隆重的婚礼。年轻的新郎在王宫里住了101个星期,渐觉生活枯燥无味,想外出打猎。国王本想阻止却不能,于是恳请他带足护卫,年轻人婉言相拒,只带上自己的马和狗去了。

他骑了很长的路,见到远处一间小屋,于是直奔过去找点水喝。他见到一位老妇人,向她要水。老妇人要求先让她用小棍子敲打他的狗,好让她取水时不被咬着。猎人答应了。老妇人拿棍子一碰,狗转眼间变成了石头。紧接着,她用棍子碰了一下猎人和马,他俩也立刻变成了石头。与此同时,猎人老家门前的那两棵柏树就开始枯萎。见状,他那位孪生兄弟立刻出发寻找他。

他首先来到孪生兄弟杀死巨人的城镇,命中注定要去他曾投宿过的老妇人家。老妇人见到他时,误以为是前者,于是对他说道:"孩子,不要误会,我本想来恭贺你和公主新婚志喜的。"

陌生人察觉了老妇人出错的原因,却只说了声:"老人家,没关系,"接着骑马前往王宫。国王和公主都错当他是其孪生兄弟,于是问道:"你咋去了那么久?我们以为你遭遇不测了。"

到了晚上,他和误以为是自己丈夫的公主同睡一床,只是中间隔着一把剑。他天亮就起床打猎去了。命运让他跟孪生兄弟走上同一条路。他老远就见着对方,知道他被变成了石像。他走进那小屋,命令老妇人给他的兄弟解除魔法。可老妇人却说:"先让我用棍子碰一下你的狗,然后再替你的兄弟解除。"

可他却命令狗逮住她,一直咬到膝盖,直到老妇人高声求饶:"叫开你的狗,我这就替你兄弟解除魔法!"

他却说:"说出咒语,我替他解除。"老妇人不肯,他命令狗一直咬到她的臀部。

老妇人随即高喊道:"我有两根棍,绿色的把人变成石头,红色的让人复活。"

猎人随即抓起红棍,替孪生兄弟、他的马和狗解除了魔法,又让自己的狗吃掉老妇人。

就在回国王城堡的路上,来者对孪生兄弟说,见自家门前的柏树枯萎,便立刻赶来寻找,还说去了对方岳父的城堡、认过公主为妻。对方一听便大怒,重击来者额头直至其死去,然后只身回到岳父的王宫。

晚上入睡时,公主问他:"昨晚你咋没跟我说一句话?"

他吼叫道:"那不是我,是我的孪生兄弟。我已经杀了他,因为在路上他无意中跟我说认你为妻!"

"你还记得杀他的地方吗?能找到尸体吗?"公主问道。

"绝没问题。"

"那我们明天骑马去那儿,"公主说道。第二天一早,他俩一同出发。一到那儿,公主随身取出一个小瓶,在尸体上洒了几滴水,人立刻活了过来。

他起身后,孪生兄弟对他道歉:"亲爱的兄弟,请原谅我一气之下杀了你。"然后哥俩拥抱在一起,一起回到了"国色天香"那儿,未婚的兄弟娶她为妻。

之后,兄弟俩把父母接过来一起住,一大家人生活得其乐融融。

10. 堪 内 特 拉

从前有个国王,他统治的国家名叫贝罗普久。非常富有、至高无上的他除没小孩外,要啥有啥。婚后多年且年迈时,王后仁佐拉终于给他生了个漂亮的女儿,取名堪内特拉。

公主长成个美人,高挑笔直如小杉树。她十八岁时,父王把她叫到身边说:"女儿,你已到结婚安家的年龄了。父王爱你胜过世上一切,除希望你幸福外别无所求。我决定让你自己选丈夫。相信你会让我满意的。"堪内特拉谢过父王的心意和关爱,却说自己无心结婚,决意独身。

国王自感年迈体弱,希望在生前能见到王位的继承人。一听这话非常不高兴,他恳求女儿别让他失望。

见父王执意要她结婚,堪内特拉说道:"那好吧,亲爱的父王,我就顺您之意,我可不想让人说我忘恩负义,但您得替我找个世上最英俊、最聪明的丈夫。"

听此,国王高兴不已,于是从早到晚坐在窗边,仔细打量来往的行人,希望从中挑到一位驸马来。

一天,国王见一漂亮小伙穿街而过,便叫来女儿说道:"快来,亲爱的堪内特拉,看那人,我看他倒是挺适合做你丈夫的。"

他们把小伙请进宫里,摆上宴席,拿各种佳肴款待。席间,小伙嘴里掉下一颗杏仁,然后迅速拣起来,藏在桌布下。

那人走后,国王问堪内特拉:"这小伙怎样?"

"真笨,"堪内特拉答道,"这么大的人,口里竟掉出杏仁!"

听罢,国王回到窗边继续观望,很快又见一漂亮小伙经过,立刻叫过女儿看如何。

"请他进来,"堪内特拉说道,"近点瞧瞧。"

又一轮丰盛筵席。等陌生人吃饱喝足离开后,国王问堪内特拉咋样。

"不咋样,"女儿答道,"穿一件披风竟要两个仆人帮忙这种人有啥用?"

"你若是挑他那点毛病,"国王说道,"我算是明白了。你是成心不找丈夫。你必须嫁人,我可不想断送自己的名声和家族。"

"那行,尊敬的父王,"堪内特拉答道,"我这就告诉您,最好别指望我,除非能找个金头金牙的男人,否则我就不结婚!"

见女儿如此固执,国王很是生气,不过仍一如既往地迁就了她,于是发布公告,大意是:任何金头金牙的男子均可前来迎娶公主,以贝罗普久王国作为陪嫁。

话说国王有个名为西奥拉文特的死敌,是个厉害无比的术士。听此布告,他就召集手下精灵,命他们给他的头和牙齿镀金。起初,精灵都说其法力不足以完成该任务,建议在他的前额上安上一对金犄角,这一来更容易,二来穿戴更舒服。但西奥拉文特却毫无妥协,坚持要上等金子做成的头和牙齿。就这样安装上后,他便前去王宫前溜达。一见人选出现,国王就叫来女儿,说道:"看窗外,包你心满意足!"

西奥拉文特正匆匆而过,国王朝他喊道:"等等,伙计,别急着走呀。你若肯进来,便可娶我女儿为妻。我会送侍从给她,马匹和仆人,你要多少有多少。"

"多谢了,"西奥拉文特答道,"我乐意娶公主,女仆就不要了,恳请赐给我一匹马,我要让公主坐在我的鞍前,带她回到我的王国,那儿朝臣、仆人一应俱全,可以说公主要啥有啥。"

国王起初反对堪内特拉以这种方式离开,但西奥拉文特始终坚持这样做。他让公主上马坐在前面,启程回国了。

傍晚时分,他下马走进马厩,然后把堪内特拉和马关在一起,还对她说道:"你这就给我听着。我要回宫去,离这里有七年的路程。你得呆在这马厩等我,不许离开,不许让人看见。胆敢违抗命令,有你好果子吃!"

公主顺从地答道:"陛下,我是您的仆人,一定听从您的吩咐。可我想知道,您回来前,我都吃啥呀?"

"马吃剩下的饲料,"西奥拉文特答道。

术士离她而去,堪内特拉深感悲惨,诅咒自己命运不济。她一直哭泣,惋惜残酷的命运将她从王宫赶到马厩,从松软的鹅绒垫赶到稻草窝,从父王餐桌的美味赶到马吃过的饲料。

如此悲惨生活,她熬了几个月,其间连给马添料、送水的人就没见过,因为这一切都是由一双隐形的手来完成的。

一天,凄凉无比的她忽见有道墙缝,透过它能见到一个美丽的花园,花园的鲜花果实可谓应有尽有。一看到且嗅到这些美味,可怜的堪内特拉无法自控,心想:"管它的,我要溜出去摘些橘子、葡萄吃。谁会向丈夫告发我呢?即使他听说我抗命,又能拿我咋样,我的处境够惨的了。"

她溜了出去,摘下园里的水果,好好犒劳了一下自己那可怜、挨饿的肚子。

不一会儿,丈夫突然回来。有匹马随即向他告状,说她趁丈夫不在溜进园子,偷吃了些橘子、葡萄。

西奥拉文特一听怒不可遏,从腰间掏出一把大刀,威胁要杀掉她这抗命的妻子。堪内特拉赶忙下跪,乞求饶命,说此举是因饥饿所迫,好歹最终软化了丈夫。他说道:"就饶你这一次,你若再抗命,我回来再听说你走出过这马厩半步,我定取你的小命。所以小心点,我又要走了,一去七年。"

他说完便一走了之。堪内特拉放声痛哭,边搓手边抱怨:"我咋这么苦的命啊!父王啊,您把苦命的女儿害惨啦!我怎能埋怨父王呢?这都是我自找的呀,我找个可恶的金头,他给我带来了厄运。我违背父命,活该遭罚!"

一年后的某天,父王的桶匠碰巧经过囚禁堪内特拉的马厩。公主认出了他,把他叫了进去。起初,桶匠没认出公主,也不知谁竟叫出了自己的名字。听完堪内特拉的心酸故事,就把她藏到自己的一只巨大的空桶里,一因他可怜这苦命的姑娘,二因他想讨好国王。他随后把桶挂在驴背上,就这样带着公主离去。他们凌晨四点才到王宫。桶匠使劲敲门。仆人匆匆开门,发现竟是桶匠站在那里,愤愤地大骂他来得不是时候,把人给吵醒了。

听到吵闹为何而起,国王派人叫来桶匠,觉得他一定有要事相告,否则不会在此刻来惊扰王宫的。

桶匠请求卸下驴子,堪内特拉从桶里爬了出来。国王起初不敢相信那竟是自己的女儿,因为她几年下来变化太大了,那瘦弱、苍白的样子,看上去怪可怜的。公主最后亮出右臂上的一颗痣,国王这才相信可怜的姑娘真是自己阔别的堪内特拉。他抱住女儿一阵亲吻,接着给她摆上一桌美味佳肴。

等女儿填饱肚子,国王问她道:"谁想到你竟落到这般境地,亲爱的女儿。我且问,这是咋的啦?"

堪内特拉答道:"那金头金牙的恶人待我猪狗不如。自从离开父王后,我多次都想一死了之,所受之苦可是一言难尽啊,说来您也未必相信。能重见父王,我知足了,再也不离开您。我宁做您的仆人,也不给人当什么王后。"

话说西奥拉文特回到马厩,有匹马立刻向他告状,说堪内特拉让个桶匠装在桶里带走了。

一听这话,可恶的术士气得发疯。赶到贝罗普久国后,他直接去了王宫正对面的一个老太婆家,对她说道:"你若让我看到国王的女儿,要啥给啥。"

老太婆索要100个金币,西奥拉文特二话没说,掏出钱袋如数给她。老太婆随即把他带到屋顶,那儿能看见宫中顶楼闺房梳理长发的堪内特拉。

公主无意间朝窗外看,忽见丈夫正望着自己,吓了一大跳,于是飞奔下楼来到父王前面:"父王,快把我锁进七层铁门的屋子,否则我就完了。"

"就这事,"国王说道,"立刻就办。"他随即下令锁上七层铁门。

见此,西奥拉文特回到老太婆面前:"你若进宫,藏到公主的床下,把这张纸条塞到她的枕头下,边塞边说'愿宫里的人酣睡过去,公主除外'。你要啥给啥。"

老妇人又索要了100个金币,接着执行术士的旨意去了。她把纸条往堪内特拉的枕头下一塞,宫里的人就睡了过去,唯有公主醒着。

西奥拉文特随即赶到那七道门,逐一打开。一见丈夫,堪内特拉失声大叫,却无人前来援救,因为宫里的人都睡得跟死人似的。术士将她从床上一把抓起,准备带走,不料老太婆塞到枕头下的纸条掉到了地上。

堪内特拉不停呼救,结果惊醒了整个王宫,人们火速援救。他们抓住并处死了西奥拉文特。他给公主设下陷阱,结果自己掉了进去——世上之事往往如此:咬人者反遭咬。

11. 巴克·伊顿萨奇家的女儿

　　从前,某某有七个女儿。一家人长期幸福生活着。一天早晨,父亲把她们全叫到跟前说:"我和你们的母亲要出趟远门,不知要去多久,所以给你们备足了三年的粮食。我们回来前,切勿为任何人开门。"

　　"好的,父亲大人,"姑娘们答道。

　　她们两年都不曾开门或出去过。一天,姑娘们洗完衣服在屋顶晾晒时,看到下面街上人来人往,对面市场铺子里摆满了新鲜肉食、蔬菜等好东西。

　　"快过来,"其中一个叫道。"一见那东西我就饿得慌!咱为啥就没份儿呢?咱去个人,到市场买肉、蔬菜。"

　　"噢,别那样,"幺妹说道,"你们知道,爸爸没回来是不能开门的。"

　　大姐扑上去揍她,二姐朝她吐口水,三姐谩骂她,四姐推搡她,五姐把她扔到地上,六姐扯破她的衣服。然后,姐几个让她躺在地上,提着篮子出门去了。

　　约一小时后,她们拎着满篮子肉、蔬菜回来了,把刚买的食品放入锅里,生起火来,却忘了门还敞开着。小妹没参与此事。晚餐做好、桌子摆好时,她溜到门厅,藏在角落的大桶后面。

　　话说姐几个正吃得欢,一个女巫经过。她见门开着,便走了进去。她来到大姐面前,说道:"我该先吃你哪个的地方,胖妹?"

　　"就从,"她答道,"打幺妹的那只手。"

　　女巫吃了她,吃完后走到二姐面前,问道:"我该先吃你的哪个地方,胖妹?"

　　二姐答道:"就从骂幺妹的嘴。"

　　她依次吃掉后面几个,这六个姐姐就此消失了。女巫吃完六姐最后一口肉,蹲在桶后的小妹吓呆了,立刻从敞开的大门跑到大街上,头也不回地飞快往前跑,直到眼前出现一座妖怪的城堡。见门边角落有口大锅,她悄悄爬进去,盖上盖子,很快睡着了。

　　不久,妖怪回来了。"嘿,呼,哈,"他喊道,"我闻到人的味道了,你是倒了什么霉才来这儿的?"他查看了所有房间,却见人。"你在哪里?"他问道,"别怕,我不会伤害你的。"姑娘仍没不出声。

　　"听我说,出来吧!"妖怪重复道,"没事的。如果你是个老头,我就当你是父亲;如果你是个男孩,我就当你是儿子;如果你和我年龄相当,我当你是兄弟;如果你是个老太婆,我就当你是母亲;如果你是个姑娘,我就当你是女儿;如果你是个中年妇女,我就当你是妻子。所以出来吧,别害怕。"

　　姑娘走出藏身之处,站到他的面前。

　　"别害怕,"妖怪又说道。后来,他出去打猎,就让她看家。晚上,他带回野兔、山鹑和瞪羚作姑娘的晚餐。他本人只喜欢她煮的人肉。他还让姑娘保管六间房的钥匙,自己留着第七间屋子的钥匙。

　　时光流逝,姑娘仍随妖怪生活。他俩以父女相称。他从没对她吼叫过。

　　有一天,姑娘向他恳求道:"爸爸,把顶屋的钥匙给我吧。"

　　"不行的,女儿,"妖怪答道,"那里没有对你有用的东西。"

　　"可我就要那钥匙,"姑娘重复道。

妖怪没再搭理,假装没听到。姑娘哭了,心想:"今天夜里,等他以为我睡着后,就偷看他把钥匙藏在哪儿。"跟妖怪吃过晚饭,她道了声晚安离开了房间,不一会又悄悄折回来,在窗帘后偷看。她很快见他从衣袋里掏出钥匙,藏进一个地洞,然后睡去。夜深人静时,她取出钥匙,回到自己的房间。

第二天,妖怪伴着第一缕阳光醒来,他首先找钥匙,却没找着,立刻猜到是咋回事了。不像多数妖怪那样大发雷霆,他心想:"我若叫醒她,只会吓着她。就让她今天保管吧,晚上回来有时间要回来。"他随后打猎去了。

等他一走远,姑娘跑上楼去打开房门,发现里面几乎是空的,仅有的窗户也关着。她推开窗格往外看,底下是王子的花园,里面没个人影,只有头公牛独自从井里取水。一听推窗声,公牛抬来对她说道:"早上好,巴克·伊顿萨奇家的姑娘!你父亲会把你养得白白胖胖,然后放烤肉叉上烤。"

这话真吓着姑娘了,她大哭着跑出房间。她哭了一天,妖怪晚上回来时,没见她备好晚饭。"你哭什么?"妖怪问道。"我的晚饭呢?你打开过顶楼的房间吗?"

"是的,"姑娘答道。

"公牛对你说啥啦?"

"他说:'早上好,巴克·伊顿萨奇家的姑娘!你父亲要把你养得白白胖胖,然后放烤肉叉上烤。'"

"那你明天去窗口对它说:'我父亲把我养得白白胖胖,绝不会吃我。我要是得到你一只眼,就拿它当镜子用,照了前面又照后面;你的肚带会松落,眼睛会瞎七天七夜。'"

"好的。"姑娘答道。第二天早上,公牛跟她说话,她就按父亲教的回答。公牛随即倒地,躺了七天七夜。由于没浇水,花园里的花全都枯萎了。

王子来到花园,发现全是焦黄的花梗。公牛躺在花梗丛中。王子一剑捅死了公牛,转身对随从说道:"再找头公牛来!"随从又找来一头强壮的公牛,从井里抽水,花活了过来,草也转青了。王子随后叫上随从离开。第二天早上姑娘听到水车转动的声音,推开窗格往外望。

"早上好,巴克·伊顿萨奇家的姑娘!"新来的公牛说道,"你父亲要把你养得白白胖胖,然后放烤肉叉上烤。"

姑娘答道:"我父亲把我养得白白胖胖,不会吃我。我要是得到你一只眼,我就拿它当镜子用,照了前面又照后面;你的肚带会松落,眼睛会瞎七天七夜。"

姑娘话音刚落,公牛立刻倒地躺了七天七夜。

七天后,公牛起身继续从井里提水浇花,才把水车转了一两圈,王子突发奇想,来花园看刚来的公牛干得咋样。他进来时,公牛正忙着干活。尽管如此,园里的花草还是一副枯萎的样子。王子拔剑冲向公牛,想杀掉它,就像杀上一头公牛那样。这时公牛跪下求情:"主人,饶了我吧,让我告诉您事情的经过。"

"咋的啦?"王子问道。

"主人,一位姑娘从那窗户探出头来,对我说了几句话,我就倒地上了,七天七夜躺着无法动弹。主人啊,她真美,一生难得见二回啊!"

"撒谎!"王子说道,"那是妖怪的家。他难道会在顶屋里藏个姑娘不成?"

"咋不会呢?"公牛答道,"您明天一早来,躲到树后就看得到。"

"我会的,"王子说,"若发现你没说实话,我就宰了你。"他离开了,公牛继续干活。第二天,王子一早来到花园,见公牛正在忙着转动水车。

133

"姑娘出现没?"王子问道。

"还没,不过快了。您藏在树枝里,很快就能看到。"

王子照做了。他刚蹲下,姑娘就推开窗格。

"早上好,巴克·伊顿萨奇家的姑娘!"公牛说道,"你父亲把你养得白白胖胖,然后放在烤肉叉上烤。"

"我父亲把我养得白白胖胖,绝不会吃我。我要是得到你一只眼,就拿它当镜子用,照了前面又照后面;你的肚带会松落,眼睛会瞎七天七夜。"

姑娘话音刚落,公牛就倒在了地上。姑娘关窗而去。王子这才得知公牛说的是实话,也知道姑娘的确美得举世无双。他从树上下来,爱的火花在心中燃起。

"妖怪咋没吃了她?"王子心想,"我今晚在宫里宴请他,跟他打听姑娘的事,看她是不是他的妻子。"

王子命人宰了头大牛,做成烤全牛,备好两口大缸,一个装水,一个装酒。临近傍晚,他叫上随从,来到妖怪院里等他打猎归来。妖怪见门前人头攒动惊讶不已,便躬身问:"各位邻居早,我何有能受此大驾光临?但愿没冒犯各位吧?"

"哪里哪里!"王子答道。

"那,"妖怪继续问道,"陛下初临寒舍到底为何?"

"想跟你共进晚餐,"王子答道。

"好啊,饭已备好,请!"妖怪边答边带头往屋里走,他那天很是走运,背包里装满了猎物。

桌子很快摆好。王子刚落座就惊叫道:"哦,巴克·伊顿萨奇,你看我做东咋样?"

"去哪儿?"妖怪问道。

"我宫里。我全备好了。"

"可那远了点。何不就这儿?"

"噢,改日吧。今晚得由我坐庄。"

妖怪随王子及随从去了宫中。

不一会儿,王子转身对妖怪说道:"你面前的我是位求婚者。我想从名门人家中寻个妻子。"

"我可没女儿啊,"妖怪答道。

"噢,你有。她在窗边我见着啦。"

"您要愿意就娶她吧,"妖怪说道。

兴高采烈的王子率随从护送妖怪回到家中。分手时,王子对客人说道:"你不会忘了咱俩达成的交易吧?"

"我可不是小孩,从不食言。"说完,妖怪进屋关上了门。

他上楼才发现姑娘正等着他,因为她不喜欢独自吃饭。

"我吃过了,"妖怪说道,"还跟王子待了一晚上。"

"您在哪儿见着他啦?"姑娘问道。

"噢,我们是邻居,一起长大的。今晚我答应把你嫁给他了。"

"我不想嫁人,"姑娘答道。她这是装的,其实心里可高兴了。

第二天一早,王子带着聘礼和华丽的新娘穿的服饰过来迎娶姑娘回宫。

临别时,妖怪叫住姑娘说:"女儿,注意千万别跟王子说话。他若跟你说话,你得装哑巴,除非他发誓'看在巴克·伊顿萨奇的分上',你才能说话。"

"好的,"姑娘答道。

他们去了。一到王宫,王子把新娘带到早备好的房间,对她说道:"跟我说话,亲爱的。"可她一言不发。王子随后离去,心想或许她这是害羞。第二天,她依旧不说话,第三天,第四天。王子最后说道:"那好,你不说话,我就去找个愿意跟我说话的妻子。"王子还真这么做了。

话说新娘子来到宫中。巴克·伊顿萨奇家的姑娘起身,对伺候新娘子的女婢说道:"来坐下。我来做宴席。"女婢听命坐下等着。

姑娘一坐下便高喊道:"柴火,过来。"柴火过来了。"火,过来。"火过来点燃柴火。"锅,过来,油,过来。"锅和油都过来了。"油,去锅里!"她说道。油照做了。当锅里的油煮沸时,姑娘把几根手指都放进去,很快变成十条煎鱼。"灶,过来。"灶过来了。"火,给灶加热。"火也照做了。灶烧到滚烫时,姑娘跳了进去,连同饰有金银的裙子和珠宝。她很快变成一根让人看了直淌口水的雪白面包。

面包对婢女们说道:"可以吃了,站近一点。"可婢女个个惊讶得面面相觑。

"你们都看啥?"新娘问道。

"看稀奇,"婢女齐声道。

"这稀奇吗?"新娘子不屑地说道,"我也会,"说完径直跳进灶里,结果一会儿就烧焦了。

婢女们随即跑去禀报王子:"快来,新娘子死了。"

"把她埋了呗!"他答道,"她干吗那样做?我可没说过让她跳进灶里之类的话。"

烧焦的女人给埋了。王子拒不参加葬礼,因为他还一门心思想着闭口不答的妻子。第二天晚上,他对她说道:"亲爱的,你是害怕跟我说话会发生可怕的事吗?你若执意装作哑巴,我只好再娶一个。"

可怜的姑娘真想说话,可对妖怪心生畏惧的她只得保持沉默。王子还真说到做到,又娶回了新娘。当新娘和女婢们端庄就座后,姑娘在地上竖起一根尖木桩,然后轻松坐上去还旋转起来。

"都看什么呀?"新娘问婢女,"你们认为那很了不起吗?我也会。"

"您不行的,"她们答道,吃惊得说话都忘了礼节。

姑娘跳下木桩后走开了。新娘立马上去,结果让锋利的木桩刺透而死。女婢们赶紧禀报王子:"快!埋掉新娘吧。"

"你们埋了她吹,"王子答道,"她干吹那样做?我可没命令她刺死在木桩上。"

她们埋了她。晚上,王子去见巴克·伊顿萨奇家的姑娘,对她说道:"跟我说话,不然我还娶。"可她还是怕跟他说话。

第二天,王子躲进房间观察。姑娘很快醒来,对陶罐和水罐说道:"快!去泉边接些水。我渴了。"

两个罐子离去。在泉边灌水,水罐撞上陶罐,碰缺了对方的嘴。陶罐哭着跑到姑娘那儿告状:"女主人,水罐碰缺了我的嘴,揍它。"

"看在巴克·伊顿萨奇的分上,我求您饶了我吧,"水罐说道。

"唉!"姑娘叹气道,"我的丈夫要是那样起誓,我打开始就跟他说话了,他就不会再去娶别的姑娘!可他就是不说,还要娶新人。"

躲藏的王子听到这话,跳将起来,冲到她的面前说道:"看在巴克·伊顿萨奇的分上,跟我说话吧!"

姑娘跟王子说话了,从此幸福生活一辈子,因为她信守了对妖怪的承诺。

12. 笑眼、泪眼和跛狐

从前有个右眼微笑、左眼泪流的人。他有三个儿子,两个聪明,一个愚笨。话说哥儿仨对父亲的眼睛颇为好奇,于是决定向他问个明白。

一天,老大去父亲房间直问缘由。父亲非但不答,反而暴跳如雷,提刀朝他扑去。年轻人惊恐地逃回原处——俩弟弟正急等那次谈话的结果呢!

可他们得到的却是:"你俩自己问去,看运气是否好点。"

一听这话,老二走进父亲房间,结果跟大哥一样的遭遇。回来后,他告诉愚笨的弟弟,轮到他去碰碰运气。

老幺大胆朝父亲走去,问道:"哥哥们不告诉我您说的话。请您这就告诉我,您为何右眼总微笑、左眼总流泪?"

父亲一样气得脸色铁青,持刀冲过来。傻瓜知道父亲没啥好害怕的,因此一步也未动。

"啊,我这才明白谁配做我儿子!"老人叹道,"他俩不过是懦夫而已。你向我证明了你的勇敢,我就满足你的好奇心。我右眼微笑,是我高兴有你这样的好儿子,左眼流泪,是我为失去的宝物伤心。我家花园原有株每小时产一桶酒的葡萄藤。自从葡萄藤被人偷走后,我便为此流泪不已。"

傻瓜回到哥哥们那儿,给他们讲了父亲宝物被盗的事。兄弟仨决定立即动身找回那株葡萄藤。哥儿仨一起上路,到十字路口后才分手。哥哥俩走一路,傻瓜另走一路。

"谢天谢地,终于摆脱傻瓜啦!"两个哥哥叹息道。"咱俩这就吃点早饭。"他们坐在路边吃了起来。

刚吃了一半,树林里走出一只跛脚狐狸,跟他俩乞讨食物。哥俩一跃而起,抄棍子就赶。可怜的狐狸拐着三条脚跑开了。狐狸跑着来到正掏干粮的傻弟弟的跟前。狐狸向他讨要点面包,傻瓜原本没带多少,但还是欣然地给饥饿的狐狸掰了一半。

"兄弟,你这是要去哪儿?"狐狸吃完分得的面包后问道。小伙子讲了父亲和神奇葡萄藤的故事。

"哎呀!真巧!"狐狸叹道,"我知道葡萄藤的下落。跟我来。"他俩一直走到某个大花园的门口。

"你在这里面会看得到要找的葡萄藤,但要弄到手可不容易。你可要听清我的劝告。你得过十二关才能到葡萄藤那儿,每关都有两名卫士把守。若见他们瞪眼看你,就大胆前行,因为他们睡着了。但若见他们两眼紧闭,可得当心,因为他们完全醒着。一到葡萄藤那儿,你会看到木铲、铁铲各一把。千万别用铁铲,因为那会发出响声,惊醒卫士。那你就完了。"

年轻人顺利地穿过花园,来到那颗每小时产一桶酒的葡萄藤。心想木铲不可能刨动硬土,他就抄起铁铲,结果响声随即惊醒了守卫。他们抓住可怜的年轻人,押解到主人面前。

"干吗偷我的葡萄藤?"主人质问道,"你怎样躲过守卫的?"

"葡萄藤不是你的,是我父亲的。你若是现在不归还,我还会再来的。"

"你要带走葡萄藤,得拿金苹果树的苹果来交换,这树二十四小时开花、结果。"说罢,他下令放走傻瓜。小伙出来后,忙找狐狸讨教。

"你瞧瞧,"狐狸说道,"这就是不听劝的后果。不过,我会帮你弄到金苹果的。金苹果长在一个花园里,凭着我的描述,你很容易认出来。苹果树旁各有一根金杆和木杆。用木杆捅,就能得到金苹果。"

傻少爷聆听着狐狸的吩咐,和上次一样躲过了所有的守卫,过花园后很快来到苹果树前。金苹果的美色使他眼花缭乱,狐狸的话早已忘得一干二净。他抓起金杆,"啪"的一声狠狠打到树枝上。守卫立刻惊醒过来,把他带到主人面前。傻瓜只得说出事情的原委。

"我可以给你金苹果,"园子的主人说道,"但要拿一匹日行全球的马作为交换。"年轻人去找狐狸。

难怪狐狸这次真生气了。"你若真听了我的话,这下该跟你的父亲在一起了。我愿意再帮你一次。去森林,你会看到有匹马的脖上套有金绳和麻绳。用麻绳牵马,否则它的嘶叫就会惊醒守卫。那你就完了。"

傻少爷终于找到了那匹马,那俊俏的样儿简直让他惊呆了。

"什么!"他心想,"用麻绳套这样的动物?我可不干!"

马嘶叫起来,守卫抓住了咱们这位年轻的朋友,押解到了主人面前。

"你若能送给我一位不见日月的金少女,"主人说道,"我就送给你一匹金马。"

"要我送给你一位金少女,你得先借我一匹金马去寻找她呀。"

"哦,"金马的主人问道,"谁担保你会回来呢?"

"我以父亲的人头发誓,"年轻人答道,"要么带回金少女,要么送回金马。"他回头去请教狐狸。

狐狸向来耐心、包容他人过失,把他带到一个深深的洞窟。里面站着一位纯金少女,美丽无比。小伙子扶她上马后,正准备骑上去。

狐狸问道:"拿如此可爱的少女去换一匹马,你不惋惜吗?但你只得这么做,因为你拿父亲的人头起誓过。我或许能替她去。"说完,狐狸变成一位金少女,跟真的没什么分别。

傻瓜带着'她'直接去面见金马主人。对方一下迷上了'她'。

年轻人取回了父亲的葡萄藤,还在这场交易中娶到了一位纯金少女。

13. 驴　　皮

从前，有位国王深受臣民爱戴，因而觉得自己是世上最幸福的君主。他心仪之物应有尽有：王宫满是奇珍异品，花园鲜花芳香四溢，大理石马厩里养着一排排乳白色阿拉伯宝马，个个长着褐色大眼。

听闻国王这些珍奇宝物，人们纷纷远道而来一看究竟，无不惊讶地发现，最气派的马厩里竟养着一头耷拉着硕大双耳的驴子。众人看得出那是头好驴，但始终不解其为何如此受宠，连离开时还犯着嘀咕。他们岂知，这头驴每晚入睡后，两耳哗啦哗啦直冒金子，天亮时由仆人捡走。

这般富庶日子持续多年后，厄运突然降临到国王头上：他深爱的王后仙去。王后去世前，一心挂念着国王的幸福，她用仅有的力气对他说道："请陛下答应我一件事。为臣民，也为陛下您，一定得续弦。不过这事急不得，耐心等待比我更美丽动人的女子。"

国王抽泣道："噢，说什么续弦啊！我愿陪你去死！"王后淡淡一笑，头朝枕上一扬去了。

悲痛数月的国王渐渐走出了阴影。大臣们意在催促他再娶一位王后。国王起初根本不听，后来逐渐同意考虑此事，但信守对已故王后的承诺，新娘必须比她更美丽动人。

大臣们欣喜说服工作取得成效，于是派出使节四处收集天下美女的画像。画师们日夜忙碌，尽力作画。唉，可惜啊！人人只得承认没哪位女子比得上已故王后。

一天，看过刚送达的一批画像后，国王失望地转过头来，目光落到了自幼生活在王宫里的养女身上。他发现，这世上比王后更动人的非她莫属！他立马表达了自己的意愿。不过，养女没有半点野心，也丝毫不想嫁给他，满心忧郁地恳请国王容她考虑考虑。当天夜里，趁着世人熟睡之际，她坐上一辆羊拉车，去找她的仙女教母求教去了。

少女一下车，仙女开口道："我知道你要说什么。你若无意嫁给国王，那我给你指点一二。跟陛下索要一件色如蓝天的连衣裙。他若做不到，你一定没事。"少女谢过仙女回到宫中。

第二天一早，父王（她一直这样称呼他）来看她。少女告诉父王，她无法答复他，除非给她弄来一件色如蓝天的连衣裙。国王一听高兴极了，立即找来国内顶级织工和裁缝，命其火速做好一件天蓝色连衣裙，否则杀头。迫于威慑，工匠们立马染布、裁剪、缝纫起来。两天后，他们就送来了连衣裙——那裙子恍如从空中剪来一般。可怜的少女惊讶得不知如何是好，于是趁着黑夜又驾车拜见仙女去了。

"没想到国王竟有这般聪明！"仙女叹道，"那就跟他要一件月光连衣裙。"

第二天，国王召见时，养女讲了想要的东西。

"宝贝儿，你要啥给啥！"国王应道，随即下令一天内做好裙子，否则全都绞死。

工匠们全力以赴，月光裙在次日凌晨摆上了她的床头。少女尽管惊叹其美丽，但还是不由得哭了起来，直到仙女闻声赶到她的面前。

"咦，他竟有这般能耐！"仙女叹道，"要一件阳光连衣裙！他要能做出来才怪呢！"

有了前两次教训，少女对仙女的话将信将疑，可别无他法，只得向父王提出那一要求。

国王没被难倒，还拿最好的珠宝和钻石缀在裙子上。新做成的裙子绚丽夺目，不戴墨镜根本不敢看。

公主见过裙子，装出一副眼睛受伤样儿回闺房去了。愧色难当的仙女已在此等候。

"这下唯有一个办法!"仙女失声说道。"国王很在乎那头驴,你就要驴皮!那是他一切财富的源头。我断定他舍不得!"

公主将信将疑,不过还是参见了国王,说不得到驴皮绝不嫁给他。这一要求让国王既吃惊又心痛,但却没有丝毫犹豫。驴给杀了,驴皮摆到了公主脚下。

一见在劫难逃,可怜的少女一边号啕,一边扯发。仙女忽然出现在她的面前。

"没事!"仙女说,"不会有事的!披上驴皮,离开王宫,走得越远越好。我会一路护着你。你的衣物和珠宝也会在地下一路随行。需要什么,你只消跺跺脚,就能得到。不过,一定要快,时间不多了。"

于是,公主披上驴皮,悄悄溜出了王宫。

公主刚一失踪,整个皇宫叫声四起,每个角落也搜了个遍。国王派出人马沿各路追踪。不过,人马一到,仙女就给公主披上隐形披风,谁也看不见她。

公主一路远去,试图找到肯收留她干活儿的人家。可所到之处,村民只是好心地给点吃的,却因她那身肮脏的驴皮不让进屋。她出逃得急,驴皮也没能及时清洗。

一天,疲惫而失望的公主正经过某大城市外的一家农场门口,忽听有人叫她。她回头见一群火鸡里有位农妇在示意她进去。

"我想请洗盘子、喂火鸡、扫猪圈的女工,"农妇说道,"瞧你那身脏衣服,干这正适合!"

少女高兴地答应了,立刻去厨房一角干了起来。农场工都来逗她,嘲笑她那身驴皮。久而久之,大家习惯了她那身驴皮,也不拿她取乐。公主很卖力,也干得不错,深得女主人喜欢。见她看管绵羊、火鸡样样在行,都以为她生来就是干这行的。

一天,她坐在小河边,哀叹自己命苦。突然,她看到自己水中的模样:驴头就像头套一样半遮着头发和脸庞,肮脏的驴皮就像席子一样裹住整个身体。她头一次见到自己在别人眼中的模样。她为此自惭形秽,接着就索性脱掉这身装束,一次次跳入河中,想把自己洗得洁净如象牙。该回农场时,她极不情愿地穿上那身似乎比任何时候还脏的驴皮。好在她聊以自慰的是明天是假日,可以忘掉自己是个农场工,再做一回几个小时的公主。

次日天刚亮,她按仙女的旨意跺了跺脚。那条色如蓝天的裙子旋即出现在她的小床上。那屋子太小,铺不开裙摆。不过,她还是一如往常地梳理、盘起美丽长发,细心别好裙摆。打扮好后,她很满意自己的模样,于是决定不失时机展示漂亮服饰,哪怕下地干活,只有绵羊和火鸡才看得到。

话说这是家皇室农场。某假日天,正当"驴皮"(人们给她起的绰号)关起门来试穿那件阳光裙时,王子骑马路过农场大门。打猎后的他问可否在此歇歇脚。花园里很快摆上了食物和牛奶。歇够后,王子起身打探这栋闻名遐迩且古色古香的房屋。他挨个打开房门,连声赞叹每间老屋。忽然,他发觉有个门把拧不动。他猫着腰,透过钥匙孔往里瞧,惊讶地发现里面有位美少女,那身连衣裙与日同辉,让他睁不开双眼。

王子一转身,原本昏暗的走廊显得更加昏暗。他回到厨房,打听谁住走廊尽头那间屋。人们说是遭众人嘲笑的洗盘女工,都叫她'驴皮'。王子虽觉其中必有蹊跷,但也明白再问也没啥用,于是骑马回到宫里,满脑子翻腾的是透过钥匙孔见到的情景。

王子整夜辗转反侧,次日一早醒来发起了高烧。王后就这根独苗,给弄得坐立不安,以为他没救了。王子突然发病,连名医也摸不着头脑,常用疗法试过后也未见奏效。最后,他们禀告王后,说王子病情背后定有难言之隐。王后跪在儿子床头,恳请他道出实情。若他意在当国王,父王会乐意免去王位之累;若是为情所困,她将不惜代价让他得到心上人,哪怕是正在交战的是敌国的公主。

"母后,"王子有气无力地答道,"我岂敢有夺父王之冠的非分之想?只要父王还健在,我就是他最忠实的子民。至于母后所说的公主,尽管我定会遵从您的意愿,但我还一个都没见到过。"

"天啦,孩子!"王后哭述道,"为了你,也为父王和我,我们将全力以赴。你没了,我们也不想活了。"

"那好吧,"王子说,"唯有一样东西能救我,'驴皮'亲手做的蛋糕。"

王后以为儿子疯了,惊呼道:"驴皮?是人?还是啥?"

"王后,"随王子去农场的一名侍从接过话茬儿,"世上除狼之外,就数'驴皮'最恶心了,她是陛下农场里一个身穿油腻黑皮的养鸡姑娘。"

"没关系,"王后说,"王子像是吃过她的糕点。人生病就会胡思乱想。快派人去让她做蛋糕!"

侍从奉命差人策马而去。

无从得知"驴皮"是否见过王子,当他从钥匙孔往里瞧或从她的小窗下路过时。且不管她是否见过或听说过王子,一得到王后的命令,她立刻扔掉那身脏皮,从头到脚洗了个遍,换上银光闪闪的紧身衣和裙子。她随后将自己关进屋子,用上等奶油、面粉和农场上最新鲜的鸡蛋,动手做起蛋糕来。

她在用盆合面时,一枚偶尔偷着戴的戒指从手指上滑入面粉里。她兴许真没察觉,兴许是装的,继续和面。眨眼间,蛋糕放进了烤炉。蛋糕烤到焦黄时,她脱掉裙子,换上那身脏皮,随后把蛋糕交给差使,同时问起王子的病情。可差使竟扭过头去,不屑作答。

差使上马,疾驰而去。一到王宫,他抓起一个银盘,赶忙给王子呈上蛋糕。病中的王子吃得很急,御医们真怕他噎着了。他的确差点儿噎着了,因为那枚戒指藏在他掰开的蛋糕里。他趁人没注意时把它从嘴里取了出来。

独自一人时,王子从枕底下取出戒指,千百次地亲吻,接着思忖如何才能见到戒指的主人——因为他也不愿承认自己从钥匙孔里见到的就是"驴皮",免得让人嘲笑"心血来潮"。可这烦心事又让他发烧起来。御医无言以对,于是禀告王后,说王子患了严重的相思病。惊恐的王后赶紧将此呈报国王,之后一同赶到儿子床边。

"儿啦!宝贝!"国王叫道,"你想娶谁?哪怕是陛下最贱的奴隶也能成为你的新娘。这世上还有我们不愿意为你做的事儿吗?"

这番话感动得王子热泪盈眶。他从枕底下掏出那枚上等的翡翠戒指。

"父王、母后,这枚戒指作证,我心仪的人绝非农家女。能戴进这戒指的手指从未碰过重活。不管她身份如何,我非她不娶!"

国王、王后细心验过那枚戒指,同意儿子的看法,戒指的主人不可能是农家女。国王随即出去,命传令官和号手访遍全城,把年轻姑娘统统召进宫来。谁能戴上那戒指,日后便是王后。

第一批是公主,接着是侯爵的女儿,以此类推。令王子高兴的是,没一个能把戒指戴过指尖。他的病也因此快速痊愈起来。所有千金小姐试过后,最后是女店员、女仆,结果不见走运之人。

"传下人、牧羊女!"王子命令道。一见那些既红且肥的手指,答案不言自明。

"女性全试过了,殿下,"侍从禀报道。王子挥手让他退让到一旁。

"替我作蛋糕的'驴皮'找过吗?"王子问道。臣子们大笑,说不敢把脏兮兮的人带进宫中。

"这就派人去请她!"国王命令道,"朕命令的是每位姑娘,不论贵贱。君无戏言!"

公主听到了号声和王令,非常清楚这都因那枚戒指而起。她倾情于王子,一想有她那般纤手的姑娘就不寒而栗。结果,当宫廷信使策马来到门前,她高兴不已。她一直期待着这次召见,于是穿上那身缀满翡翠的月光连衣裙,精心打扮起来。当来人传唤时,她急忙披上驴皮,说自己准备好晋见王子。

她被直接带到王子等着的大厅。见到那身驴皮,王子心一沉。难道是他弄错了?

"你,"王子边问边转眼别处,"你住的是农场内院最边上那屋吗?"

"回殿下,是的,"她答道。

王子觉得说话就得算数,于是继续说道:"那伸出你的手。"让在场人吃惊的是,从又黑又脏的驴皮下面伸出了一只纤细而白净的手!戒指非常轻松地戴进了那根手指。那驴皮顿时滑落在地,一位天仙般的姑娘站在众人眼前。王子不顾虚弱之躯,跪在她面前,国王和王后也为二人送上祝福。面对如此热烈的欢迎和费解的拥抱,公主反倒无以言对。就在这时,大厅天花板豁然敞开,乘着丁香花车的仙女教母降临。她三言两语道明了公主的身世及其到此的由来。这场婚礼的盛大活动随即展开。

各国君主都在受邀之列,自然包括公主的养父(他这时已娶了位寡妇),人人都欣然前往。

这次盛会真稀奇!国王们都以自觉最显赫的方式出行:乘滑竿者有之,坐千奇百怪的马车者有之,骑大象、老虎,甚至老鹰者有之。这是一场前所未有的婚礼。婚礼一结束,国王便宣布加冕仪式,说他和王后已经疲于王位,新婚夫妇将接任其位。

喜庆活动持续了整整三个月,新任国王和王后继而管理国家。他俩深得臣民拥戴,在其仙逝100年后,还被人们当作父母祭拜。

14. 仙子惹的祸

从前,有位仙子名叫丁德内特,世间心肠最好者非她莫属,可就缺些见识,总在做善事,却总给人带来伤害。体会最深的莫过于某地远处某海中央的岛民。仙界法律赋予她特别保护这世间最漂亮的岛屿,她也为使该岛成为最宜居之地而昼思夜想过。

事情的经过是这样的:仙子隐身光临各家各户,结果听到各地孩子都渴望"长大",去做自己想做的事,还听到老人追忆往事,希望再年轻一次。

"难道无法让这些可怜的人们心想事成吗?"她想。某晚,她灵感忽现:"哦,有了。有人试过。他们借古老的'青春泉'让人重返年轻,我打算做得更好些。我要给果园里那眼冒泡的泉水施法,孩子一喝就长大成人,老人一喝回到童年。"

丁德内特没征求过本可以给他建议的其他仙子的意见,就匆匆前往泉边施法。

试想想,岛上淡水泉仅此一处,每天清晨男女老少来此地喝水。想到这让岛民快乐的计划,兴奋的仙子藏在玫瑰丛中,每当脚步声传来,她都探头一望。她很快得到了施法成功的足够证据。差不多就在她眼前,孩子拥有了成人的个头和力量,而老头、老太变成了无助的婴儿。事实上,她对自己工作成效非常满意,竟走出隐藏之地,逢人便讲其所作所为,领受人们的不尽感激。

然而,得愿的喜悦一过,神水之奇效不禁让人不寒而栗。身处力量和美貌顶峰倒是件美事,但人人都想永远如此!这正是仙子一直急于安排的。老人刚成人即变成婴儿,孩子一成年就以惊人的速度走向衰老!仙子意识到了出错,想纠正却为时已晚。

这事一发生,岛民们绝望之极,竭力想摆脱这可怕的命运。他们就地打井,不取神水,可砂土中没水,雨季也早已过去。他们把露水、果汁、植物液储存起来,但这不过杯水车薪而已。一些人跳入大海,希望海流——他们无船可乘——能将其带往别的海滩,少数等不及的人当场自杀。其他人则盲目地听天由命。

施法最糟糕的地方也许是,年龄段的跨越太快,让人猝不及防。国民议会上就和平或战争发表建议的人,只要能谈出成人的真知灼见,就算貌似婴儿也不要紧。唉!貌似婴儿之人,又带着婴儿的无助和愚蠢,而却能教他改变一切。结果不出一月,人口逐渐消亡,丁德内特仙子为此蠢行深感羞愧和悲伤,离岛而去。

许多世纪后,身体欠佳的瑟尔诺左拉仙子,遵医嘱每星期周游世界两次,旨在呼吸到空气。其中一次旅行中,她发现自己来到泉岛。瑟尔诺左拉从不只身出行,逢游必带那对可爱的儿女:十四岁的科尼雄和小几个月的突佩特。儿子是幼年时从贩奴市场买回的,女儿则由监护人科里思托波托守护神委托代管。瑟尔诺左拉有心让科尼雄和突佩特在成年后结为夫妇。与此同时,孩子俩随母亲乘小飞船旅行,其空中穿行速度相当于当今最快船只的 1950 倍。

深受岛屿美景的吸引,瑟尔诺左拉让飞船着陆,由留守此地的龙看管,自己则随儿女一起上岸。仙子吃惊地发现,偌大个城镇的各条大街和房屋荒无一人,决定施法术一探究竟。她正忙于此事时,科尼雄和突佩特溜达开了,慢慢来到泉边,炎热天,那咕嘟直冒的泉水十分诱人。他俩刚猛喝一口,刚查明原因的仙子赶了过来。

见此,她高喊道:"噢,小心!小心!别喝那致命的毒水,否则一生就毁了!"

突佩特问道:"毒水?我喝过的水就数这最提神,科尼雄也是这样认为的。"。

"我来晚了,不幸的孩子!你们干吗离开我呀?听着,听我说,发生在可怜的岛民身上的事,也会发生在你俩身上。众仙之力盖莫大焉。"说完,她补充道,"不过,他们无法毁掉其他神仙的工作。你俩很快会进入年迈者的虚弱、痴呆状态,我能做的,不过是尽力让你俩容易承受一点儿,不像他们那样死时身边无人。"

法力开始显现!科尼雄比一小时前更高大、成熟,突佩特也不像个小姑娘。

两位年轻人果然像瑟尔诺左拉说的并不难受。

"别可怜我俩,"科尼雄劝道,"若注定很快变老,那我俩就别再推迟婚礼。我俩在期待死亡时也期待幸福,那有啥关系呢?"

仙子也觉得科尼雄说得有道理,见突佩特脸上亦无惧色,于是说道:"就这样,但不是在这可怕的地方。我们立刻回到巴格塔,搞一场空前的庆祝活动。"

他们回到飞船,几小时就从岛屿回到4500英里外的巴格塔。见这对年轻人短时间的变化如此之大,人人惊讶不已。由于仙子承诺只字不提这次历险,别人也不知原委,只是忙着为新人赶制次日婚礼用的服饰。

次日清晨,守护神科里思托波来到宫廷,他每次来访,都习惯探视被监护人。一见孩子突然长大,他也大为震惊。他一直喜欢她,这下便狂热地爱上了她。他心急火燎地求见仙子后,提出了求婚,丝毫不怀疑对方会不成人之美。可瑟尔诺左拉根本听不进去,甚至暗示他最好做别的打算。守护神表面答应,结果直奔突佩特的闺房而去,竟在楼下新郎等待时带她破窗而去。

获知此事,仙子气愤万分,接二连三派使节前往守护神位于拉提布夫的宫殿,命其立刻送回突佩特,否则向他开战。

对仙子的使节,科里思托波不予明确答复,而是把突佩特关进守卫严密的塔里。在那儿可怜的姑娘尽其口舌之能极力延迟婚礼。然而,若不是悲痛及神水的魔力在几天之内完全改变了她的容貌,连科里思托波对此也大为惊讶,加上她要求得到娱乐、新鲜空气、独处,因为他的出现让她烦心,那她的所有努力都是白搭。但有一事他拒不执行,就是把她送回巴格塔。

与此同时,双方都忙于召集军队,科里思托波把指挥权交给了一位名将,而瑟尔诺左拉让科尼雄统帅全军。正式宣战前,突佩特的父母被守护神召至拉提布夫。自婴儿起,父母就未曾见过她,倒是来往于巴格塔的旅行者不时跟他俩提起过女儿的美貌。因此,让父母吃惊的是,眼前的女儿不是个可爱的小姑娘,而是个中年妇女,虽然模样不错,但容颜不再,比自己还年迈。这突然的巨变让科里思托波一样吃惊,认为是某个臣子开玩笑,故意把突佩特藏起来,拿个老年妇人顶替。气急败坏的他立刻叫来城中所有仆人和卫兵,盘问谁如此放肆地作弄他,抓来的姑娘到底怎么啦。众人都说,从突佩特交由他们负责,从未见她蒙面离开屋子半步,还说,她的饭菜是她在花园散步期间送上桌的,因为她喜欢单独吃饭,没人见过她的脸,或者长什么样。

仆人显然没说假话,科里思托波也只得相信。"不过,"他想,"如果他们没插手此事,那准是仙子干的。"一气之下,他下令军队出征。

瑟尔诺左拉自然明白守护神会怎么想,一听说是她想出的卑鄙诡计,气不打一处来。她起初真想立刻向科里思托波开战,好在大臣们费尽九牛二虎之力才拦住了她。她派出大使去科里思托波处,力求妥善管理各项事宜。

泽普拉蒂王子受命前去拉提布夫宫,途中会晤了屯兵巴格塔大门外的科尼雄。王子向他出示了暂时保持和平的手谕。科尼雄渴望再次见到突佩特,请求陪同泽普拉蒂王子一起去拉

143

提布夫执行这一使命。

守护神此时见自己惹出乱子,对突佩特的激情已完全消失,尽管他告诉王子自己仍旧认为是仙子让这姑娘发生可怕的变化,但还是乐于接受泽普拉蒂提出的和平条件。王子当即答道,那姑娘就是突佩特,有人足以证明这一点,遂授意把科尼雄叫到现场。

得知就要见到昔日恋人,突佩特满心喜悦,她很快回想起了所发生的一切,她记得的科尼雄也会一样变化。情人的见面时刻并不全是幸福,尤其是无法忘怀容貌自己消逝的突佩特,还有在场的守护神,他这下终于相信没人骗自己,于是在侍从的陪同下出来签署了和平条约。

就剩下情人俩时,科尼雄叫道:"啊,突佩特,亲爱的突佩特!咱俩又重逢了,忘掉往日的痛苦吧。"

"往日的痛苦,"她接过话来,"那咱俩失去的容颜和可怕的未来呢?你像比我上次见到时老了50岁,我知道命运对我也好不了哪儿去!"

"噢,别那么说,"科尼雄拉着她的手答道,"你真的不同,各年龄段自有其风韵,60岁的女人肯定没一个比你漂亮!你若双眼依旧明亮,跟衰老的皮肤也不配呀!我看你布满皱纹的额头,就知道你的双颊曾经饱满过,你那枯萎的喉咙透出衰变的雅致。你老化的五官同样和谐,这正是昔日风采的最好证明。"

"噢,鬼老头,"突佩特大哭起来,"你就只能给我那点安慰吗?"

"突佩特,"科尼雄答道,"可你曾说过,只要能得到我的心,你是不在乎自己容貌的。"

"没错,"她承认道,"可是你还依然在乎跟我一样衰老、不中看的人吗?"

"突佩特呀,突佩特,"科尼雄答道,"你尽在胡说,我心依旧,世上万物都无法改变它。"

谈话间,泽普拉蒂王子走进屋里,带来守护神的无尽歉意,说他完全同意科尼雄带着突佩特随时回到巴格塔,还说请原谅没能替他俩送行,希望不久后会去巴格塔看望他俩。

恋人俩当晚无法入睡——科尼雄因要回家而高兴,突佩特则惧怕其虚荣在巴格塔让受到打击。旅途中,科尼雄试图用头一天的理由安慰她,但不见效,反倒使她心情越来越糟。一回到宫里,她直奔原来的住所,恳请仙子让她和科尼雄躲起来,谁也不见。

在他俩返回后的那段日子里,仙子一直忙于庆祝和平及接待希望重修旧好的守护神等活动,科尼雄和突佩特被完全晾在一边。他俩虽希望如此,但仍有被忽略的感觉。

一天上午,他俩终于透过窗户见到臣子簇拥的仙子和守护神,气派十足地朝着他们走来。突佩特立刻藏到屋子最黑暗的角落,科尼雄却忘了自己不再是14岁的少年,跑过去迎候,却给绊倒在地,还重重地伤着一只眼睛。见恋人无助地躺在地上,突佩特急忙赶过去,可她那虚弱的双腿不争气,差一点倒在对方身上,结果在他额头上磕掉了三颗松动的牙齿。刚好进门的仙子哭着聆听守护神的讲话,他暗示这一切可望逐步得到纠正。

"上次的神仙大会,"他说,"对各路神仙的行为都予以了审查、讨论,还给出了建议,尽力减少丁德内特施法于泉水带来的危害。鉴于她并无恶意,大会认为她应该有能力解除一半的魔法。当然,她本该把那口致命的泉毁掉才是上策,可却没有想到这一点。即便如此,她的心依然是善良的,我相信,一旦她得知需要她的帮忙,她会赶来的。在此之前,得先恢复其中一位的力量和美貌,这交由夫人您来决定。"

听完这话,仙子心凉了。对她来说,科尼雄和突佩特一样亲,自己怎能厚此薄彼呢?就臣子来说,没人明白她会在选择突佩特上犹豫不决,但女性都赞同选择科尼雄。

仙子虽难以抉择,可科尼雄和突佩特却想得不一样。

"哦,我的宝贝,"科尼雄叹道,"我看中你的心灵胜过外表,这下终于有了可向你表白忠诚的最佳证明！尽管宫里最美的女子会醉心于我的年轻和力量，但我只想怎样才能让她们拜倒在你的脚下，向你的年迈和皱纹表示衷心的敬意。"

"别急，"突佩特打断他，"我不明白你咋啥都占全，让我独自承担屈辱？不过我相信仙子是公平的，她绝不会那样待我。"说罢，她回屋去了，拒不出来，哪怕科尼雄不停的祈求给她解释。

丁德内特来前的几天里，宫中没人谈论别的事。人人期待她一来就能拨乱反正。可是，唉！她也不知咋办才是上策，总是谁建议啥她就采信啥。最后，她想到了一个主意，似乎是满足双方意愿的唯一办法。她让仙子召集所有臣子、臣民听取她的想法。

"补救恶行者是快乐的，"她开始讲道，"不曾作恶者更快乐。"

见无人反驳此言，她继续讲道："我对造成的危害，只能消除一半。"她对科尼雄说，"我能恢复你的力量，"又转向突佩特，"或者你的美貌。我要么都做，要么都不做。"

人群中发出奇怪的低语，科尼雄和突佩特惊讶得颤抖不已。

"不行，"丁德内特继续说，"我可不忍心你俩一个衰弱下去，而另一个尽享荣耀。由于我无法同时让你俩恢复原样，你俩各自一半的身体可恢复年轻，另一半却要继续萎缩。我让你俩选择各自的那一半——比如我会在腰部或身体正中间画一条线。"

她傲视四周，期待自己的妙计得到鼓掌。失望的科尼雄和突佩特气得直发抖，其他人发出阵阵大笑。出于对不幸情侣的同情，瑟尔诺左拉走上前来。

"除了那建议，"她说，"你不觉得让他俩轮流享受一段昔日的青春和容貌更好吗？"

"这主意甚妙！"丁德内特叫道，"哦，那当然最好！你俩我先触碰谁？"

"她，"总是迁就突佩特的科尼雄答道，"我熟悉她，因此经得住任何突变。"

这位仙子弯着腰，用魔环碰了碰突佩特，老妇人立刻变成小姑娘。见此，整个宫廷喜极而泣。突佩特朝科尼雄奔去，对方惊奇得跌倒在地。她承诺会常去看他，并告诉他自己所参加过的舞会和水上宴会。

两位仙子尽其口舌之能各回住所，守护神也跟上她俩道别。

"哦，天啦，"丁德内特失口叫道，打断守护神的告别演说，"我差点忘了为科尼雄确定变年轻的时间。我真蠢！我恐怕这下晚了，我本该在用魔环触碰突佩特时就宣布的。哦，天啦，干吗没人提醒我呀？"

"你太匆忙了，"瑟尔诺左拉答道，她其实早察觉丁德内特又在捣鬼，"我们这下只好等到科尼雄衰弱到极点时再说，他到时还会喝水，再变成婴儿，突佩特就只好一生当保姆、妻子和看护人啰。"

长期饱受身心焦虑、虚弱之苦，突佩特似乎觉得怎么娱乐也不够，尽管她依旧喜欢可怜的科尼雄，但的确很少抽出时间看他，或对他温情一些。虽然没跟他在一起，她依然相当快活，尽管那可怜人儿因年老而几乎耳聋、眼花，但并非啥都看不见。

处理丁德内特的未尽事宜、让科尼雄重获青春等，最终落到了科里思托波的身上。当守护神偶然发现科尼雄其实是他的儿子，因此非常乐意去做这件事。他正是因这一请求才参加了一年一度的仙人盛会，鉴于他曾经帮过许多会员，他这一祈求才得以批准。类似的请求在仙界前所未闻，还招来不少老资格仙人的反对。不过，因科里思托波和瑟尔诺左拉的威望极高，反对的声音被搁置一边。最近那位喝过着魔的泉水者据说已被解除了魔咒。作为回报，守护神要求能陪着仙子回到巴格塔，目睹儿子重现原身。

他们决定只告诉突佩特，说给她找了个丈夫，在于次日婚礼上给她惊喜。她听到这消息大为吃惊,一想到科尼雄将让位于人的伤心样儿,更是自责不已,但她绝不能违抗仙子的意愿,整天琢磨这新郎会是谁。

时辰一到,一大群人聚集在仙子的宫中,里面装饰着唯仙境才有的芳香花卉。突佩特就位,可新郎在哪儿?

"有请科尼雄!"仙子吩咐管家。

突佩特插话道:"哦,夫人,饶了他吧,求您啦,别让他露面,让他独享自己那份安宁吧。"

"他一定得到场,"仙子答道,"保准他不后悔。"

她正说着,科尼雄被领了进来,面对欢快的人群露出垂老者的憨笑。

"领他到这儿,"仙子边命令,边朝吃惊、退缩的突佩特挥手。

瑟尔诺左拉随后握住那可怜老人的手,守护神走上前来,用自己的戒指触碰了他三下,科尼雄马上变成了英俊小伙。

守护神说:"愿你长寿、夫妻幸福、热爱父亲。"

仙子丁德内特惹的祸就此终结!

15. 摘花奇遇记

从前有位妇人，家有三个宝贝女儿。一天，大女儿在河边草地走动，忽见溪流中开着一朵石竹花。她弯腰去摘，刚碰到花就不见了人影。第二天早上，二女儿去那片草地，看能否找到失踪姐姐的线索。见一枝漂亮的玫瑰横在小道上，她弯腰想把它移开，同时禁不住摘了一朵，结果也突然消失了。幺女不知姐姐俩发生啥事，于是寻其足迹而去，结果成了一枝芳香的白色茉莉花的牺牲品。老妇人的几个女儿这下全没了。

她没日没夜地哭，哭到姐仨失踪时的小儿长成一位高大的小伙。一天夜里，儿子问母亲怎么回事。

儿子听完后便说："祝福我吧，母亲。我寻遍各地也要找到她们。"

他出发了，平淡无奇地走了几英里后，遇仨大男孩在打架，便止步问其缘由。一个说："先生，家父去世前留给我们兄弟仨一双靴子、一把钥匙和一顶帽子。谁穿上靴子，想去哪儿去哪儿，谁拥有钥匙，世上大门任他开，谁戴上帽子，没人能看见他。大哥想独吞这三件宝贝，我俩希望靠抓阄来定。"

"噢，那好办！"小伙说道，"我把这石头尽力扔远些，谁先捡到，三件宝贝就归谁。"说完，他捡起石头扔出去。哥几个朝石头落地处飞奔而去。小伙赶紧穿上靴子，说道："靴子，快带我去大姐那儿。"

转眼间，小伙来到陡峭山上一座坚固的城堡门前，上面由门闩、铁链把着。他掏出钥匙打开一道道门，穿过无数大厅和走廊，最后见到一位衣着华丽的美女。一见他，对方吃惊地问道："噢！先生，你咋来此地的？"小伙说是她的弟弟，还说是如何打开那些门才到的。她也跟小伙说她很幸福，只是丈夫受控于咒语，要处死不死之人方可解脱。

姐弟俩攀谈了很久，之后女子劝弟弟离开，因为她猜丈夫随时可能返回，未必愿意见到他。但小伙请她放心，说他有顶隐身帽。姐弟俩谈得兴致正浓，门突然开了，飞进来一只鸟儿，好在没发现什么异常，因为小伙一听声响就戴上了帽子。女子赶紧起身，端来一个巨大的金盆，鸟儿飞了进去，紧接着走出一位俊男。他转向妻子大叫道："我确信屋里有人！"女子吓着了，声称就她本人。丈夫一再坚持，女子最终实话相告。

"果真是你的弟弟，藏他干吗？"丈夫追问，"我看你在撒谎。他若再来，我非杀他不可。"

听此，小伙摘下帽子，走上前来。丈夫见他酷似妻子，立刻信了，还高兴地拥抱内弟。他从身上拔下一根鸟毛，说道："如遇危险，叫声'快来帮我，鸟王'，包你万事大吉。"

小伙谢过姐夫后离去。一出城堡，他命令靴子带他去二姐的住处。

小伙照旧来到大城堡门前。里面的二姐跟姐夫过着恩爱的生活，却渴望见到他能摆脱半人半鱼魔咒的那一刻。妻子介绍内弟后，归来的丈夫热情相迎，还送给他一片鱼鳞，说："如遇危险，叫声'快来帮我，鱼王'，包你万事大吉"。

小伙谢过二姐夫离去。一出大门，他让靴子带他去幺姐的住处。靴子把他带到铁梯通达的一个黑洞。

瘦得不成样儿的幺姐坐在里面，一个劲儿地抽泣。见有人站在面前，她立刻起身，高喊道："无论你是谁，请救我离开这可怕的地方！"小伙随即表明身份，还跟她讲到两位姐姐和姐夫受困咒语等不幸。她也讲了自己的经历：一怪物从河边草地带走她、逼她成婚、她因不从而被多

147

年囚禁于此。

妖怪每天来央求她,还告诫她绝无获释的希望,因为他的忠贞举世无比,还是永生之人。听罢,小伙想起了受困魔咒的姐夫俩,便建议幺姐要对方拿永生之谜作为交换条件。这时,四周突然摇晃,好似遇上旋风一般,那老头随即进来、跪在姑娘面前,问道:"你还是执意不嫁给我吗?那你只好坐着哭到世界末日,我非你不娶,永不改口。"

"那我答应你,"姑娘说道,"但你得说出你的永生之谜。"

老头发出一阵狂笑:"哈!哈!哈!你在想怎么杀掉我?那你先得找到藏在海底的某个铁匣子,里面有只白鸽,你还得找到白鸽下的蛋,拿到这儿砸我的脑袋。"说完,他又是一阵大笑,自信没人去过海底,即使去过也找不到那铁匣子,或将其打开。他然后还对她说:"你既然知道了我的秘密,那就非得嫁给我不可。"

姑娘苦苦哀求将婚礼推迟到三天之后,他同意了,然后得意地离去。怪物消失后,姑娘的弟弟摘下那顶隐身帽,叫她别灰心,三天后定能获得自由。小伙随后穿上靴子,意念着自己在海边,即刻就出现在那儿。

他掏出鱼鳞,高喊道:"快来帮我吧,鱼王!"二姐夫游过来,问要帮什么忙。小伙讲了幺姐的经历。听完,姐夫当即招来所有的鱼儿。

最后来到的是一条小沙丁鱼,道歉说头被海底里的一只铁匣子撞伤。鱼王令几条最强悍的大鱼随沙丁鱼去弄回铁匣子。它们很快将其驮了回来。小伙随即掏出钥匙,说道:"钥匙,打开铁匣子。"尽管大伙围着抓白鸽,可还是让它飞走了。

小伙明知追不上,心都凉了半截,忽想起身上有根鸟毛。他掏出鸟毛,高喊道:"快来帮我吧,鸟王!"鸟王'嗖'的一声落到他的肩上,问他要帮什么忙。内弟讲了经过。听完,鸟王让其所有臣民即来听令。顷刻间,各种鸟儿顿时让整个天空黯淡了下来。最后到来的是一只小白鸽,道歉说在巢中接待一位老朋友。

鸟王令一些鸟儿把小伙带往白鸽巢穴。一到那儿,那只破除魔咒、让人恢复正身的蛋就在里面。小伙揣好蛋,叫靴子径直带他去幺姐正等着他的洞穴。

老头把婚礼定在三天后,那一天已过了不少时辰。戴着隐形帽的小伙一进洞,发现妖怪在场,正催促幺姐兑现立刻完婚的承诺。一见弟弟打手势,幺姐坐下,让老妖把脑袋枕在她的怀里。老头欣然依从,站在身后的弟弟悄然递过蛋。她接过来就砸向那恶心的脑袋。妖怪惊起,随着一声地震般的呻吟,翻身毙命。

随着那口气离开老头身躯,两位姐夫恢复了正身,继而让人接来转悲为喜的岳母。一家人欢聚一堂。幺女找到了老妖藏在洞穴的宝藏,富足一生。

16. 哈里三子的故事

小宁吉尔在乡下一直快乐地生活到18岁。村庄离康斯坦丁堡约40英里。穆罕默德和兹内比夫妇养大了他,他自然认为他们就是自己的亲生父母。

宁吉尔虽不富贵,但还算满足自己的命运,不像同龄人那样想出门。一天,穆罕默德哀叹着说他该去康斯坦丁堡谋生,难怪他大吃一惊。从军、当法学博士、给人讲解《可兰经》等职业由他选择。"那本圣经你几乎熟记于心,很快就能教人。要写信啊,告诉我们你的近况,我们忘不了你。"说完,老人给他4块皮阿斯特,算是去大城市的零花钱,还求人让他搭乘即赴康斯坦丁堡的大篷车。

大篷车一般走得慢,经过几天旅行,首都的城墙和塔楼终于依稀可见。车一停,乘客就各奔西东,让宁吉尔举目无亲、孤独不堪。他胆量过人、容易结交。可他毕竟是第一次离开村庄,没人给他提起过康斯坦丁堡,因此连一条街或一个人的名字都不知道。

宁吉尔站了一会,边东张西望,边想接下来该怎么办。突然,一位热心人走过来,边鞠躬边问愿否先赏光住他家,再作打算。见别无他法,宁吉尔接受了建议且随他而去。

他俩走进宽敞的房间,一位约十二岁的姑娘正摆放供三人用餐的碗筷。

"泽丽达,"主人说道,"我告诉你要带朋友回来吃晚饭,没说错吧!"

"好爸爸,"姑娘答道,"您每次都说得准,也从不蒙人。"她正说着,一位老仆人往桌上搁上一盘东方人特爱吃的肉饭。给每人摆上一只啤酒杯后,老仆人悄声离去。

吃饭间,主人瞎侃一通,可宁吉尔只是望着泽丽达,尽量不显得过分放肆。

姑娘脸红了,不自在起来,最后面朝父亲。"这位客人老看着我,"她犹豫地低声说道,"哈森要知道,会醋意大发的。"

"不会的,"父亲答道,"不是让你跟这小伙好。我没说过让他跟你姐姐阿静蒂娜好吗?我这就设法让他爱上她。"他起身打开橱柜,取出一些水果和一罐酒,连同一只不大的珍珠母银匣子,放在桌上。

"尝尝这酒,"他边跟小伙说话,边往杯里倒酒。

"也给我来点,"泽丽达喊道。

"不行,"父亲答道,"前几天你和哈森就喝到点了。"

"那您自己喝吧,"姑娘说道,"要不他以为我们会毒害他。"

"既如此,我就喝点,"父亲说道,"这长生药对我这年龄没啥危害,你却不然。"

宁吉尔喝干后,主人打开珍珠母匣子让他看,里面那美若天仙的少女肖像让他欣喜若狂。他目瞪口呆地望着,一种从未有过的感觉在心中翻腾。

父女俩逗趣地望着宁吉尔,他醒悟过来后说道:"我有几点不明,烦请指教:为何请我来?为何让我喝这让人热血翻涌的危险液体?为何让我看这让人几近失去理智的肖像?"

"我能解答一部分,"主人答道,"而非全部。你手上拿着的是泽丽达姐姐的肖像。它让你完全爱上了她。去找她吧。你找到她,就等于找到你自己。"

"我去哪儿找她呢?"宁吉尔边问边吻那张让他目不转睛的小肖像。

"我只能点到为止,"主人戒备地答道。

"我知道,"泽丽达急迫着插话。"明天,你得去犹太集市,从右手边第二家商店买一块表。

半夜……"

半夜会发生什么,宁吉尔没听到,因为泽丽达的父亲赶忙捂住她的嘴,喊道:"哦,孩子,住嘴!你不想因不慎而引来姐姐们的霉运吧?"老人刚说完,周围腾起一股浓雾,原来他情急之下弄翻了那宝瓶。老仆人惊叫着跑进来。宁吉尔让这场奇遇弄得很烦心,于是离开了。

那一夜他在清真寺外的台阶上度过。天刚亮,他从头巾折缝取出肖像。一想起泽丽达说过的话,他打听到了去集市的路,直奔她说的那家商店而去。

听宁吉尔说想看表,商人出示了几块,还指了指他认为最好的那一块,价值为3个金币,宁吉尔欣然照付,可商人故意刁难,说除非知道他的住处,否则不给。

"这我也不知道,"宁吉尔答道,"我昨天才来,找不着去先前住过的那家。"

"好吧,"商人说,"那跟我来,我给你找家不错的穆斯林旅馆,一应俱全且便宜。"

宁吉尔同意了。两人穿过几条街,最后来到了犹太商人推荐的旅馆。依他的建议,年轻人把仅有的一块金币预支为食宿费用。

宁吉尔吃过饭,关上房门,伸手进头巾折缝,欲取钟爱的肖像,结果还触碰到一封密封好的信,显然是在他不知情下放进去的。见是养母兹内比自己的笔迹,他匆匆拆开。试想他读到如下文字时会是怎样惊奇:

"我最亲爱的孩子,这封你迟早会在头巾里发现的信,旨在告诉你并非我们亲生。我们相信你父亲曾是某远方的大老爷,这信瓢里有他的来信,我们如不将你归还于他,他扬言要报复我们。我们永远爱你,但别再找我们,也别写信,因为这都没用。"

同一信封里还有一张纸,宁吉尔并不熟悉笔迹的几句话如下:

"骗子,你们肯定和那些术士串通一气,拐走不幸的希罗科家俩女儿,夺走其父赠与她们行的护身符。你们让我父子分离,可我获悉了你们的躲藏地,我向圣祖起誓要惩罚你们的罪行。我的弯刀快如闪电。"

读完这两封莫名其妙的信,可怜的宁吉尔感到越发伤心孤独,也很快意识到,自己准是致信穆罕默德夫妇那人的儿子,却不知去哪儿找他,当然也更思念收养自己却不能再见的恩人。

为摆脱郁闷心情,以便从长计议,宁吉尔走出旅馆,在市里轻快地转悠到夜幕降临。他原路返回,正跨过门槛,忽见月光下有东西闪烁。他捡起来,发现是块金表,宝石光芒四射。他朝大街两头张望,看能否见到失主,但却不见人影,便将其裹进腰带,与当天早上从里面的犹太人那里买来的银表并排放着。

捡来的好运让宁吉尔心情舒畅了些,"因为,"他想,"这对宝贝至少可卖1000金币,能维持到找着父亲之时。"受此安慰,他把两块表放在旁边,准备睡觉。夜间,他突然醒来,听到一块表好似在耳语什么。

"奥萝拉,好姐姐,"那表悄声说道,"他们记住半夜给你上发条了吗?"

"没呢,亲爱的阿静蒂娜,"对方答道,"你呢?"

"也把我忘了,"第一个声音答道,"现在一点钟,我们得等到明天才能摆脱囚禁,如果那时不被人忘掉的话。"

"咱俩这下没事可干,"奥萝拉说道,"我们只得认命咱走吧。"

宁吉尔惊呆了,忽地坐了起来,借着月光看到两块表滑到地上,然后从猫窝滚出了房间。他追到门口,又跑到楼梯边,不等他看见,两块表已经溜到楼下,然后上街。他想开门去追,可钥匙拧不动,只好放弃,回到床上。

第二天,所有痛苦加倍袭上心头,觉得比以前更孤独、更可怜。在一阵绝望中,他匆匆把头巾往脑袋上一按,别上宝剑,离开旅馆,决定去找卖银表的商人讨个说法。宁吉尔赶到集市,发现要找的那人不在店里,顶班的是另一个犹太人。

"你找的是我哥,自己的哥"对方说道,"我俩轮流守店、进城办事。"

"啊,办什么?"宁吉尔气冲冲地说道,"你那混蛋兄弟卖给我的表昨夜跑了。我会想法找回来,否则你这当弟弟的就得赔偿!"

"你说啥呀?"犹太人说道,一群人围上来,"表跑了。如果你说的是一桶酒,编得倒还像。可是表不可能!"

"可能不可能,法官说了算,"宁吉尔答道,忽见要找的人走进集市。他一个箭步上去,抓住那人手臂,要拽他去见法官,但守店的家伙瞅准机会跟兄弟耳语了句:"啥都别招,不然我俩就完了"。那声音大得足让宁吉尔听得清楚。

法官得知此事,按土耳其方式鸣哨几声让人群离开,之后让宁吉尔讲述事情原委。听完他的陈述,法官觉得这事非同寻常,转身询问犹太商人,对方不仅没回答,反而抬眼望天,随即晕倒在地。

法官没理会晕倒者,他告诉宁吉尔,说他的陈述离奇得令人难以置信,还说他得找人把商人抬回去。宁吉尔一听气坏了,忘了对法官应有的尊重,扯起嗓门吼道:"把这家伙弄醒,让他从实招来。"他边说边朝犹太人一剑刺去,痛得那家伙发出一声刺耳的惊叫。

"您看见了,"犹太人对法官说道,"这家伙疯了。我原谅他那一剑,但别把我交由他处置。"

这时,巴萨老爷碰巧经过法院,听到一阵嘈杂声,于是进来看个究竟。听过解释,他仔细打量了一番宁吉尔,还温和地问他咋会发生这种奇事。

"老爷,"宁吉尔答道,"我发誓说的是实话。等我讲完,您也许就会相信,我就是他们符咒的受害者,这群本该清除出地球的人渣。我被变成一只三足罐长达三年,直到我被盖上头巾那天才才得以恢复真身。"

听完这话,巴萨高兴得撩开袍子,边拥抱宁吉尔边叫喊:"哦,我儿,我儿,我这不是找着你吗?你是不是从穆罕默德和兹内比家来的?"

"是的,老爷,"宁吉尔答道,"我倒霉时全靠他俩照顾、言传身教,让我不配做您儿子。"

"感谢始祖,"巴萨叹道,"在我最没想到时,你们知道,是始祖给我送回其中一子。"接着,他继续对法官说道:"我婚后前几年,我和美丽的赞芭卡生了仨儿子。他三岁那年,一位圣洁的苦行僧给我家老大一串上等珊瑚珠,还嘱咐道:'看好这宝贝,笃信始祖,你就会快乐,'又给站在您面前的老二一只铜盘,上面用七种文字刻着穆罕默德的名字,告诉他真正的信徒绝不能摘下头巾,说他会体验到最大的快乐,还给老幺的右臂戴上手镯,祈祷孩子的右手纯洁,左手无瑕,从而永不遭受磨难"。

"老大忘了苦行僧的教诲,可怕的灾难降临到他和老幺的头上。为免老二招致类似厄运,我在对敌作战时,把他交由忠实老仆人古娄库看管,带到一个偏僻之地养大。从连连的战事中返回后,我赶过去想拥抱儿子,却不见他俩的踪影。数月前,我打听到孩子住在一个叫穆罕默德的家里,便怀疑他偷走了我的儿子。孩子,快告诉爸爸是咋落入他手中的。"

"老爷,"宁吉尔答道,"除跟老仆人住在某海滨城堡外,我对少年期间没啥记忆。准是在我约十二岁的某天,我们出门散步,碰上一个跟这犹太人很相像的人,他蹦跳着走近我们。我突然发晕,试图抬手碰头,可惜僵硬无比。一句话,我被变成一只铜罐,双臂变成了两个把子。我至今不知老仆人发生了什么。我当时觉得是被人扯上肩扛走的。

"几天后,我觉得被人搁到了一道浓密树篱边上。一听抓我的人在边上呼呼大睡,我决定逃走。我尽力穿过刺丛,坚持走了约一小时。

"您想不到,老爷,三条腿走路多别扭,尤其是膝盖僵硬无比的时候。我历尽艰辛,终于来到一块菜园,钻进白菜丛中,静静地过了一夜。

"第二天日出时,我发觉正有人弯腰审视我。不远处传来一名男子的声音:'干嘛待那儿不走呢,兹内比?'

"'世上最漂亮的罐子!'我旁边的妇女答道,'谁能想到在自家白菜丛中发现这个!'穆罕默德把我从地上抱起来,欣赏了一番。我太高兴了,谁都希望被人欣赏,罐子也一样!我被他俩带回家中,装上水,放在火上烧煮。

"我过了三年平静而有益的日子,每天被当时年轻漂亮的内兹比刷得亮铮铮的。

"有天早晨,兹内比把我放在火上,炖了一块上好的牛肉作午饭吃。由于担心炖汤蒸汽会穿过盖儿后走味,她四周找东西捂住盖子,可除丈夫的头巾外,没有发现啥顺手的物件。她把盖儿周围牢牢系住,随后出门了。三年来,我第一次觉得脚底发烫,于是挪开脚步——这比当时逃到穆罕默德家菜园轻松多了。我咋觉得自己在长高,事实上,几分钟又变成了人。

"三小时祷告之后,穆罕默德夫妇回来了,见厨房里的不是铜罐而是个小伙,那吃惊样儿可想而知。我讲了自己的经历,但他俩起初不相信,不过我最终说服了他们相信我说的是实话。我被他俩当作亲生儿子,继续生活了两年,直到他俩有天打发我来这城市自谋生路。现在,各位老爷,我这儿有两封信,是在头巾里找到的,这或许也能证明我的经历。"

宁吉尔正说话,犹太人伤口的血渐渐止住。就在这时,门口出现一位可爱的犹太姑娘,二十二岁上下,头发和衣服凌乱不堪,仿佛刚逃离巨大危险的样儿。她来时手里还拿着两根白木拐杖,后面跟着两名男子。宁吉尔认出第一个是受剑伤那人的兄弟,觉得第二个是在自己被变成罐子时一旁站着的那人。这俩人各自大腿上缠着一条宽大的亚麻布带,手里拿着大棒子。

犹太姑娘走到受伤男子的面前,在他旁边放下两根拐杖,然后望着他大哭起来。

"可怜的伊佐夫,"她呜呜道,"你干吗冒险自找麻烦呢?你瞧给自己和俩兄弟带来啥麻烦啦!"说完,她转向同来的两名男子——他俩这时已坐在犹太人脚边的垫子上。

巴萨老爷和在场的人都被这犹太姑娘的美貌和言语打动了,恳请她说出事情的原委。

"各位老爷,"她开口道,"我叫苏弥,是著名拉比莫瓦兹的女儿。我太爱伊扎夫了,"她边说边指着最后进来的那位,"尽管他忘恩负义,我还是忘不了他,我那冤家!"她转身面朝伊扎夫,继续说道:"你给各位绅士说说你和俩兄弟的经历,争取以忏悔获得谅解。"

"我们兄弟仨是三胞胎,"那名犹太人征得法官同意,且经苏弥要求讲开了,"是著名的纳善·本·萨迪家的孩子,分别叫伊兹夫、伊佐夫和伊扎夫。我们仨自幼学会了巫术秘诀。由于我们出生相同的星座,于是有福同享、有难同当。"

"我还没啥记忆,母亲就去世了。兄弟仨15岁时,父亲病重,念啥符咒都不见效,觉得自己来日不多,便把我们叫到病床前,给我们留下了下面这些话:

'孩子们,除那些巫术秘籍外,我没财富留给你们,这你们都知道。你们已经得到了些石头,上面刻有一些神秘的符号,我早就叫你们再多刻些。但你们现在还差几个最宝贵的护身符——希罗科家女儿的三枚戒指。要想法弄到手,不过见到姑娘仨要注意,谨防被其美貌所迷住。她们跟你们信仰不同,此外,她们是海滨巴萨老爷公子的未婚妻。千万别陷入情网,那只会让你们痛苦。如遇危险,我建议你们找莫瓦兹拉比的女儿,她暗恋伊扎夫,手头有她父亲写成的《符咒秘籍》,《塔木德经》用的就是那种墨水。'说完,父亲往软垫后一仰去了。这使我们哥仨迫切想得到希罗科家女儿的那三枚戒指。

"我们料理完丧事后,就着手打听三位姑娘的下落。一番周折后,我们得知其父亲希罗科身经百战,这名扬全国的仨美女分别叫奥萝拉、阿静蒂娜和泽丽达。"

第二个名字让巴萨父子不禁一惊,但却没吱声,伊扎夫继续往下讲。

"我们先化了装,携专门租来的一批上等宝石,扮成外国商人去接触这几位姑娘。唉,可惜纳善·本·萨迪警告过我们别为其美貌所倾倒!美丽绝伦的奥萝拉身着缀满闪光珠宝的金色外套;金发的阿静蒂娜身着银色连衣裙;最可爱的小泽丽达是一身波斯小姐打扮。

"我们随身携带的宝物还有一壶长生不老药,谁喝谁心中就会荡起爱情涟漪。这宝物是美丽的苏弥给我的。她曾试过,还让我也喝,好回报她的激情。因为我拒绝喝,她非常生气。我让仨姑娘看这种液体,可她们却忙于查验宝石、挑选自己最心仪的宝贝。我正把液体倒入水晶杯,泽丽达的目光便落到酒壶包装纸上的文字上:'注意:此水仅限跟未婚夫一起喝!''啊,骗子!'她嚷道,'你给我下什么套?'我朝她指的地方一看,认出了苏弥的字迹。

"这时,我那兄弟俩拿奥萝拉和阿静蒂娜俩渴求的东西,换走了她俩的戒指。两枚神奇的戒指一离手,俩姐妹立马不见踪影,原地留下的只有金表和银表。就在这时,被买通放我们进去的老仆人匆忙进来,说泽丽达的父亲回来了。我那兄弟俩吓得发抖,赶紧把两块表藏在头巾里。趁仆人照料晕倒在地的泽丽达,我们溜掉了。

我们害怕恼怒的希罗科会追来,没敢回到寄宿地,就躲进了苏弥家中。

"'可怜的家伙!'她叫道,'你们是这样听从父亲忠告的吗?今早,我查阅过一些巫术书籍,发现你们沉迷于迟早会毁掉你们的激情。不行,别以为我会乖乖地忍受这种侮辱!阻止泽丽达喝那药的人正是我!至于你,'她转身面朝我的兄弟俩继续说道,'你们还不知道会为那两只表会付出多大代价!不过,你这下明白了,了解真相会让你们的日子更悲惨。'

"她边说边拿出莫瓦兹写的圣书,指着下面文字念道:

'两块表若在半夜用金银钥匙拧上发条,当日前一小时会恢复正常状态。两块表永远由一位女士保管,无论表在哪儿,都会回到她那儿。表的指定保管者是莫瓦兹的女儿。'

"我那兄弟俩发现自己的企图遭到挫败,除气愤外别无办法。他们把两块表送到苏弥手中,然后继续赶路,我好奇地想知道会发生,于是留了下来。

"随着夜深,苏弥给两块表上了发条。半夜钟声敲响,奥萝拉和妹妹现身了。她俩对发生的事一无所知,以为刚从睡梦中醒来。苏弥的故事让她俩明白了自己可怕的命运,于是绝望地抽泣起来。好在苏弥答应决不抛弃她们,这才让她俩感到了些许安慰。一点的钟声刚敲响,姐妹俩又变成了手表。

"难言的恐惧整夜缠绕着我,觉得被某种隐形物推着走——说不清去哪儿。我清晨起床出门,在街上碰上同病相怜的伊兹夫。我俩认为康斯坦丁堡再也没法待了,于是让伊佐夫陪我俩离城而去,不久后决定分开走,以免被希罗科的探子认出来。

"几天后,我发现自己来到某海滨古城堡门口,见一高个仆人在门前来回踱步。送上一两块低廉的珠宝,他就开了口,说他受雇照看海滨巴萨老爷的儿子。巴萨当时在遥远的国家作战。仆人说,小伙跟希罗科的女儿订了娃娃亲,而兄弟俩则将娶她的两个姐妹,他还提到了被托管人身上的护身符。我当时心里只想着美丽的泽丽达,自以为把持住的激情却完全复苏了。

"为清除危险的情敌,我决定绑架他。为此我开始装疯,起劲地又唱又跳,还喊仆人把少爷带来看我耍把戏。他同意了,主仆二人被我那些滑稽的动作迷住了,笑得泪流满面,甚至还模仿起我来。我之后声称口渴,请仆人给取点水喝。仆人一离开,我劝说少爷摘下头巾,好让脑袋凉快些。他高兴地做了,眨眼间变成了一只罐子。仆人的喊叫惊醒我,要保命,就得跑。我抓起罐子,飞奔而去。

"各位老爷已获知了罐子的事儿。这下我只能说,我醒来时,罐子不见了。但一见俩哥哥还在附近睡得正香,才得到些许安慰。'你咋到这儿的?'我询问道,'自我们分手后你出啥事了?'

"'唉!'伊佐夫答道,'我们正经过一家路边旅馆,里面传来歌声和笑声。我们真傻,竟然就进去、坐了下来。切尔卡西亚美女正为几名男子跳舞助兴。他们客气地接待了我们,还让我们坐在最可爱的两位姑娘旁边。我们很快乐,不觉时间已逝。这时,一位姑娘倾身对姐姐说道:'他们的兄弟跳了,他们也得跳。'我不知道她说这话到底是啥意思,也许你能告诉我们?'"

"'我知道,'我答道。'她们在想我偷走巴萨儿子的那天,为少爷跳过舞。'

"'你兴许是对的,'伊佐夫答道,'因为那俩女士拉起我俩的手,跳到我们精疲力竭为止。最后我们又坐在桌边,喝多了点。我们晕头晕脑时,几个男子跳将起来扬言要杀我们,我们无力反抗,只得让他们抢个精光,包括希罗科女儿那两个稀有的护身符。'

"我们仨无计可施,于是回康斯坦丁堡请教苏弥,结果发现她从莫瓦兹的书中读到了我们的不幸之事。这位善良之人听过我们故事后痛哭流涕,因为贫穷的她对此爱莫能助。阿静蒂娜变成的那块银表,除非用银钥匙上过发条——这似乎不大可能——每晚都会回到苏弥那儿。我最后建议,每天上午就把它卖出去。苏弥同意了,唯一要求我们先弄明白表的去处才能卖,或许这样便于她把奥萝拉带走,让神秘时刻碰巧上过发条的阿静蒂娜不会孤独。几周来,我们一直靠这种方式过日子,希罗科的两个女儿每晚都回到苏弥那儿。伊佐夫昨天把这块银表卖给个这小伙,在他晚上走进旅社之前,又按照苏弥的吩咐,把那块金表放在台阶上,两块表今日清晨就从旅馆回来了。

"'要是早知道!'宁吉尔叫道,'要是再镇定些,我就见到了可爱的阿静蒂娜。她的肖像都那么漂亮,那真人肯定差不了!'

"'错不在你,'法官答道,'你不是术士,咋能猜到表必须在那时候上发条呢?不过,我会下令,让商人把表还给你,你今晚一定不会忘记上发条的。'"

"'你今天是得不到了,'伊佐夫说道,'因为表已卖出。'

"'既如此,'法官说道,'你得把这小伙掏的三块金币还给他。'

一见如此轻易走掉,犹太人高兴地伸手掏钱,宁吉尔却拦住了他。

"'别,别,'宁吉尔叫道,'我不要钱,我要可爱的阿静蒂娜。没有她,啥都没用。'

"'尊敬的法官,'巴萨说道,'他说得对。我儿子失去的是无价之宝。'

"'我的老爷,'法官说道,'您的智慧,我望尘莫及。此事烦请您定夺。'"

巴萨旨在让他们陪他回家,并命仆人看住这犹太仨兄弟。

一到家门,巴萨见旁边长凳上坐着两名捂得严实、着装漂亮的女子,宽松的裤子镶着银线,薄纱袍质地细腻无比。其中一位拎着一个绿带封口的粉色手袋,里面像有东西在动。

见巴萨走近,她俩起身相迎。拎袋人说道:"尊敬的老爷,请买下这袋子,别问里面装着什么。"

"你要多少钱?"巴萨问道。

"300金币,"对方答道。

听罢,巴萨轻蔑大笑,二话没说往前走。

"这交易不会让您后悔的,"女子继续说道,"咱们明天再来,您也许乐意掏400,后天就

500啦!"

"走吧,"同伴抓住她衣袖说道,"咱俩别逗留了。它可能会叫,那咱俩的秘密就泄露了。"说完,她俩离开了。

仆人看管着的仨犹太人留在前厅,宁吉尔和苏弥跟着巴萨老爷走进华丽的屋子。在明亮而宽敞的房间一角,一位约三十五岁的女士靠在沙发床上,美丽的面孔仍透出忧伤。

"美丽无比的赞芭卡,"巴萨边招呼边走向她,"快来谢我,因为我带回了失踪的儿子,你可没少为他流泪。"不等母亲拥抱他,宁吉尔跪倒在她的面前。

"让家人随我欢呼吧,"巴萨老爷继续说道,"快告诉义卜拉辛和哈森,让他俩来拥抱自己的兄弟吧。"

"唉!我的老爷,"赞芭卡说,"您忘了哈森和义卜拉辛这时在擦泪、捡珊瑚珠?"

"还是遵守原祖的旨意吧,"巴萨答道,"那咱就等到晚上吧。"

"请原谅,尊敬的老爷,"苏弥插话道,"这有啥神秘呀?借助《符咒秘籍》,我也许能帮点忙呢。"

"苏弥,"巴萨答道,"我一生的幸福多亏了你,请跟我来,我的难处,等你看过我那两个痛苦的儿子后,比我的任何解释都管用。"

宁吉尔和苏弥紧跟着巴萨从长沙发处站起。巴萨一把拉开隔着大厅的帘子。他们见到两位年轻人,分别在十七到十九岁之间。年幼那位坐在餐桌边,右手托着前额在流泪。父亲进去时,他抬头看了看。宁吉尔和苏弥都看到了那只乌黑的手。

另一位忙着捡拾满地散落的珊瑚珠,他捡起后放到兄弟坐着的那个餐桌上。他已拣回98颗,以为都全捡齐了。当珠子突然从桌上滚走,他又得重捡一遍。

"你知道,"巴萨悄声说道,"每日三小时,一个捡珠子,另一个为变黑的手伤心。我弄不明白这两起不幸是咋回事。"

"咱们别待这儿,"苏弥说道,"以免徒添他俩的悲伤。请允许我去取回《符咒秘籍》,我肯定它不仅能告诉我们疾病的起因,还能提供诊治的方法。"

巴萨欣然同意苏弥的建议,可宁吉尔强烈反对。"苏弥若离开我们,"他对父亲说,"等可爱的阿静蒂娜跟美丽的奥萝拉今晚回来,我就见不着了。我要等啥时候才能见到她呀。"

"请放心,"苏弥答道,"日出前我会回来。我留下心爱的伊扎夫作担保。"

"犹太女子刚离开宁吉尔,年迈的女仆就走进严密看守仨犹太人的大厅。宁吉尔一下认出她是泽丽达的奶妈,但起初没认出她后面那衣着华丽的男子,原来是两天前接待他的那家主人。"

他急忙上前,但不等开口,女仆转身面朝自己领来的军人。"先生,"她说道,"就是他们。我从法院一直跟踪到这儿。他们是一伙的,我不会搞错。你就揍他们一顿报仇吧。"

陌生人一听,脸气得绯红。他拔剑就朝仨犹太人扑去,结果让宁吉尔和巴萨家的仆人给拦住了。

"你想干啥?"宁吉尔叫道,"你竟敢袭击受巴萨保护的人?"

"噢,孩子,"军人答道,"巴萨要知道是这几个家伙抢走我所有珍贵之物,他会收回保护权的。他不了解他们,也不了解你。"

"他非常了解我,"宁吉尔答道,"因为他认了我这个儿子。这就跟我去见他。"

陌生人弯腰穿过宁吉尔撩开的帘子。见父亲奔过来拥抱军人,宁吉尔很是惊讶。

"天啦!亲爱的希罗科,是你吗?"他叫道,"真主的追随者被赶跑时,我以为你死于那场可怕的战斗。你眼里干吗还燃烧着那天释放出的火焰呢？请镇定，告诉我有啥可以效劳。瞧，我已经找到了儿子，愿这也成为你幸福的吉兆吧。"

"我没猜到，"希罗科答道，"你痛失多年的儿子回来了。几天前，光环笼罩的真主出现在我梦里，还对我说，'明天日出时，去嘎拉塔大门，你会见到一个年轻人，一定得把他带回家，那是你老朋友海滨巴萨老爷的二儿子。你别弄错了，把手指放进他的头巾，你会摸到那块牌子，上面用七种不同文字刻着我的名字。'"

"我按吩咐做了，"希罗科继续说道，"我当时被他的外貌和礼貌迷住了，因此就给他看阿静蒂娜的肖像，让他爱上了她。我正沉浸在眼前的幸福、并期待把你儿子带回时，几滴春药洒在桌上，一股浓雾气腾升而起，伸手不见五指。雾气散去时，年轻人不见踪影。我家年迈的女仆今早告诉我，说她发现拐走我女儿们的骗子，于是匆匆寻仇而来。我既来此，自然就听你吩咐。"

"我深信我们会交上好运的，"巴萨说道，"就今晚，我可望得到金表和银表。所以这就把泽丽达请来跟我们一道见证吧。"

丝质品的'沙沙'声引得他们朝门口望去，已做完每天忏悔的义卜拉辛和哈森进来拥抱自己的兄弟。喝过春药的宁吉尔和哈森只想着两位心仪的美女，得知莫瓦兹的女儿有望从《符咒秘籍》中找到解除他捡神珠的咒语，义卜拉辛也兴高采烈起来。

几小时后，苏弥带着圣书返回。

"瞧，"她边说边跟哈森招呼，"你的命运记录在此。"哈森弯腰去读那些希伯来文字："他的右手是因为碰过不洁动物的脂肪才变得黑如乌木，只有当这种动物在海中淹死完后才能恢复。"

"唉！"可怜的年轻人叹道，"我现在想起来了，一天，赞芭卡的仆人在做蛋糕。她警告过我别碰，因为蛋糕拌有猪油，可我没理会她，手很快就变成了现在的乌木色。"

"圣洁的苦行僧！"巴萨叹道，"您的话真灵啊！您在给我儿子送手镯时就警告过他，可他没听，这下受到重罚。请告诉我，聪明的苏弥，到哪儿能找到给我儿子带来灾难的最后那只动物？"

"这儿写着呢，"苏弥边回答边翻书，"那只小黑猪在两个切尔卡西亚人拎着的粉色袋子里。"

一读到这儿，巴萨绝望地跌入软垫里。

"啊，"他说，"就是早上要我掏300金币买走的那袋子。准是她俩让伊兹夫和伊佐夫跳舞，然后从他们身上取走希罗科女儿的护身符。她俩可以解开附在我们身上的咒语。快找到她俩，我愿意拿出一半财产。我真傻，竟把她俩打发走了！"

巴萨叹息自己的愚蠢，义卜拉辛依次翻着这本书。他红着脸读如下文字："珍珠圈已被'单双'游戏亵渎。其主人一直用隐藏某个数字的方法进行欺诈。让那不虔诚的穆斯林人寻找那丢失的珠子吧。"

"哦，天啦，"义卜拉辛叫道，"倒霉的那天浮现在我眼前。在和奥萝拉玩游戏时，我弄断了珍珠线。她握着我手中的珠子，猜说'单'，为了让她输，我从手里漏掉一颗珠子。自从那天起，我每天一直在找，但就没找着。"

"圣洁的苦行僧！"巴萨叫道，"您的话真灵！自珍珠圈不完整时起，我儿子就一直蒙受惩罚。《符咒秘籍》不一样能教我们如何拯救义卜拉辛吗？"

"您听，"苏弥说道，"这是我查到的：'珊瑚珠子在黄缎裙子的第五个折缝里。'"

"啊,真走运!"巴萨叹道,"我们很快就会见到美丽的奥萝拉,义卜拉辛马上就能在黄缎裙子的第五个折缝里找到,因为书里提到的无疑是她。"

犹太女子刚把莫瓦兹的书合上,泽丽达在一群仆人和年迈的奶妈陪同下出现了。她刚进来,欣喜若狂的哈森'扑通'一声跪下,亲吻她的手。

"老爷,"他对巴萨说,"请原谅我这激动之举。我的心不曾需要春药来煽动!赶紧举行结婚仪式,让我俩成为夫妻吧。"

"儿子,你疯了吗?"巴萨问道,"你兄弟俩的灾难还持续着,你有心情独自快乐吗?有谁听说过黑手新郎的?再等等,等黑猪淹死海里后再说吧。"

"对呀,亲爱的哈森,"泽丽达说道,"等我姐姐俩恢复真身后,咱俩的幸福会增加十倍。我带来的春药在这儿,因此她俩的幸福就如同咱俩的。"她把酒壶递给巴萨,巴萨让人当面封存起来。

一见泽丽达,赞芭卡满心欢喜,愉快地拥抱她,之后她邀上所有朋友,带头走进花园,坐在一棵漂亮、茂密的茉莉树枝下。她们刚坐下,就吃惊地听到墙外传来气冲冲的男子声音。

"忘恩负义的姑娘!"那声音说道,"你们就这样待我?让我永远藏起来!这洞子对我来说,可不够黑、不够深!"

唯一的回应是一阵笑声。那声音继续说:"我干啥了要遭来这样的鄙弃?我设法给你俩弄来美丽的护身符,难道就这样回报我?我把带来好运的黑猪赐给你俩,难道就得到这样的回报?"

这番话让听者的好奇心达到了顶点。巴萨命令仆人立刻拆墙,之后却不见说话人,只见两位绝色美女,十分从容而欢快地跳上一个平台。跟她俩一起的是个老仆人,巴萨认出是宁吉尔以前的监护人古娄库。

一见巴萨,古娄库吓得直退缩,因为宁吉尔就是从他手上被抢走的,这回落在巴萨老爷手里除了一死,没别的指望。但巴萨做了原谅他的手势,还问起他投崖后是咋逃生的。古娄库说是一位苦行僧救了他,为他疗伤,还把他送给在场的两位女子做仆人至今。

"可,"巴萨老爷又问,"刚才那声音提到的小黑猪在哪儿?"

"我的老爷,"其中一位女子答道,"您一下令墙拆,您听到说话的那人吓惨了,抓起猪跑了。"

"立刻追上他,"巴萨喊道,但两名女子笑了。

"别紧张,老爷,"另一个说道,"他会回来的。您只消下令把住洞口,他进去就出不来了。"

这时天快黑了,大伙回到宫里。女眷们住宿楼附近的一个气派长廊里,摆着咖啡、各种水果。巴萨接着命令把仨犹太人带到他的面前,借此问问在旅馆里强迫他们跳舞的是不是这两个姑娘,可让他心烦的是,当几个看守去推墙时,仨犹太人趁机逃跑了。

听此消息,犹太女人苏弥吓得苍白,看了一眼《符咒秘籍》,她马上露出笑容。她半大声朗读道:"不必担心,他们会抓到苦行僧的。"这时,哈森却大声痛惜,说刚到的好运又丢了。

一听到这回忆,巴萨的一个差使大笑起来。"老爷,一个好运跳着来,另一个好运拄拐去。别害怕。好运不会走远。"

一听这离题的插话,巴萨大吃一惊,命他离开,没叫不准回来。

"遵命,老爷,"差使说道,"我一回来就是一大群,您会高兴迎接我的,"他说完出去了。

没旁人时,宁吉尔转身请求两位漂亮的生人帮忙。"我兄弟和我,"他大叫道,"对三位绝色姑娘充满爱意,其中两个却受到残酷的咒语控制。如果她们的命运碰巧掌握在你俩手里,你们会全力恢复她们的幸福和自由吗?"

小伙的请求却把她俩惹火了。"什么,"其中一位嚷道,"恋人的痛苦对我姐妹俩意味着什么?命运夺走我俩的恋人,如果由我俩决定来这事,全世界都该跟我俩一样痛苦!"

这意想不到的回答让在场者吃惊不小。巴萨恳请她讲讲自己的经历。她征得姐姐同意后讲开了:

17. 切尔卡西亚美女的故事

"我俩出生在切尔卡西亚的穷苦人家。姐姐叫苔兹拉,我叫黛莉。我俩除靠姿色外,别无所倚。我俩在娱乐方面受过良好训练,一学就会,自幼会演奏各种乐器,能歌更善舞。另外,尽管至今仍处逆境,我们一样活泼、快乐着。

"我俩很快活,十分满足居家日子,可一天早上,苏丹王的寻妻官一见我俩就被外貌打动。我俩一直以为这种事迟早会发生,只好听天由命。可巧的是,这时两个小伙走进我们家。年长者约二十岁,头发乌黑、眼睛明亮,另一位顶多十五岁,清秀得让人误认为是女孩。

"他俩迷了路,怯生生地敲门,恳请我父母给予容留。短暂犹豫后,父母答应了,还把他俩请进我俩的闺房。如果说我父母为其外貌所动,那我和姐姐更不用说了。可想到第二天就得启程进宫,姐妹俩就痛苦万分。

"我夜梦惊醒,见年幼的那位生人坐在我床边,觉得他握着我的手。

"'可爱的黛莉,'他悄声说,'不必害怕见你才知爱为何物的人。我是,'他继续说,'德利凯特王子,黑色大理石岛王的儿子。与我同行的朋友是我国最富有的贵族之一,他所知道的各种秘密正是苏丹王想得到的。我俩之所以逃离祖国,全因为父王执意要我娶一位两眼大小不一的美女为妻。'

"见迅即征服爱慕者,我的虚荣心得到满足,也被小伙示爱的方式迷住。我两眼慢慢朝他移去,可那一瞥几乎让他失去理智。他晕眩倒地。我没法走开,苔兹拉匆忙穿好衣服,和王子提过的那位年轻贵族塞拉米斯跑来帮忙。

"回过神后,想到当天得赶往康斯坦丁堡的旅行,我们自叹命运不济。塞拉米斯承诺和王子会紧随身后,并设法跟我俩说上话,我俩才得到一点安慰。他俩吻我俩的手,然后从侧门离去。

"不一会儿,父母告诉我们护卫已到。道别父母后,我俩坐进固定在骆驼两侧的箱子里。这些箱子很大,足以舒服躺下。箱子上方留有窗口,我俩可沿途欣赏乡村风景。

"我们连续几天旅行,不免为即将发生的事忧伤、焦虑起来。一天,我正望着窗外,忽听有人叫我的名字,同时看到一个衣着漂亮的女孩从骆驼另一侧箱子里跳出来。我一眼认出是王子,激动的心怦怦直跳。他说是塞拉米斯想出的主意:他让王子打扮成这样,而自己则扮成贩奴者,打算将此绝色少女献给苏丹王。他还说服骆驼队的主管让他租下这空箱,所以王子才轻易地爬进我俩的箱子。

"这一妙计让我俩惊讶,可随从打断了我们惬意的谈话,他们发现骆驼行走歪歪扭扭,便过来检看情况。好在其行动并不快,王子及时返回其箱中,骆驼又恢复平衡,确保计谋没露馅。

"王子和朋友无意让我俩进入苏丹王的宫殿,却不知如何帮我俩逃走,之后又咋办。快到康斯坦丁堡的那一天,我俩终于从王子那儿得知,塞拉米斯在路上结识了一位圣洁的苦行僧,跟他说我俩是他的妹妹,不忍看着成为贩卖的奴隶。苦行僧对此颇感兴趣,当即答应,如果我们能逃离护卫视线,他给我们找个避难处。这风险虽大,但却是我俩的唯一选择。

"当晚,骆驼队刚入睡,塞拉米斯打开我俩的箱子顶部,我俩悄悄爬出后,沿着来时的路往回跑了一段,继而拐进一条岔路,最后来到苦行僧为我们提供的避难处。在那儿我们有吃有住,重获自由的幸福自不待言。

"苦行僧很快也被我俩的美貌俘虏了。逃出后的第二天,他建议我俩随他去不远处的一个小旅馆找两位犹太人。他俩持有非法弄来的珍贵护身符。'去试试,'苦行僧说道,'设法弄到宝物。'

"那家旅馆不在去康斯坦丁堡的正道上,但饭菜可口,商人们都喜欢去。我们一到,发现至少已有六到八人正等着吃茶点。他们客气地招呼我们,然后一起坐下来吃饭。

"不一会儿,苦行僧提到的两人走进来。经他暗示,我和姐姐各让出一个空位给他俩。

"苦行僧碰巧说过'他俩的大哥都跳舞了',我俩当时没在意这话,可随即想起来了,于是决定也让他俩跳舞。为达此目的,我俩使出浑身解数,很快让他俩言听计从。那天下来,我俩弄到了护身符,把他俩丢到一边。王子和塞拉米斯越发爱我俩,还说我俩是世上最美尤物。

"我们离开旅馆时,太阳已经下山,不知随后该去何处,便欣然听从了王子的提议:立刻乘船去黑色大理石岛国。那都是啥地儿啊!黑如煤玉的岩石耸立岸边,让整个国家笼罩在一片浓黑中。水手都没去过那儿,因此跟我们一样吓得不成样子,多亏塞拉米斯为我们领航,我们才得以安全抵岸。

"一离开煤玉墙般的海岸,我们来到一个漂亮无比的国度,这里田野更葱郁、溪流更清澈、太阳更明亮。人们拥过来迎接深受爱戴的王子,不过也告诉他父王仍在气头上,一因他拒不娶表妹奥金帕尔公主为妻,二是他私自逃离。人们纷纷恳请他保命要紧,别回首府去。我尽管很想拜访心爱的王子家,但还是恳求他听取明智的建议,与我们一道去塞拉米斯位于密林的宫殿。

"我和姐姐在农舍长大,塞拉米斯的宫殿美如仙境。它取材粉色大理石,光洁度极好,四周雕刻着花朵和溪流,恰似镜中之物。我有特意配备的套房,黄色丝绸和银器与我的黑发相配。我们俩每天有新衣服穿,还有奴仆伺候着。哦!可惜这幸福昙花一现!

"塞拉米斯嫉妒姐姐,这打破了大伙的平静生活,他知道王子的心有所属,仍忍受不了她对王子的友善。我们每天面对温和的责备和解释,不过苔兹拉的眼泪总让塞拉米斯跪地乞求原谅。

"我们就这样过了几个月,突然有一天传来国王病危的消息。我请求王子立刻回宫,既为见父王,又为在议员和贵族面前露面。他爱我胜过对王冠的渴望,因此犹豫不决,好像预知到后来会发生的事儿似的。最后,苔兹拉当着塞拉米斯的面,对王子讲了一番严肃的话,让他决定回宫,并答应天黑前返回。

"黑夜到来,王子却没到来,劝说王子回宫的苔兹拉表现出种种焦虑情绪,塞拉米斯顿生嫉心。我无法言表痛苦的滋味。无法入眠的我起床、沿着王子常来常往的路漫步进入森林。突然,我听到远处传来马蹄声,王子随即跃身下马,站在我身边。'啊!我太崇拜你了!'他赞叹道,'非塞拉米斯的爱所能及。'他刚说完,我就听到身后传来轻微的噪音。不等转过身,我俩的头就在面前不停转动,这时传来了塞拉米斯的吼声:

"'伪君子,回答我,还有你这不忠的苔兹拉,你们为何这样背叛我?'

"我这才明白过来,盛怒之下的他竟把我误认为是我的姐姐。

"'唉,'我脑子微弱回应道,'我不是苔兹拉,是黛莉,你把我和你朋友的生活全搅乱了。'一听这话,塞拉米斯停住思考了一会。

"'别怕,'他的话平和了些,'我能让你俩完好如初。'他在我俩舌头上涂了点魔粉,然后把我俩的头放回到脖子上。转眼间,我俩的头与身体连接得天衣无缝。可因生气而糊涂的塞拉米斯却错放了我俩的头!

"这奇怪的改变带来的怪异之感,我无法描述。我俩本能地举起手——他触摸到的自然是女式头发,我则取掉盖着前额的头巾。不过,于是漆黑一团,王子和我都不知道发生了什么事情。

"这时,苔兹拉出现了,后面跟着一群捧花的奴仆。借助他们火把的亮光,我们明白了咋回事。事实上,我俩的第一感觉是交换过了衣服。

"可无论咋说,我俩还是更喜欢自己的身体。尽管我俩仍然爱着对方,但起初还是有些怨恨塞拉米斯。王子对我的一往情深,很快使他为此改变深感庆幸。'我幸福至极,'他说道:'美丽的黛莉,我心一直属于你,现在又得到了你的头。'

"尽管王子试图朝好的方面去想,但塞拉米斯却为其愚蠢深感羞愧。'我,我,'他支吾道,'还有两支蜡笔,跟前面用过的那两支一样具有魔力。让我再砍下你俩的头,一切问题都能解决。'这提议听起来非常诱人,但有一点风险。经过一番商量,我俩决定不换头。'如果你俩不接受我的帮助,'塞拉米斯继续说,'那就别责备我。不过,请接受这两支蜡笔,如果你俩一旦再遇砍头,就按我讲的做,你俩的头就会回到原位,'说完,他把蜡笔交给我俩,随后一起回到城堡。

"然而,这不幸的交换带来的麻烦才刚开始。我的脑袋不由自主地带着王子的身体回到自己的住所。女仆们只看到我穿的连衣裙,径直说我走错了走廊,还让几个男仆把我领到王子殿下的住处。这已经够糟糕的了——因为当时还是夜里,我的奴仆开始给我脱衣服,我既惊讶又茫然,差点晕倒,不用说,王子的头在城堡的另一端也遭受过同样的煎熬!

"到次日一早,各位不难猜到,我俩几乎没睡觉,但已部分适应了怪异的处境。照镜子时,王子已是棕色皮肤、黑头发,而我却是满头金色卷发。那天一过,宫中的人习惯了这一变化,也就不再去想它了。

"几周后,我们听说黑色大理石岛国的君王驾崩。我那王子的头本来雄心壮志,渴望跨马直奔首府宣布自己是国王。但问题是:哪个贵族认得出带着女儿身的王子呢?我们事实上还在想:哪个是王子,哪个是姑娘呢?

"最后,一番激烈争论后,我的头获胜,我俩一同出发,不料国王早已宣布奥金帕尔公主为继承人。大部分议员和贵族公开声称,他们更拥护合法的继承人。由于他们无法确信王子是在自己身上,还是在我身上,因此把我俩当作骗子投进了大牢。

"几天后,随我俩赶来首府的苔兹拉和塞拉米斯告诉我俩,说新女王控告我俩犯有叛国罪,还亲自听审对我俩的缺席审判。该对我俩怎样量刑,他们一直惶恐,好在我俩将被斩首。

"我跟姐姐说,我看不出有哪点好,可塞拉米斯粗暴地打断我:

"'什么!'他惊呼道,'我当然会用这两支蜡笔,而且……'。可带我俩去大广场行刑的官员过来了——因为奥金帕尔决定此事不便再拖。

"广场上挤满了年龄不同、阶层各异的人,中心位置搭着一个平台,上面立着绞刑架,旁边站着蒙上黑面罩的行刑者。经他示意,我首先登上平台,我的头很快在他脚下呼呼直转。姐姐和塞拉米斯一个箭步冲到我旁边。塞拉米斯闪电般从刽子手那儿夺过砍刀,砍下王子的头。这一奇怪的行刑程序惊呆了众人,不等他们回过神来,我俩的头和身体回到原位,蜡笔也放到我俩的舌头上。紧接着,塞拉米斯领着王子来到平台边上示众,说道:'看好啦,诸位的法定国王在此!'

"话音刚落,阵阵欢呼声响彻云霄,那声音传到王宫的奥金帕尔那儿。受到绝望打击,她跌倒在阳台上,人事不省,随即被奴仆抬回房间。

"我俩这时转喜为悲。我跑过去深情抱住王子,可他脸色突然苍白、步履踉跄。

"'我对你至死不渝,'他望着我,喃喃地说,'我死也是国王!'他的头耷拉在我肩上,静静停止呼吸,因为他颈部的一根动脉血管被割断了。

"我木然走向旁边的砍刀,想尽快随心爱的王子而去。就在塞拉米斯(赶巧)抓住我的手时,我却把砍刀疯狂地对准他。心脏被刺中的他倒在我脚下"。

人人屏吸聆听着故事,黛莉显然再讲不下去,苔兹拉则一头扎进软垫堆里。赞芭卡吩咐女仆尽全力照顾好这姐妹俩,希望把她俩带去她的房间。

姐妹俩正处此景,精明的易卜拉欣跟父母建议:鉴于两位切尔卡西亚姑娘意识模糊,这无疑是搜身的好时机,看能否在其身上找到属于希罗科女儿的护身符。想到如此冷漠对待客人,巴萨不禁感到震惊,拒绝这样做,还补充道,希望第二天说服她俩自愿交出护身符。

这时临近午夜,站着犹太人苏弥旁边的宁吉尔取出阿静蒂娜的肖像,很高兴听人说她比肖像更漂亮。人人翘首以盼,等着12点钟响时,那两块手表会来寻找苏弥。这事可不能耽误,巴萨命令敞开每道门,结果进来的不是期盼已久的两只手表,而是被打发出去的差使。

巴沙愤然起身。"阿兹米,"他吼道,"我没命令你别出现在我的面前吗?"

"老爷,"阿兹米谦卑地答道,"我躲在门后,听到了两位切尔卡西亚姑娘的故事。因为我知道您喜欢听故事,那就让我也给您讲一个吧,我保证长话短说。"

"快讲,"巴沙答道,"但说话留心点。"

"老爷,"阿兹米讲开了,"我今早正走在街上,注意到一男子带着奴仆与我同向而行。他进了一家面包房,买了些面包让奴仆拿着。我看着他,结果发现他还在其他地方买了不少食品。当奴仆拿不了时,主人命令他回家在午夜前备好晚饭。"

"没旁人时,那人沿街往前走,拐进一家钟表店,我看他出来时手里拿着的是块银表。刚走出几步,他弯腰捡起脚边的一块金表。我这时跑过去对他说,他若不把那表一半的钱分给我,我就到法官那儿告他。他同意了,把我领到他家中,给了我400金币,说那是我该得的一半。我得到了自己想要的那一份后就离开了。

"那正是伺候老爷的时候,我回到家,陪您去法官那儿,在那儿才得知仨犹太人的故事,于是意识到留在陌生人处那两块表的重要性。我赶到他家,他却出去了,我只好去找那个奴仆,告诉他我是给他主人送去重要消息的人。他以为我是主人的朋友,恳请我稍等,还把我领进一个房间,在那儿我看见那两块表就在桌上。我把表放进口袋里,留下价值金表一半的400金币,另加三块金币,我知道那是另外一块表的价值。各位都知道,两块手表从不会呆在购买者中,可这人也许会觉得自己幸运地拿回了自己的钱。我已经把两块表绑在一起,此刻,奥萝拉和阿静蒂娜稳妥地锁在我的房间里。

听此,人人激动起来,阿兹米差点让人拥抱窒息。宁吉尔虽不知这差使睡在哪间屋里,但也抑制不住冲进门来。

差使请求去带回两位小姐,很快牵着她俩回来。

可喜的忙乱持续了几分钟,义卜拉辛趁机跪在奥萝拉拉跟前,在她连衣裙的第五个褶缝寻找那颗遗失的珊瑚珠。《咒语秘籍》已道出真相,那珠子真在那儿!由于念珠一颗不少,这年轻人日复一日寻找的日子就此结束。

一片欣喜中,唯独哈桑还绷一张脸。

"唉!"他说道,"人人都幸福,你们眼前这可怜的人除外。我曾觉得自己有个难兄难弟,我这伤感中唯一的慰藉都没了!"

"放心,"巴萨答道,"偷走粉红袋子的苦行僧一定能找到。"

这时晚饭已备好。他们吃过自认为是世上最美味的珍奇水果后,巴萨吩咐把春药酒瓶端上来,让几个年轻人喝下。他们眼里随即燃烧起新的火焰,发誓至死彼此忠诚。

1点的钟声敲响时,仪式接近尾声,奥萝拉和阿静蒂娜突然消失,她俩站过的地方留下的是两块表。沉寂笼罩着人群——原来他们忘了魔法。此时传来阿兹米的声音,问可否让他把两块表保管到第二天,拿自己的人头担保解除魔法。经苏弥同意,他的请求得到批准。巴萨给阿兹米一个钱包,里面装着1000金币,作为他替自己一家人操劳的报酬。之后,大伙各自回了家。

阿兹米从没拥有过这么多钱,高兴得一夜没合眼。他早早起床,来到花园,想着怎样解除希罗科两个女儿的魔法。突然,一个温柔的女子声音传到耳边,透过灌木丛,他看见苔兹拉正往妹妹的头发里插花儿。树叶的沙沙声使黛莉先是一惊,随即一跃而起,准备逃走,阿兹米恳求她留下,告诉他她俩在情人死后又发生的事儿,以及她俩怎么找到苦行僧的。

黛莉答道:"奥金帕尔女王对我俩的惩罚令是,我俩必须带着悲伤,在她为臣民即将举办的盛大节日上唱歌、跳舞。这残忍的命令几乎让我俩崩溃,我们郑重起誓,要让所有情侣跟我俩一样悲惨。这个计划推行得非常成功,都城里女子很快跑到奥金帕尔面前,趁还能挽救所有人的生活,恳请她把我们逐出王国。她同意了,于是下令把我俩、连同奴仆古娄库装上同一条船。

"一上岸,我们见一老人边忙着淹死一些小黑猪,一边不停跟它们说话,好似它们能听懂他话似的。

"'该死的种群,'他说,'都怪你们造成他的不幸,我可给过他魔法手镯。你们都死去吧!'

"我们好奇地靠近他,最后认出了他——我姐妹俩从篷车逃走后帮过我们的苦行僧。

老人很高兴认出我俩,还拿他住的山洞庇护我们。我们乐意地接受了他的帮助,带着他送给我们的那头唯一活着的小猪,一起去了山洞。

他补充道,'你俩要啥,海滨巴萨老爷都会给的。'

"我没问这猪为何这么金贵,于是接过来,一直装在工装袋里。我俩昨天向巴萨老爷兜售,结果遭到他的嘲笑。我们把气发在苦行僧身上,趁他熟睡时剪了他的胡子,到现在都不敢出来见人呢。

"啊,"差使叫道,"把你们的美貌浪费在折磨他人上很不适合。忘掉不幸的过去,想想未来。因此请你收下这块金表,珍惜未来更美好的日子。"说完,他把金表放在她膝盖上,然后转向苔兹拉,"还有你,丽人,请允许我送给你那块表。它确实只是银的,但这是我唯一能给你的。不过我确信,你一定在什么地儿放有一张正好跟这表匹配的银牌。

"哦,你有,"黛莉叫道,"那就把牌固定在你的表上,我会把我那块金牌挂在我的表上。"

牌子拿了出来,正如阿兹米所猜的那样,正是这姐妹俩从伊兹夫和伊佐夫那儿拿走的嵌着金银的两块护身护。那两块表如闪电一般从苔兹拉和妹妹手中滑落下来,奥萝拉和阿静蒂娜站在她俩面前,各自的手指上挂着一张护身护。

对这突来的变化和许久未见的阳光,她们起初也一副困惑样儿。当她们逐渐明白身上魔法已解除时,那高兴劲儿真是难以言表。

让切尔卡西亚姐妹从失去护身护中得到安慰,可能有些困难,不过奥萝拉和阿静蒂娜恳求她俩擦干眼泪,因为她们的父亲希罗科是亚历山德里亚的州长,一定会如姐妹俩的期望予以回报的。这一承诺很快得到希罗科本人的确认。他在巴萨和两个儿子的陪同下来到花园,很快和家里女眷们聚到一块儿。只有哈桑没在,因为他正为自己那只乌黑的手痛苦着。

令所有人诧异的是,此刻从平台角落传来嘈杂声,哈桑在一群奴仆的簇拥下出现了,他拍着手,高兴地呼喊。"我像往常一样哭泣,"他叫道,"当所有泪水突然间不再流出时,我低头看自己的手,我发现黑色已经消失。可爱的苔兹拉,我的心一直属于你,这下没什么能阻止我向你求爱啦。"

哈桑压根儿没想询问或关心自己是怎么痊愈的,但其他人却非常感兴趣。那只小黑猪明显已死——可它怎么死的?什么时候死的?对此奴仆们回答道,当天早晨,他们见有人被三人紧追不放,还说这人去过他们看守的山洞庇过难,他们后来遵命推石头堵上了入口。

一阵刺耳尖叫打断了故事,这时,一个人——切尔卡西亚姐妹认出是那个苦行僧——冲着转过台阶角落,跟在后面的就是那仨犹太人。逃命者一见这么多人聚在一起,立刻向转另外一条路。但奴仆们把他们四个一起抓住,带到了主人的面前。

让巴萨惊奇的是,他发现那个给他仨儿子念珠、护身符和手镯的人,正是这位年迈的苦行僧。"不要怕,圣父,"他说道,"在我这儿你是安全的。但请告诉我,你是怎么到这儿的?"

"老爷,"苦行僧解释道,"我睡着后,胡子被两个切尔卡西亚人剪掉了。我羞于见人,于是就带着那粉色丝袋悄悄溜走了。这三人晚上偶然碰到我,我们闲聊了一会儿。可是,就在清晨,天色亮到足能看见彼此的脸时,他们其中一个叫道,说两个切尔卡西亚美女从犹太人那儿偷走了护身护,我就是与她同行的苦行僧。我立即起身,试图逃回自己的山洞,但我跑不过他们。正当我们经过您家花园时,他们把装着小黑猪的袋子抢过去,扔进海里。正是这一举动解救了您的公子。我想祈求您原谅他们可能对您做过的任何坏事,不仅如此,您还该为这事给他们一点儿补偿。"

巴萨答应了圣僧的要求,见俩犹太人迷上了切尔卡西亚姐妹的美貌,他准许他们结合,且在伊扎夫与聪明的苏弥婚礼的那天一起举行。他请来法官,犹太人用本族帽子换来穆罕默德追随者的头巾。在经历众多的不幸之后,巴萨的仨儿子也恳求父亲别再耽搁他们的幸福,法官在正午时分为这六对新人主持了婚礼。

References

[1] 曹顺发,陈福宇.灰色童话故事书[M].四川:四川文艺出版社,2010.
[2] 陆谷孙.英汉大词典[Z].上海:上海译文出版社,2007.
[3] 何桂金,周开鑫.高级英语语法教程[M].重庆:重庆出版社,2000.